COUNTIES OF MODERN ENGLAND

Scotland

NORTH SEA

Isle of Man

IRISH SEA

Wales

Humber R.

The Wash

Severn R.

Thames R.

Isle of Wight

ENGLISH CHANNEL

0   40   80
Scale of Miles

1. NORTHUMBERLAND
2. CUMBERLAND
3. DURHAM
4. WESTMORLAND
5. LANCASHIRE
6. YORK
7. CHESHIRE
8. STAFFORD
9. DERBY
10. NOTTINGHAM
11. LINCOLN
12. SHROPSHIRE
13. LEICESTER
14. RUTLAND
15. NORTHAMPTON
16. HUNTINGDON
17. CAMBRIDGE
18. NORFOLK
19. SUFFOLK
20. HEREFORD
21. WORCESTER
22. WARWICK
23. BEDFORD
24. MONMOUTH
25. GLOUCESTER
26. OXFORD
27. BUCKINGHAM
28. HERTFORD
29. MIDDLESEX
30. ESSEX
31. SOMERSET
32. WILTSHIRE
33. BERKSHIRE
34. SURREY
35. KENT
36. CORNWALL
37. DEVON
38. DORSET
39. HAMPSHIRE
40. SUSSEX

THE ENGLISH LANGUAGE

An Historical Introduction

THE
ENGLISH
LANGUAGE

An Historical
Introduction

JAMES D.
GORDON

University of Pennsylvania

Thomas Y. Crowell Company
New York Established 1834

Manufactured in the United States of America

Acknowledgments are gratefully made to the following authors and publishers who have granted
permission to use selections from copyrighted
publications.

Alvarez, G. A., "Speaking Out" (*Saturday Evening
Post*, Sept. 9, 1967). Copyright © 1967 by The
Saturday Evening Post Company.

Churchill, Winston S., "Harrow," in *A Roving
Commission* (New York: Charles Scribner's Sons,
1930). Reprinted by permission of Charles
Scribner's Sons and the Hamlyn Publishing Group.

Hodgson, Phyllis, and G. M. Liegey, eds., *The
Orcherd of Syon* (Early English Text Society, o.s. 258
[1966]).

Trevelyan, G. M., *History of England* (London:
Longmans Green & Co., 1945).

Yeats, William Butler, "The Indian upon God,"
in *The Collected Poems of William Butler Yeats* (New
York: The Macmillan Company, 1934). Copyright
1906 by The Macmillan Company; renewed 1934
by William Butler Yeats. Reprinted by permission
of M. B. Yeats, The Macmillan Company, and
Macmillan & Co.

Preface

This treatise proposes to give an account of the English language in its historical development for the benefit of young students new to serious linguistic study, most of whom are likely to think of their main interests as literary or generally cultural. In the experience of the author, relatively few students who present themselves in courses in the history of the language have had any introduction to modern linguistic study or intend to specialize in linguistics. They are generally quite unsophisticated beyond the type of normative grammar that remains rooted in the practices of lower-school English instruction.

The point of view maintained in this volume is, therefore, primarily pedagogical. Lest we be dismissed for not producing what we had every intention to avoid, let it be said that we do not attempt to present an original venture in linguistic history—neither a new construction of the historical course of the language nor a rigorously structured analysis such as would appeal to readers of some proficiency in both historical and descriptive linguistics.

On the other hand, the advances in linguistic methodology which all of us have seen in the last half-century, especially since the Second World War, have had so great an influence upon all serious linguistic study that their relevance to even the most elementary historical account cannot be set aside. It would be a blessing if all young students interested in the history of English were acquainted with the terminology, basic concepts, and methods of structural linguistics, but lacking such advantage, we have attempted to include these elements to the extent we have thought necessary or useful for our purposes.

In accord with the general aim of this book, we have selected and arranged our material according to the following specific purposes:

1. To accustom students to the notion that language is in constant change and that permanent and intrinsic standards of linguistic etiquette are an impractical ideal.

2. To inform them of the various types and processes of change and to show that many of these processes have led to the present state of the language, are still in operation, and may reasonably be expected to result in further permanent change.

3. To impart some elementary acquaintance with the characteristics of the language in the most important literary periods of the past and to show what causes led to the transition from one stage to the next.

4. In consequence of the general neglect of the history of England among both secondary and college students, to refer briefly to conditions in the political and social history of England which have most radically affected the state of the language.

5. In keeping with our primarily pedagogical purpose, to multiply concrete examples and to employ repetition even at the sacrifice of a strict and orderly chronological progression.

6. To restrict footnote references and bibliography to books in the English language and a few articles of unusual importance in learned journals.

Undoubtedly there is a great need today for more rigorous applications of structural analysis to historical states, and a number of such essays have appeared or are in preparation. Their ultimate value will be very great, but the profits will accrue mostly to advanced specialists. The experience of this author is that the unavoidably high level of abstraction in such presentations alienates the very students whom we should be most eager to attract: that is, students whose main interests are centered in literary study but who will one day compose the main body of teachers of English in school and college and are therefore most likely to perpetuate what Professor Kenyon once called "the still abundant quackery based on eighteenth century knowledge and twentieth century ignorance of standards and correctness."

It is impossible for me or, I think, anyone else today to write on this subject without acknowledging a debt to many pioneers in linguistic history whose names we may not even recall. I am particularly conscious of such prominent names as Wyld, Wright, Luick, Horn, Zachrisson, and Jespersen; of the more recent contributions of Campbell, Brunner, Mustanoja, Dobson, and Kökeritz; and, of course, of those whose work requires the highest degree of self-abnegation, the editors of the *Oxford English Dictionary*, the *Middle English Dictionary*, and the many volumes of the Early English Text Society. I have had the advantage of other historical surveys and owe much to the example of Pyles, Robertson, and Kennedy, and especially to that of my former teacher, Professor Albert C. Baugh, whose personal influence, added to that of Professors Harold Stine and the late P. V. D. Shelly, has communicated to me an enthusiasm quite in excess of my native ability. I am also indebted to Professor Harold B. Allen, who has read the manuscript and made invaluable suggestions.

I owe a word of thanks also to the many students who by choice or requirement have studied this subject with me over the years, whose youthful spirits have been a source of renewed vitality, and who have taught me by their unabashed candor as well as by their enthusiasms what to them is important and interesting to learn. For better or for worse they have shaped this text. If its merits outweigh its faults, I am happy to acknowledge my debt to them.

J. D. G.

Contents

ix

Chapter 1

LINGUISTIC HISTORY

All human things change with time, and the record of this change is history. If there were no change there would be no history. Usually when we say "history" we are thinking of the larger and noticeable changes that take place in human affairs: social and economic conditions like the drift of population from the country to the city in modern times and the improved standard of living in America among the lower middle classes; governmental behavior like acts of Congress or the far-reaching decisions of the United States Supreme Court; international changes like the fortunes of the United Nations and the growing independence of the former colonial peoples. As these activities recede from us into the past, they become part of the past story of mankind, and we call them history.

There are, also, special histories of very particular forms of human behavior: of warfare, of transportation, of costume, of photography, of literature. For almost every form of activity, someone has written a history, and among these special histories is the history of the mother tongue.

Like most histories, however, the story does not lie ready to hand. It must be recovered. Where do these materials lie, from which we are to build our picture of the past? Because of the way in which the young student usually studies history of any kind, he can be pardoned for believing that it is something essentially to be read in textbooks. Actually any textbook of history is an individual statement, containing not only a presentation of facts but much reconstruction and reinterpretation. At best it is one man's view of things, limited by his knowledge of the facts and the quality of his imagination. At the worst it may be incomplete, biased, or even erroneous. In any case it must be tentative, since the advancement of knowledge will sooner or later reduce it to minor importance. The student must, therefore, know something of the nature of the changes that modify the state of things, where the evidence is to be found, how the data may be assembled, and how valid conclusions may be drawn. In other words he must, if he is to be a really educated person, learn to think like an historian. In this book, then, we shall examine not only the chronology of change in the English language but also the nature of the processes that have resulted in past changes, are still in evidence, and will undoubtedly generate new states of language for generations to come.

Language may be said to have two histories: one in the life of the individual person and one in the life of the speech community. One's first steps in learning to use language are imitative. We hear and reproduce, at first slowly and with many failures, as in all learning, but later with skill. By the time, however, that we are old enough to reflect on our own actions, our language has become so much a part of us that we think of it as "natural." We have lost all memory of how we learned this apparently simple skill. But language is not "natural," at least not in the same sense as seeing or breathing or walking. It has been invented by man, and apparently by different people at different times. What is more, any child could learn any language with the same facility as another if he were reared from his earliest years in that particular linguistic culture, for the simple reason that the hereditary factor in human intelligence is the apti-tude for learning *a* language but not one particular language.

Now, just as the individual has lost all memory of his first encounter with the mystery of speech, so the human race has lost all recollection of when, where, and how language was invented. So far as we know, many centuries elapsed between the beginning of speech and the beginnings of a permanent system for representing this auditory form of language in visible form—in other words, in writing. It is well to keep in mind this fact that in all civilizations the spoken language existed long before the begin-ning of written records. In some cultures even today written language does not exist and never has existed. From this fact we may draw certain useful distinctions.

It is sometimes said that one language, Latin, for example, is older than another, English, for example. Strictly speaking, this could be true only if the earliest ancestors of the Latin people had invented their language at an earlier period than the ancestors of the English. We have good reason to believe, however, that this did not happen. At the time when Cicero and Vergil were writing their accomplished prose and poetry in the first century B.C., the unnamed ancestors of the Anglo-Saxon tribes were speaking a not totally dissimilar language, but they had not yet become so self-conscious as to want to preserve the memory of their thoughts and actions in writing. Latin *literature*, then, is older than English literature and illustrates a more primitive *state* of language than modern English, but the language itself does not have an earlier origin.

Furthermore, the system of writing by which a language is represented is not identical with the language itself. It is only one aspect of the language, and not the most important. In fact, the same language might conceivably be represented by different alphabetical schemes. When the earliest attempts at writing were made by the Germanic tribes of Europe, they used an alphabet, now extinct, called the Runic alphabet, but because their culture was heavily influenced by Latin civilization and learning, the Roman alphabet eventually replaced it. This Roman alphabet was a modification of the Greek, which in its turn was an adaptation of the alphabet used in Semitic writing. In modern times the Roman alphabet is in general use in Western Europe and the New World, whereas in Russia a form of the Greek alphabet is used. The original choice of one over the other, however, was not due to the fact that one was linguistically better suited than the other to the languages which used it. The choice was merely an accident of history. The lands in which Latin Christianity prevailed used the Roman alphabet, and those in which the Greek Church was supreme used the Greek.

Thus, the relation between a language and its written forms is what we call "arbitrary" or "conventional." The symbols *r* and *s* are not better suited to the sounds they represent than any other symbols. We could, in fact, reverse their use, and if everyone followed the same practice no difficulty would arise. Their values depend entirely on general custom.

But more important still, the relationship between the written and spoken language is a very imperfect one. There are many more sounds in our language than letters in the alphabet. Hence letters may signal different sounds at different times; notice, for example, the value of the letter *a* in *hate*, *hat*, *all*, *father*, and *about*. Or the same sound may be represented by different letters, as for example the final consonants in *off* and *cough* or the vowels in *deign*, *wane*, *main*, and *say*. Furthermore, these relationships may not only vary from one region to another, but may also change from one generation to another, since the written language tends to change more slowly than the spoken. Many parts of the English-speaking world continue to spell final *r* in words like *mother* or *r* before a consonant in words like *arm*, though the words are no longer pronounced as formerly, just as we all continue to spell *know* and *right* as they were pronounced several hundred years ago.

[margin note: author pronounces differently]

From such imperfect and only partially reliable systems of writing, however, we must deduce our knowledge of the sounds of language in past times. We have some knowledge of the appearance of a few famous people of the past of whom pictures were made in their lifetime, but no one today knows from actual experience the sound of English on the tongue of Thomas Jefferson, William Shakespeare, or Geoffrey Chaucer. By the careful use of written records we can arrive at a very good knowledge of what their sounds must have been, but the farther back we go the less complete our knowledge becomes. Eventually we reach a point in antiquity earlier than any existing written records. This is the period of prehistory, about which our knowledge rests upon conjecture. We know, for example, that English and German are evolutions of what was once the same language. We call it **Proto-Germanic,** but not a scrap of written evidence remains to show us what Proto-Germanic really was. Only by comparing the common characteristics of the different languages which have evolved from it and noting their likenesses and differences can we form some notion of the sounds that composed it. This is a subject of study known as **comparative grammar.** That part of language study which describes the sounds of a language and their history back to and through prehistoric periods is called **phonology.**

[margin note: first]

However, it is not only the sounds that change, but the larger elements as well. Fortunately, in historic periods the history of these elements is somewhat easier to recognize than the history of sounds. New words come into a language and old words are forgotten **(lexical change).** Or words remain but change their meaning **(semantic shift),** or they undergo grammatical variation, as in number, case, or tense **(morphological change).** All of these phenomena we shall have occasion to speak of in discussing the past, but an observant student will be interested also in the manner in which similar changes are going on all about him in the living language. In fact, events of the past can often be more vividly comprehended by comparison with current events.

Finally we shall discover that the larger events of history have an interest to us. Invasion and conquest, repopulation and intermixture, the rise and fall of social classes, education or the lack of it, distribution and redistribution of wealth, learning, science, and inventions—all of these are likely to have linguistic aspects. Those who participate in these events or whose lives are modified by them express their experiences and aspirations in language, and their language is modified to suit their changing needs.

Discussions of language are often made confusing by the fact that the terms are ambiguous, in particular because they are used sometimes with popular and sometimes with technical meanings. The word *language* itself may be extended to cover communication noises among subrational animals as well as certain noises among human beings which express attitudes in a quasi-verbal form, such as those expressions somewhat inaccurately spelled *tsk-tsk* and *uh-huh*. An exhaustive treatment of language would include these phenomena, but our account will be limited to the items more conventionally thought of as speech sounds, words, and groups of words.

Various words are inaccurately used by the literate public to refer to what they think are unacceptable forms of speech. For example, **vernacular** occasionally turns up in reference to the lowest forms of popular speech. Here it will always mean the native speech of a person in contrast to the same person's use of Latin as a second language. **Colloquial** very commonly refers to "ungrammatical" or uneducated usage, but we use it to refer to those characteristics of speech which are not found in dignified literary style but may be heard in speech, even in the speech of those whom we term "cultivated" or "educated." The literary style varies according to the writer's purpose and his reading public. Therefore it is sometimes **formal;** that is, very obviously self-conscious and mannered, scrupulously preserving the standard spelling and employing variety and complexity of sentence structure. At other times it is **informal,** approaching within limits the ease and familiarity of the speech of educated people. This is the kind of writing one expects to find in the better class of journalism. Colloquial language, however, varies according to the social background and education of the speaker; its usual divisions are into upper or **cultivated,** middle or **popular,** and lower or **vulgate.**

Dialect speech is generally recognized as regional, though the term is also applied to social levels. As used by linguists, however, the term does

to make worse

the US; to be avoided

not carry a pejorative connotation. In England, at least in the recent past, regional or provincial speech has been regarded as substandard, but in the United States this distinction is not valid. The common notion that regional speech, insofar as it deviates from spelling pronunciations and rules of school grammar, is inferior is especially to be avoided here.

The term **substandard** is variable in meaning. In England it has been applied to deviations from the type of English known as "Received Standard."[1] In the United States it may be applied to characteristics which would be avoided by educated folk generally. However, since standards vary to some extent from region to region and are often difficult to establish objectively, it is perhaps preferable to use the less pejorative term **nonstandard.**

It is also pertinent at the beginning of any study of the history of the language today to make clear that there are two methods by which linguistic study can proceed. The older method, with which we are here mainly concerned, is historical or **diachronic.** In this process we examine a language as it has changed from one period to another to find answers to the question: How have things come to be what they are? The other method ignores this question, looks only at the state of language as it is, and asks: Assuming that language is relatively static, how can it be analyzed? How is it structured? How does it work in this one period? This is a purely **synchronic** or descriptive method. The two methods suppose two distinct points of view. Thus to the synchronic analyst *lady* and *window* are simply two irreducible base forms, and the historic fact that they originated as compounds is not at all relevant to his purposes.

Synchronic and diachronic linguistics may, of course observe the same data, but for different purposes. The difference is not a matter of which is right and which is wrong, but of which is more appropriate to a given investigation. In fact, there are times when one method supports or confirms the other. Suppose, for example, we are examining the parallelism in *handiwork, handicraft,* and *fisticuffs.* How would their forms be analyzed synchronically? A first step might be to compare the first two with *handyman* and assume the compounds *handy* plus *work, handy* plus *craft,* and *fisty* plus *cuffs.* All six of these items are recognizable separate words which might well enter into composition. To be sure, *fisty* is not as

---

[1] Also "Received Standard Pronunciation" or simply "Received Pronunciation," abbreviated RP.

common as the others, but it is sufficiently attested. A little further consideration, however, reveals that *handi-* of *handiwork* does not mean the same thing as *handy-* of *handyman;* that is, they are not semantically equal. *Handiwork* and *handicraft* have semantic equivalents in *handwork* and *handcraft*, but there is no **handman* or **fistcuffs*.[2] Eventually we are led to the conclusion that the three compounds are made up of base forms bound by the empty connective form *-i-*. Looking now into the history of the words we find that *handiwork* has historical priority, deriving from Old English *hand-geweorc*, by phonetic reduction of the prefix *ge-*, which is nowhere else preserved in English and which has no longer either semantic or grammatical function. *Handicraft* and *fisticuffs* were formed later on the analogy of *handiwork*. Thus the historical and descriptive explanations supplement each other.

However, new concepts have been developed in modern synchronic studies which have led to many exciting discoveries about language. These have so enriched our understanding of historical periods that we must make use of them, and as the occasion arises they will be explained.

---

[2] An asterisk before a word indicates that it is a hypothetical reconstruction of which no written record remains.

Part I

THE PROCESSES OF LINGUISTIC CHANGE

Chapter 2

WORDS AND
LEXICAL CHANGE

The evolution of language can be more clearly understood if we know something about the "mechanics of change." Let us begin with changes that affect whole words (lexical and semantic change), since these are easier to recognize and comprehend than changes in the individual sounds of words.

Lexical Change

A thorough discussion of lexical change might conceivably begin with the question, "What is a word?" Most people take the existence of the word for granted because in our eye-minded attitude toward language we are accustomed to word divisions in print. To some, however, it is puzzling to be told that many linguists consider the word indefinable, and some even doubt that it exists as a separate linguistic entity. Nevertheless, we shall be satisfied here to accept the existence of the separate word as it is commonly understood. We may, of course, recognize that the boundary that separates word from phrase is sometimes blurred and that there is a temporary middle period between word and phrase. The expression *howdy-do* may be in such a transition, just as *good-bye* was a few hundred years ago.

The **lexicon** (that is, the total word resources of a language) is modified through the loss of old words and the introduction of new. One of the principal causes of loss is social change. Old ideas are given up and old customs give way to new. Words relating to horse-drawn vehicles in daily use in the horse and buggy days are now seldom used, and were they not preserved in older literature, and therefore in dictionaries, younger people would find them quaint, if not unfamiliar. Interest in horse-racing may have kept alive such words as *colt* and *filly*, but few young people growing up in our large cities today would know the referent for *crupper*, *sorrel*, *brougham*, or even *hansom cab*. On the other hand, *carburetor* and *windshield* are now commonplace, though a hundred years ago they would have been considered very strange words. Even *garage* was unknown in 1901 to the compilers of the *OED*,[1] and the earliest occurrences in the Supplement that was in use in 1902 were then printed with inverted commas. And, of course, *helicopter, spaceship, television, aeronaut,* and *count-down* have become new household words in the present generation. Extreme popularity is no guarantee of a word's survival. In fact, popular terms may be as short-lived as popular acclaim. In the first half of this century the terms *fox-trot* and *two-step* were universal in the vocabularies of the young and gay. Now they are probably as evocative of the past as the family album.

Words pass out of use also for reasons that are not altogether clear. It is only occasionally in the United States, and then among older people, that we hear the word *fetch*, except perhaps in the semiproverbial phrase *fetch and carry*. Yet we have by historical descent no other word of the same connotation, 'go and get and bring back,' unless we consider that *bring* is now a satisfactory substitute. Another dying term is *lief* in "I had as lief stay here as go elsewhere." One indication of its passing character is that when used at all it is becoming confused with *leave* in "I would just as 'leave' stay here as go elsewhere." And if *lief* is obsolescent, its comparative and superlative forms, *liefer* and *liefest*, are so seldom heard as to be obsolete, like Shakespeare's *wight* and *wot*.

Sometimes words are saved from oblivion by being used in special familiar contexts that one expects to be old-fashioned, like the language of the Bible or of prayer, where we still recognize *thou speakest, he speaketh, abide* (in the sense of 'dwell'), *bier;* or like certain phrases alluded to above which have become proverbial tags, such as "to work with might and *main*," "to have neither *kith* nor kin." Obviously some of these expressions, like the last two pairs, owe their survival to their occurrence

---

[1] *OED: Oxford English Dictionary,* also called *New English Dictionary* (*NED*). On its general character and outstanding importance, see pp. 263–64.

in easily remembered alliterative groups, such as *friend or foe*, *widow's weeds*, *wend one's way*, *bed and board*, etc. Expressions of this class may appropriately be termed **archaic.**

New words which come into a language result from borrowing, from new combinations of older elements, from modifications of older elements, and from coinage.

BORROWING

One cause of borrowing from another language is that large populations speaking different languages live side by side. As we shall see later, borrowing from neighbors is illustrated by the introduction of Scandinavian words into English after the Viking invasions and by the heavy influx of French words into English after the Norman Conquest. In modern times also, with the spread of the British Empire into all parts of the world, English-speaking communities borrowed words from people of other languages with whom they lived in close proximity, such as the American Indians, the Spanish Americans, German immigrants, the Dutch colonists in America, the Boers in South Africa, and even, in the case of *boomerang* and *kangaroo*, the aborigines of Australia.

Another cause of borrowing is the recognition of superior values in other linguistic cultures; such borrowing is sometimes called **cultural exchange.** The most notable influence of this type on English has been Latin, which for the whole course of the recorded history of English has been revered as the language of learning. In addition, it was for centuries the international language of Europe and the language of the Western Christian Church, so vital a part of European civilization. French learning and literature, too, have from time to time been extensively cultivated by large numbers of educated Englishmen, thus strengthening the influence which began with the invasion of the Normans. Less in bulk but still significant are borrowings occasioned by special kinds of cultural superiority. Thus we have from German education: *kindergarten, seminar, semester;* from Italian art: *cadence, stanza, concerto, symphony, sonata, piano, soprano, tempo, fresco, studio, prima donna;* from medieval Arabic learning: *algebra, alchemy, alkali, cipher, zenith;* and, of course, from Hebrew in the sphere of religion: *alleluia, amen, cherub(im), jubilee, seraph(im), shibboleth.* Finally, a large number of familiar household words have come to us over the centuries with the importation of foreign commodities: *banana, ketchup, chocolate, coffee, ginger, lemon, molasses, pepper, pongee, quinine, sherbet, sugar, taffeta, tea, tobacco, turban.* Even place names connected with the production of commodities have become a common part of our working vocabulary: *calico, cashmere, champagne, china, cologne, copper, damask, lisle, milliner, muslin, parchment, shantung, sherry.*[2]

COMPOUNDING

New combinations are continually being made to refer to new objects or experiences. In fact, this is one of the earliest and most ingrained tendencies in our language, though to some extent it was lessened by extensive borrowing during late medieval times. A glance at Old English poetry will show how picturesquely this resource could be used. Here compounds of the following type are abundant: *broad-gabled, folk-hoardings, heaped-up, land-dwellers, mead-hall, ring-prowed, whale-road.* Compounding continues to be a familiar device in modern English despite the influence of Latin and Greek, as we see in many well-established forms: *ashpit, bookkeeper, dishcloth, floorwalker, frying pan, handyman, housekeeper, living room, typewriter.* In more recent times compounding has continued: for example, *airborne, airport, boiling point, car wash, clothes dryer, dishwasher, driving range, jet-propelled, landing field, time purchase, windshield.* If anything the pace is accelerated in popular speech: *disc jockey, hot dog, top dog, hepcat, drag race, twin bill, snow job.*[3] In sports language, even the well-established *consecutive* has recently given place to *back-to-back.* One might lament here the waning influence of the literate minority in public affairs, but it cannot be denied that such figurative expressions flow from the same imaginative use of language that brightened the pages of Old English poetry.

In compounding it is interesting to observe a process at work. The tendency in English from ancient times has been to move the accent to the first syllable of nouns and adjectives but in the opposite direction in verbs. When nouns like *moustache* or *cigarette*, for example, appear first in

---

[2] The origins of these words may be found in the etymologies given in such convenient reference books as *Webster's Collegiate Dictionary* or *The American College Dictionary.* See also references on p. 16.

[3] It will be noticed that some of these terms are printed as one word, some as two words, and some hyphenated. There is no perfect consistency in this matter. See below.

English they retain their foreign stress on the second or later syllable. In the course of time the stress shifts to the first syllable, unless the change is impeded by insistence upon "correct" pronunciation. In the latter event, practice will vary. In the United States *moustache* is stressed on the first syllable by many respectable speakers, and *cigarette* is commonly so stressed, though the more educated speakers avoid it. Among educated speakers of England, stress is preserved on the later syllable of both words. On the other hand, *garage*, which in the United States maintains the foreign stress on the second syllable, is commonly heard in England with stress on the first syllable. More recently, the popular term *hi-fi*, which sprang into general use in the fifties and sixties as a clipped form for *high fidelity*, was used first with the stress proper to the original noun phrase, but is now heard with stress on the first element, especially among less educated speakers, who thereby give the word welcome in the language as a new compound noun. At all events, when a new combination of words approaches the status of the compound noun, shift of accent to front element commonly testifies to the development.

It is sometimes difficult to tell, however, when the elements of a new formation are closely enough tied to be regarded as one word. The spelling practice among printers is not consistent enough to be a safe guide to linguistic fact. For example, *icecup* and *iceman* are printed as one word; but, despite the fact that *ice pack* and *ice water* are invariably stressed in the same way, and *ice cream* rather commonly so, they appear as separate words.[4] From the point of view of linguistic history one would be justified in giving all of these the same status. That is to say, when in a new compound noun the stress shifts from the second to the first element, it is being used by the speech community as one word, whatever the custom of printers may be.

Some old compounds are so modified by phonological change that their character is concealed. In medieval and early modern times our numeral *one* was pronounced without the initial sound that makes it sound like *won*. In that period it was compounded in *alone* (all-one), *atone* (at-one), and *only* (one-ly). Such forms, sometimes called **amalgamated com-**

---

[4] It will be noticed, however, that in the formative stages of compounding, these five words are not all alike. In the first three *ice* was originally a noun and would normally carry stress, whereas in *ice cream* and *ice water* it was first adjectival in the form *iced*. In the general use of these words, however, this distinction is forgotten.

pounds, are also illustrated in *Christmas, daisy, doff, don, holiday, lord, lady, sheriff, window.*[5]

Affixing

Another familiar method of word formation is the use of **affixes,** that is, prefixes and suffixes. In the oldest periods of the language these were of the native Anglo-Saxon stock. The prefix *on-* was then very frequent, and survives today in its modified form *a-,* in words like *about* and *among.* In this form it has continued to be used since Old English times to make many new compounds: *abroad, aflutter, afoot, afoul, aside.* Similarly *æfter-* (after), *be-, mis-, of-, ofer-* (over-), *un-, under-, up-, ut-* (out-) were extensively used in word making and continue to be so used today. In this group also we should include *with-* as represented in the modern forms *withdraw, withhold,* and *withstand,* but the meaning of the prefix *with-* has changed so far from its Old English (OE) meaning, 'against,' that it cannot now be used to form new compounds. Likewise *to-,* as used in *today, together, tomorrow,* has ceased to be active. The others, however, are called upon continually in modern word formation: *belittle, overdraft, outmaneuver, outboard, afterthought, underdone.*

From this early period also come some of the most useful suffixes in the languages: *-dom* (kingdom), *-en* (oaken), *-er* (baker), *-ful* (wonderful), *-fast* (steadfast), *-hood* (manhood), *-ing* (dwelling), *-ish* (childish), *-less* (beardless), *-ness* (holiness), *-some* (winsome), and others as well. Two call for special comment. From OE *-lic* we derive both *-like* and its weakened form *-ly.* The latter of these has been from early times a standard suffix, a means (but not the only means) of forming adverbs from adjectives and adjectives from nouns. Thus we have *manly* besides *mannish* with different connotations. In later times, however, the strong form *-like* came also to be used as a suffix, giving us again double forms, *childish* and *childlike,* also with different connotations.

One other interesting suffix is *-s,* originally a genitive (possessive) ending, but used also to form adverbs as in *nowadays* and *sometimes.* It was

---

[5] The original form of these compounds can be found in an etymological dictionary: for example, C. T. Onions *et al., Oxford Dictionary of English Etymology* (Oxford, 1966); Eric Partridge, *Origins: A Short Etymological Dictionary of Modern English* (London, 1958); or Ernest Weekley, *A Concise Etymological Dictionary of Modern English* (New York, 1952).

used frequently as an ending in *-ways* to form such adverbs as *always* and *sideways*, or, with a variation in spelling, in *once*, *twice*, and *thrice*. Unfortunately Dr. Samuel Johnson, the great lexicographer of the eighteenth century, made the blunder of labeling the adverbial genitive *-ways* a corruption of *-wise*, as in *crosswise*, and since his time it has been regarded by many people as inferior to *-wise*, or has been used, if at all, without the *-s* ending, as in *straightway*. However, *-ways* is of ancient lineage and has been accepted by many great writers, such, for example, as John Keats in "La Belle Dame Sans Merci":

> *For sideways would she lean, and sing*
> *A faery's song.*[6]

In very recent times *-wise* has caught the public fancy in a special way, and our ears are now almost daily abused by its needless, if not ludicrous, repetition (*wealthwise, percentwise, salarywise*).

As Latin and French became more and more influential in English word formation, affixes of Latin origin began to multiply. These are so commonly taught in elementary English instruction as scarcely to require mention. Every schoolchild, sooner or later, learns to recognize prefixes like *ab-*, *ad-*, *circum-*, *con-*, *contra-*, *inter-*, *intra-*, *per-*, *re-*, *sub-*, *super-*, *trans-*, or suffixes such as *-ary*, *-ate*, *-ion*, *-tion*, *-ist*, *-ite*, *-ory*, *-tude*.

One effect of the multiplication of Latin forms in the Middle Ages was the disuse of some of the native English forms. We have already noted the loss of *with-*, meaning 'against,' in *withdraw*, *withhold*, and *withstand*. The same fate overtook *for-*, an intensive prefix which we find in the word *forlorn*. Here the particle was prefixed to an original English verb *leosan* 'lose,' of which the past participle form was *loren*. Hence *forlorn* meant 'utterly lost.' This explains our modern use of the word in the sense of 'desolate.' Other familiar combinations of early origin are *forbid*, *forget*, *forgo*, and *forsake*; but this prefix, like *with-*, is no longer used to make new words.[7]

In the modern era Greek has played an increasing part in English word formation, largely but not exclusively to provide new words for our

---

[6] Some texts of Keats's poem give *sidelong* for *sideways*, but there is good reason to believe that the latter is authentic.

[7] The prefix *for-* must not be confused with *fore-* 'before,' as in *forearm, forecast, foreground, forejudge, foretell*.

ever-expanding scientific language, as the student in biology, chemistry, and physics very soon learns; and among the many new words of all kinds are to be found the prefixes *a-*,[8] *amphi-, anti-, apo-, arch-, di-, dia-, epi-, eu-, hemi-, hetero-, homo-, neo-, pen-, peri-, proto-, pseudo-, syn-*.

Perhaps mention should be made here of *-ize*, which was originally a Greek suffix, but came into English directly from French. Many words with this suffix have been in the language in good standing for centuries (*authorize, civilize, colonize, humanize, realize, terrorize*), but a new stimulus has been given to it in the last few decades, resulting in new formations like *concertize, tenderize, finalize*. So popular has this suffix become that, like *-wise*, it has provoked resistance among people of conservative taste. If, however, history can be counted upon to repeat itself, some, at least, of these verbal experiments will eventually be accepted with good grace.

MODIFICATION

Another general process of word change is the modification of existing forms, of which **shortening,** or **clipped forms,** is one type. Usually this tendency is of popular origin and is especially common among the young. Like many other innovations it is frowned upon by the champions of good usage, and has been since at least the time of Jonathan Swift, who was quite severe upon such specimens in his day as *incog, rep,* and *mob,* though, as we see, the last of these was to achieve unquestioned respectability.

The remarkable vitality of this tendency is indicated by the current word *cab,* as in "to call a cab." The word began life in our language as a clipped form of *cabriolet,* used especially in *hansom cab,* a two-wheeled, horse-drawn public vehicle, now only a memory among those who were born about the turn of the century. When horses were supplanted by the internal combustion engine, the vehicle became a *motor cab.* A little later the *taximeter,* invented in Germany, was added and the name became *taximeter cab,* whence *taxicab,* and now back to *cab,* used without a trace of odium.[9] Similarly respectable are *ad, auto, flu, bike, bus, pants, phone, pike* (*turnpike road*), *sub, taxi, zoo,* though, to be sure, some of these would not be used by conservative writers.

---

[8] As in *asexual, asymmetric, amoral;* not to be confused with *a-* from OE *on-*.

[9] Notice also *cabulance,* a portmanteau word, on which see below, p. 21.

Other clipped forms somewhat less dignified abound in school and college jargon: *chem lab, comp, dorm, exam, gym, lit* (*literature*), *math, prof, psych,* and the dubious specimens *soc* (*sociology*) and *sec ed* (*secondary education* as a subject of study). In addition to the *bra* and the *hanky,* we have on the domestic scene the *hi-fi,* which may be either *mono* (*monophonic*) or *stereo* (*stereophonic*).

A second variety of modification is the **back formation,** a new base from which a word in the established tradition is falsely assumed to have been formed by affixing. Three interesting samples have been cited from literary usage.[10] Readers of the Bible remember *firstlings* in the account of Abel (Genesis 4:4), that "he also brought the firstlings of his flock." Shakespeare, perhaps remembering the word from the Coverdale translation, put it into the mouth of Macbeth in the murderous resolution

> *The very firstlings of my heart shall be*
> *The firstlings of my hand.*

[IV.i.147]

Here *-ling* is a suffix similar to *-long* in *endlong* and *headlong,* meaning 'state' or 'condition.' This suffix added to the base in Middle English *groof* or *grufe* gave the adverb *grufeling,* 'in a prone condition.' Shakespeare knew the spelling *groveling* and, assuming the *-ing* to be a participial suffix, used the hitherto nonexistent verb *grovel* in the line

> *If so, gaze on, and grovel on thy face.*

[2 *Henry VI:* I.ii.9]

Sideling, another adverb with the same suffix, meaning 'sidelong' or 'sideways,' was understood by Swift in his *Argument against Abolishing Christianity* as a gerund, " . . . not without stooping, and sideling, and squeezing his body." However, a contemporary of his, Vanbrugh, eleven years earlier in 1697, had written in *Aesop,*

> *She could not bear to see her go*
> *Sidle, sidle, to and fro*

And since that period *sidle* has been accepted as a verb in standard usage.

Also lovers of Keats will remember a line in the "Ode to a Nightin-

---

[10] Thomas Pyles, *The Origins and Development of the English Language* (New York, 1964), p. 285.

gale" in which he used *darkling* in its traditional meaning, 'in darkness.'
Like *groveling* and *sideling*, however, it was strongly suggestive of a verb
with participial suffix. Byron used it so twice in *Don Juan*, once to rhyme
with *sparkle*, a verb of more ancient lineage; but he could not have invented
the form, for Thomas Moore, a friend whose works Byron surely knew,
had already used it in 1800 in his "Ode to Anacreon" to make the same
rhyme:

> *Now with angry scorn you darkle,*
> *Now with tender anguish sparkle.*[11]

Today, however, *burgle* from *burglar* is considered substandard, and
enthuse(d) from *enthusiasm* and *complected* from *complectioned* are still looked
on by some with suspicion, though all of them are as legitimate in origin
as *grovel*, *sidle*, and *darkle*.

In earlier times the sound *-s*, occurring finally in the pronunciation
of *pise*, an Old English singular, and of *cherise*, anglicized from the Old
French, was mistaken for a plural ending, and thus arose the spurious
singulars *cherry* and *pea*. A similar misapprehension resulted in *Chinee*,
first recorded in a famous poem by Bret Harte. Other back formations of
various levels of respectability are *baby-sit, bootleg, edit, housekeep, jell,
launder, laze* (from *lazy*), *peeved* (from *peevish*), *typewrite, student-teach;* many
more can certainly be found in current popular speech.

A third process of modification is known as **folk etymology,** in which
an unfamiliar word is changed by the illiterate or the unwary to a more
common form and thus becomes associated with a false word ancestry.
When the separate elements of Old English *tit* + *mase* 'small bird' passed
out of use, the compound became *titmouse*. In the same way *shamefast*
became *shamefaced*, and *hiccup* was respelled *hiccough*, although the original
pronunciation has remained. The introduction of French words among
the illiterate majority gave rise to a number of such novelties. For example,
berfray, originally a tower built for simple protection, became *belfry* when
put to a different use; *carriole*, originally a *carriage* for four persons, became
carryall; chartreuse became *charterhouse; appentis*, originally a small outhouse
built against a wall, became *a penthouse; picois* became *pickaxe; primerole*
became *primrose;* and *salière*, an instrument dispensing salt, entered into a
compound word *saltcellar*, with the second element modified on the model
of *wine cellar*. From Spanish by the same process *cucaracha* gives us *cockroach*.

---

[11] See *OED*, s.v. "grovel," "darkle," "sidle."

If there is less of this type of change today, it is because people are more widely schooled, at least to a superficial extent. Nevertheless, it is not unknown. Among the unsophisticated *chaise longue* frequently turns up as *chaise lounge*, and *cole slaw* (Dutch, 'cabbage salad') as *cold slaw*. Occasionally there is offered on a menu a dish of hot shredded cabbage designated *hot slaw*, apparently in the mistaken belief that *slaw* refers to cabbage.

COINAGES

We have now come close to the last source of new words—**coinages.** Very recent coinages are sometimes called **neologisms.** Modern neologisms are often purely technical terms made up of Greek forms, but many such terms pass into the everyday language of educated people, and some even become common household terms. These may range from the very familiar *telephone* and *phonograph* to the somewhat more learned *orthodontia* and *eugenics.* As these examples indicate, neologisms are commonly made up of preexisting forms. A new word under these circumstances is a fusing of known elements, native or foreign, or an imitation of one of these. Very few are completely new.

A type of modern neologism, in part resembling amalgamated compounds, results from the deliberate telescoping of two words. Blends of this kind are sometimes called **portmanteau** words. Familiar examples are *brunch, cabulance, cheeseburger, medicare, motel,* and *smog.*

Under the influence of modern advertising and retail selling, many trade names have been constructed from recognizable elements, though their future is impossible to predict. *Victrola,* once in daily use, has, with great changes in recorded music, disappeared from the contemporary vocabulary. *Frigidaire* for a time was used as a common noun for electric refrigeration in the home, but today it has retreated to less general use. On the other hand, *Vaseline* (1874), *aspirin* (1899), *cellophane* (1921), and *zipper* (1925) maintain their vitality and may be accounted at least relatively permanent. Other words familiar to this generation may well become quaint if not unknown to the next: *simonize, Brillo, Coke, Kleenex, Band-Aid,* and *nylon* and its followers, *Orlon,* etc.

A common mode of word formation for trade purposes is the **acronym,** a word made from initial letters or syllables. Currently used acronyms are *Alcoa, Amoco, Pebeco, Philco, Socony, Sunoco.* The process has now spread to other more general uses, of which *radar* (ratio detecting and ranging) is an outstanding example. Names of agencies and organizations are particularly given to this device, as it is an easy way to circumvent a cumbrous organizational title. Thus we have *WAAC, WAVE,* and *WASP*,[12] used as names of women's auxiliary groups in the armed services, and *UNESCO* and *CARE*, post–World War II service groups. The practice has now become so widespread that official titles are sometimes chosen specifically to provide an attractive acronym.

In addition to acronyms simple sets of letters, separately pronounced, sometimes take on the force of words. An impressive example is *OK*, of uncertain origin but surely a hundred years old, and perhaps the most widely known Americanism in the world. In the 1930s government agencies began to be known by initials (*NRA, WPA, OPA*), and the tendency has not since declined; but government is by no means the only stimulus to such activity, as the following list illustrates: *AAU, AFL-CIO, COD, FM, GI, IQ, LP, NAACP, SOS, TB, TV, VIP, WCTU*. The process is also subject to extension by functional shift: the term *master of ceremonies,* once connected with more dignified uses but now designating the central figure in variety entertainment on television and in night clubs, was first shortened to *MC*; now the individual is said to be *emceeing* the program.

The various neologisms mentioned so far are new only as combinations of older forms. Pure coinage, or **root creation,** as we have said, is relatively infrequent, though it does occur to some extent and must have occurred in the past, for new words do suddenly appear in earlier written records, seemingly without discoverable etymons (that is, earlier roots from which they were derived). Thus we see for the first time in the

twelfth to the
fourteenth century: *bad, big, cut, dog, fog,*
lad, lass, pig
sixteenth century: *bet, crease, dodge, gloat, jump*
seventeenth century: *blight, chum, hump, job*
eighteenth century: *bore* ('cause ennui'), *donkey, fun,*
hoax, jam
nineteenth century: *slum, loaf* ('be idle'), *blizzard,*
bogus, rowdy[13]

---

[12] *WASP* is also used now in the United States to mean 'White Anglo-Saxon Protestant.'

[13] Simeon Potter, *Our Language* (London, 1950), pp. 78–79. To the sixteenth-century inventions we might add *drizzle* and to the seventeenth, *gas* and *pun*. In the first group a few of the words may have had a somewhat earlier beginning; for example, some vestiges remain that point to etymons for *dog, cut,* and *pig*.

Some new roots have surely sprung up by the process of echoism, that is, making a word that seems to imitate the sound referred to. In this way *barbarous* is said to have been coined in ancient Greece, and *murmur* even earlier. Certainly *bang, buzz, hiss, pop, slap, splash*, and many other such vivid words originated in this way.[14] But, of course, not all root creations refer to auditory experience; *blurb, fink, goof, jazz, jive* have various explanations. Many such terms are, to be sure, of slang origin and do not survive, but for the term of their lives they are often very expressive. They owe their origin and popularity to the same intuitive word sense that gave to Charles Dickens such appropriate names as Uriah Heep, Murdstone, and Chuzzlewit.

---

[14] A further extension of echoism is found in some infantile forms using reduplication, as *mama, choo-choo, boo-boo*, etc. **Infantilism** is also seen in the current vogue of the diminutive suffix −*y/ie* as in *nightie, hanky, girlie, all righty*, etc.

Chapter 3

WORDS AND
SEMANTIC CHANGE

Denotation and Connotation

Words that remain in the language may hold to their meanings without change over a long period, as is true of words whose referents are things of perennial and commonplace familiarity: *man, woman, eat, drink, live, die, sky, earth,* etc. But even words of this type may shift their significations, as we see in the past meanings for *boy, girl, friend, infant, ladies, gentlemen.* Or words may retain their basic value while taking on special meanings, more or less permanent. *House,* for example, has been stable in its general use for a long time, but we also have special meanings in the common expressions "the house will come to order" and "a full house." The commonest cause of change is the development of new **connotations.** In this discussion let us say the **denotation** is the general or basic meaning. Thus *intangible, impalpable,* and *untouchable* have the same denotation. But one cannot be substituted for the other because by common usage they have acquired an appropriateness to a particular context. They suggest, therefore, more restricted associations than their etymological meaning. The same kind of distinction, or difference in connotation, has developed in *invaluable* and *valueless,* and in *unspeakable, unmentionable,* and *indescribable.*

Connotation arises from the common use of a word, often in ways that give it emotional coloring, more or less heightened. Words that remain in purely technical or learned use seldom gain such coloring. Thus *psittacosis, phoneme, chiaroscuro* probably remain simple referential terms, though quite similar terms such as *tuberculosis* or *grammar*, which are associated with the experiences of pain, fear, or frustration, or which are the occasion of bitter controversy, may develop important connotations. In this connection the histories of *anemic* and *propaganda* are significant, for both of them were originally of learned use and quite innocent of the connotations which they now bear.

In the usual process of change, then, words acquire extended or secondary meanings, which grow in importance to the point of either rivaling or overshadowing the older meanings. In the latter event the original meaning may be forgotten and the process repeated on the secondary meaning. When Coleridge referred in *The Ancient Mariner* (l. 297) to "The silly buckets on the deck," he was reviving an older meaning of *silly* as 'innocent' (here equivalent to 'useless'), but this sense resulted from the specialized use of a word whose earlier meaning was 'blessed' or 'blissful.'[1]

In some instances a word may come to mean (or suggest) the opposite of an earlier meaning. In *Hamlet* (I.ii.256) the words "I *doubt* some foul play" mean 'I fear there has been some foul play,' whereas the present meaning would be 'I suspect there has *not* been foul play.' A somewhat similar development is seen in a word which, for our purposes, takes its beginning in the Latin *cognitum*. From its later form in Old French, *cointe*, it came into English as *queynte*, a spelling which reflected the French pronunciation of that time. The meaning when applied to persons was 'wise,' 'skilled,' or 'clever'; as applied to things, 'ingeniously or cunningly contrived.' In a later specialization the word came to mean 'fine,' 'elegant,' or 'dainty'; still later, and with more restriction in meaning, 'picturesque or pleasing in an old-fashioned way.' In current colloquial use the word now occurs in the derogatory sense of 'odd' or 'ludicrous.'

Semantic shift must not be confused with **functional shift,** though the two often go together. A *star* is a heavenly body noted for brilliance. The word is applied metaphorically to a person who is distinguished for expert performance. When we then say, "She starred in the play," we are using a noun in a different function. Such a functional shift lies behind the use of *sail* and *man* as verbs in senses that no longer contain the original

---

[1] Some of the various meanings of *silly* remained in use side by side over long periods. See *OED*, s.v. "silly," "seely."

denotations: "The Pacific fleet *sailed* out of Pearl Harbor"; "The defenses were *manned* by mere boys."

Euphemisms also play a part in semantic change, though the first step is rather a change of word than of meaning. We tend to shy away from unpleasant facts by substituting a word with less painful or embarrassing connotations. Unhappily the fact and its unpleasant associations overtake the substitute word, which was perhaps not a precise synonym in the first place, and it then becomes freighted with new values, as did *hose, abdomen, powder room, napkin* (for *diaper*), *linen* (for *underwear*), and many others.

Contamination is a shift in meaning sometimes accompanied by confusion of forms. It results from a more or less close accidental resemblance between words of different meaning. For instance, in the thirteenth century the Old French *defouler* was adopted into English with its original meaning 'trample under foot.' Soon, however, its resemblance to the native verb *foulen* 'become foul' (OE *fulian*) suggested the form 'defoul' with the meaning of modern *foul*. In a second stage the native verb *filen/fylen* 'make foul' led to *defilen*, eventually with the modern sense 'defile.' *File* 'make foul' survived into the earlier modern period but ironically was often mistaken as an apheFic form of *defile* and spelled *'file*.

This process can be illustrated today in the verb *demean*, used by discriminating speakers in the neutral sense 'behave' as in *demeanor* but by many other speakers and writers in place of *degrade. Connive*, whose earlier meaning was 'to acquiesce tacitly in evil' seems to have been contaminated by *conspire*, and is now rather generally understood as 'to participate actively in evil scheming.' In this instance the shift results in a very definite loss, for we have no satisfactory word to replace *connive*. From time to time, also, one hears even professional news announcers use *counsel* for *consul*.

Another type of contamination, which is altogether psychological, is the tendency to shy away from words which bear an accidental resemblance to 'taboo' words. A good up-to-date instance of this is the word *niggardly*, which, though completely innocent of any pejorative reference to the American Negro, would probably be avoided by sensitive people in public utterance.

DIRECTION IN SHIFT

Semantic change, like most linguistic phenomena, is difficult to predict, but historically the change can often be seen to follow a direction. One of these is **generalization;** that is, a word extends its application to many more things.

For instance, Chaucer might have said, "Whether I go or ride," that is, "walk or ride." Now *go* is any form of movement from one place to another. Originally *place* was a specific open space; a *thing* was a legislative assembly; a *miscreant* was simply a misbeliever.

With generalization we commonly have **fading,** that is, loss of precise meaning of any kind, so that a word serves merely to express a general attitude or to fill out a syntactic structure. It would be difficult, for example, to relate the meaning of the nouns in the following phrases either to their usual definitions or to their etymological origins: *under the circumstances, a tough proposition, in this case, in the first place, on the other hand, at any rate, at all events, another matter.* Adjectives likewise suffer such loss, particularly in the worn-out hyperboles of popular speech: *lovely, grand, great, gorgeous, stunning, fabulous.* Paradoxically, however, a number of verbs used in forceful idioms in which the meaning of the verbs themselves eludes definition do not show a loss of concrete value: *to go mad, to turn coward, to take sick, to make out.*

Specialization is the reverse of generalization. For example, the earlier meaning of *starve* was simply 'to die.' The word was sometimes found with qualifying phrases like *starve with cold*, recorded by *OED* through the nineteenth century. Currently, however, except in regional speech, we use the word for only one kind of death. *Meat* was food in general, as preserved in the expressions *meat and drink* and *sweetmeats.*

In Chaucer's romance *Troilus and Criseyde*, the heroine, in proposing to send a ring to her uneasy lover, says to Pandarus

> *Wol ye don o thyng*
> *And ye therwith shal stynte al his disese.*
>
> [III. 883–84]

Disese here means 'discomfort,' not 'physical illness.' In a passage better known another famous lover, Juliet, commenting on her sudden falling in love, says

> *In truth, fair Montague, I am too fond.*
> [*Romeo and Juliet:* II.ii.98]

But she does not mean 'too affectionate,' for *fond* in its earlier form *fonned* was the past participle of the Middle English verb *fonnen*, which meant 'to be foolish.' The participle became the adjective *fond*. This was Juliet's meaning and also Hamlet's when he resolved to "wipe away all trivial fond records." The current meaning springs, no doubt, from the notion that love is a special kind of folly. A *doom* was formerly any kind of 'judgment,' a *mansion* simply a 'place of residence'; *to spill* was 'to destroy or subvert'; and *deer* were 'wild animals' of any species, as Edgar in *King Lear* knew when he complained

> But mice and rats and such small deer,
> Have been Tom's food for seven long year.

[III.iv.144-45]

Some specialized meanings are peculiar to a business or occupation. Thus *machine* is not the same thing to a typist as to a seamstress. *Iron* has different referents for golfer and housewife, *stone* for mason, jeweler, typesetter, and surgeon, and *gas* for cook, motorist, and chemist.

Elevation and **degradation** are another pair of opposite trends in change of word meaning. If a word is applied to some person or thing more highly esteemed than its earlier referent, it has undergone elevation. Thus a *chamberlain* was once a servant who performed menial household chores, but later the name could refer to so dignified a person as the Lord Chamberlain, an officer of great authority in the royal government of England. *Constable* and *marshal*, once applied to servants who tended the horses, likewise came to signify positions of some dignity. *Steward* and its variant *Stuart*, as the former royal family of Scotland and England was named, meant originally 'sty-ward' or 'keeper of the sty.' From a Latin beginning in *nescius* 'ignorant,' the English *nice* has risen to the meaning of general commendation, while *penthouse*, once a lean-to shack, has risen in the world in more ways than one.

Somewhat commoner than elevation is **degradation**. As we have said, the process refers not to the use of the word itself but to a change in its signification. *Uncouth*, for example, is a word used only by discriminating speakers, but its meaning has fallen from simply 'untaught' to 'ill-mannered.' The title of a medieval book, *A Mirror for Lewd Men and Women*, would surprise the modern reader, especially if he were told that its contents, far from being pornographic, were of the most serious moral and religious nature. In this title the word *lewd* meant 'illiterate,' the book having been composed for the use of clergymen who preached to the uneducated laity. *Harlot*, which once meant a rascal of either sex, perhaps exhibits both degradation and specialization, as does *lust,* which once meant simply 'pleasure.' Other examples whose earlier meaning is instructive to study are these: *villain, churl, wench, caitiff, cunning, crafty, sly, counterfeit, knave.*

Of course, a word may develop many different uses without losing its central meaning. This process, called **radiation,**[2] is illustrated in the various uses of the word *power,* such as "the power of the king," "the power of his right arm," "water power," "turn the power off," "a power in the community," and, in mathematics, "to the fourth power." Radiation is a very common phenomenon, instances of which can be found by simply turning the pages of a dictionary. The meanings of the words *head* and *charge,* both verb and noun, will repay close study. The effects of radiation are achieved by the forces of imagination in the use of language which lead to metaphor and metonymy. Thus we speak of "the *foot* of a hill," "a *head* of steam," "an *arm* of the sea," "the *face* of the heavens," "the *bowels* of the earth," "the *hand* of Fate." In the popular language the most common figure is hyperbole, as in "you slay me," "it's out of this world"; but, as we have seen, such a development in single words leads to generalization and sometimes fading.

Influence of Individuals

To what extent have words and meanings been influenced by prominent individuals and successful authors? "It is a truth often overlooked," wrote Henry Bradley,[3] "but not unimportant, that every addition to the resources of a language must in the first instance have been due to an act (though not necessarily a voluntary or conscious act) of some person." However true this may be as a general assumption, it is difficult to prove in specific cases. There are, however, examples of the role of an individual in vocabulary trends to illustrate the point. In one of his famous "fireside chats" of the 1930s, President Franklin D. Roosevelt gave a boost in national prestige to the word *chiseler,* meaning 'a cheat,' and was criticized by some very proper persons for stooping to the use of recent slang. In fact, however, as *OED* amply illustrates, the verb *chisel* in the same mean-

---

[2] James B. Greenough and G. L. Kittredge, *Words and Their Ways in English Speech* (New York, 1900), pp. 259 ff.

[3] *The Making of English* (New York, 1904), p. 215.

ing had been used much earlier, both here and in England, though it had not the wide acceptance that the popular president's blessing gave it.

Earlier in the century when President Warren Harding's words and actions were in the center of national attention, his use of *normalcy* was extensively noticed and imitated, but here also we have evidence (*OED*) that he did not invent the form. If these two instances had occurred in earlier times for which the written remains are less complete, we might be tempted to view them as inventions of the two presidents. It is therefore the part of caution to remember that the first written record of a word is not necessarily its first use in the language, nor, on the other hand, is it evidence of wide general use. Words like *fain*, *forestall*, and *scathe* were used in the sixteenth century; yet, as Archbishop Trench reminded us,[4] they were included in the glossary of archaisms appended to Edmund Spenser's *Shepherd's Calendar* by E. K. (sometimes said, though without proof, to have been Spenser's friend Edward Kirke).

SPENSER

Spenser is an excellent example of the influence of an important individual in word making. Chaucer's influence is subject to some difference of opinion, but we know that Spenser, as a matter of conscious technique, strove to establish new forms (*elfin*, *horsey*, *shiny*) and to reestablish old ones (*yclept*). It is somewhat surprising to the modern reader to learn that E. K. considered *askance*, *bevy*, *dapper*, and *sere* as archaic in his time. Apparently Spenser restored them to currency, and a few other words such as *blatant*, *chirruping* (n.) and *sunshiny* may also have been his contributions.

THE BIBLE

The early translators of the Bible from Tindale and Coverdale to the King James or Authorized Version of 1611 have also left their mark upon our language, a fact which should surprise no one, considering both the superb linguistic quality of their work and its long familiarity to all classes of readers. According to Henry Bradley[5] we owe to them either the origin,

---

[4] Richard C. Trench, *English Past and Present* (New York, 1855), p. 72 and *passim*.

[5] Pp. 219–26. But Bradley somewhat overstated the facts, for *beautiful* is recorded earlier than Tindale. See Hans Kurath and Sherman Kuhn, *Middle English Dictionary* (Ann Arbor, 1954—; hereafter abbreviated *MED*), s.v. "beautiful."

the survival, or the general acceptance of such words and expressions as *apparel*, *beautiful*, *damsel*, *elder* (in the ecclesiastical sense), *filthy lucre*, *loving-kindness*, *peacemaker*, *prodigal*, *quick* (i.e., 'living'), *raiment*, *scapegoat*, *tender mercy*, *travail*. One curious specimen is the result not of the genius of the translators so much as of the wrongheadedness of many unwary readers, for whom the phrase *an help meet for him* was persistently misunderstood so as to give the absurd compound *helpmeet*, later folk-etymologized as *helpmate*.

SHAKESPEARE

Shakespeare is commonly regarded as the greatest single benefactor of our language, and in some senses this evaluation is just. Like the English Bible, his plays are so familiar to so many that our cultivated tradition, both literary and colloquial, is studded with felicitous phrases of his creation: "coign of vantage," "tower of strength," "sound and fury," "yeoman service," "sere and yellow leaf," "to the manner born." He had a way also of turning the meanings of common words to such bright and imaginative use that they have a quality of newness: "*cudgel* your brains," "*well-apparell'd* April," "too *flattering-sweet*," "*flecked* darkness," "*fettle* your fine *joints*," "*sharked up* a list of *landless resolutes*," "a violet in the youth of *primy* nature," "revisits the *glimpses* of the moon."

It does not appear, however, that Shakespeare had the same kind of interest in words for their own sake that Spenser had. *OED* records a number of words as occurring earliest in Shakespeare,[6] but it is in every instance possible that the word was known to him from oral circulation. On the other hand, it is highly probable that in an age that was remarkably conscious of linguistic effect and daring in experiment a far-ranging imagination like his was acutely aware of this trend and shared in its activity. It is reasonably certain, therefore, that new word forms, and

---

[6] George H. McKnight lists *bump, dwindle, credent, illume, orb, inauspicious, baseless, multitudinous, cerements, courtship, dickens, lonely.* See *Modern English in the Making* (New York, 1928), p. 188. George Gordon supplies a longer list of such first occurrences, including *aerial, auspicious, control, countless, exposure, fitful,* and others, to the number of about fifty. He also calls attention to the various reactions of Richard Puttenham, Thomas Nashe, and Ben Jonson to the contemporary "liberties taken with the English vocabulary." See "Shakespeare's English" (Society for Pure English, Tract 29, 1928; reprinted in the same author's *Shakespearean Comedy* [Oxford, 1940]), pp. 129–54.

especially functional and semantic shifts, were original with him. An illustration of the point is *boy*, which when used before his time as a verb had the meaning 'to call one a boy,' perhaps insultingly, but his line in *Antony and Cleopatra* (V.ii.220), reflecting his own experience on the contemporary stage, was a new use:

> *. . . and I shall see*
> *Some squeaking Cleopatra boy my greatness. . . .*

In another passage in *King Lear* (I.i.205–08),

> *Will you . . .*
> *Dower'd with our curse, and stranger'd with our oath*
> *Take her, or leave her?*

two words, *dowered* and *strangered*, were newly used as verbs. Instances of this kind are abundant in Shakespeare, but many others, occurring in passages less memorable, remained nonce words, or at most, had only limited currency.   *only once for a special occasion.*

MILTON

We know also that Milton frequently exploited etymological meanings already obsolete, though his experiments were not quite so extensive nor so influential as Spenser's. Examine, however, the origins of the words set in roman type in the following passages from *Paradise Lost*.

> *Thither let us tend*
> *From off the tossing of these fiery waves . . .*
> *And reassembling our* afflicted *powers,*
> *Consult how we may henceforth most* offend
> *Our enemy.*

[I.183–87]

> *Here we may reign secure; and, in my choice,*
> *To reign is worth* ambition, *though in hell.*

[I.261–62]

> *But wherefore let we then our faithful friends . . .*
> *Lie thus* astonished *on th' oblivious pool . . . ?*

[I.264–66]

. . . *underfoot the violet,*
Crocus, and hyacinth with rich inlay
Broidered the ground, more colored than with stone
Of costliest emblem.

[IV.700–03]

Advanced in view they stand—a horrid[7] *front*
Of dreadful length and dazzling arms, in guise
Of warriors old . . . .

[I.563–65]

In courts and palaces, he [Belial] *also reigns,*
And in luxurious *cities, where the noise*
Of riot ascends above their loftiest towers. . . .

[I.497–99]

SCOTT

In the nineteenth century two influential authors of Scottish origin are known to have experimented with our vocabulary. Sir Walter Scott was interested in medieval things and therefore in the older English vocabulary as well as in the English language of Scotland, which preserved features not known in other varieties of English. To him we owe the revival of *glamour*, a doublet of *grammar*, and its variant *grammarye*. Both *glamour* and *grammarye* connoted knowledge of a strange or occult kind. The Old English *rād*, which became *road* in the standard language, retained the original vowel in Scottish English, often spelled *ai* to indicate length. In this form it developed the meaning we express by *inroad*, but had died out after the sixteenth century until revived by Scott, who is thus responsible for *raid*, an invaluable item in the current lexicon.

CARLYLE

Thomas Carlyle's contribution seems to have been more in new compounds, many of which have not taken hold, but it is surprising to think, considering how widespread and commonplace their use is, that *environment, outcome,* and *self-help* were not in use in the modern standard language before his time.[8]

---

[7] So also Spenser, *The Faerie Queene:* I.vii.31.

[8] For a fuller account of the contributions of individuals to the English vocabulary, see Stuart Robertson and F. G. Cassidy, *The Development of Modern English* (New York, 1954), pp. 215–31. See also ch. 16 below on Renaissance scholarly activity in coining words from Latin.

Chapter 4

PHONOLOGY

The Sounds of Language

The development of the lexicon of a language and changes of meaning are usually not the result of changes in individual sounds. Other kinds of development, however, are dependent upon sound changes, and we must therefore learn something of the phonology of a language in order to understand what is going on in its history.

Some Misconceptions

The more fully educated a person is when he first attempts to analyze the sounds of his language, the more likely he is to be confused. As a result of his schooling he reads extensively. In fact, an overwhelming proportion of all that he learns in a formal way comes to him through language that he sees. When his attention is called to language, it is usually presented as something seen. The circumstances of modern culture, therefore, make us eye-minded about language, but we must learn to think quite differently about it if we are to understand what is happening in linguistic change. To this end several cautions are necessary.

1. School experience makes educated people feel that the written or literary standard is the most excellent form of a language, and for some purposes it certainly is; but we have no warrant to view it as the most suitable for all occasions. The spoken language is earlier in the experience of both the race and the individual, and it maintains its own vitality in all ages independently of literary activity. Even in the most civilized of cul-

tures literature remains only a fraction of the whole linguistic activity. The language of literature, moreover, is constantly adjusting itself to keep up with the growth of the spoken language, but the influence of literature upon speech is less persistent. Whether this is a good or a bad state of affairs is not the point. If we are to understand the life history of a language, we must understand how it is used by the mass of the people who speak it as well as by the well-educated minority.

2. Ordinarily we assume that we know what a word is, but much of this knowledge is the memory of conventional forms as they are presented to us by the printer and reinforced by the attention to spelling that absorbs so much of our energies in early schooling. Established spelling and word divisions are, to be sure, very useful, for they enable us to maintain a common written language in all sections of the vast English-speaking world. Nevertheless, the conventional written forms do obscure the real facts.

For example, a piece of homely juvenile dialogue might be written thus:

> What do you want to use them for?
> I'm going to take them apart.

The real stream of speech, however, as far as it can be represented by common symbols, might well be closer to:

> Wahdaya wanna yusum for?
> Ahm gawna takum apart.

3. When speech is represented in such realistic fashion, the inference is sometimes drawn that it is slovenly or illiterate and therefore to be avoided. Actually the speech sounds of all native speakers are somewhat different from those suggested by conventional spellings and word divisions, though not all differ in the same way. There have been, it is true, some instances in which the spelling has permanently influenced the common pronunciation. In *fault* and *vault* the *l* originated as a spelling affectation in words originally borrowed from French and remained silent for a long period, but since the eighteenth century the pronunciation has followed the spelling. Similarly, an unnecessary *c* added to the spelling in *perfect* is now pronounced, though in *debt* and *doubt* the *b*, which originated in the same way, remains silent. Generally speaking, however, the effort

to maintain a strict correspondence between spelling and pronunciation is misguided and pretentious.

4. Finally, it is generally assumed that a word is made up of a number of separate sounds roughly corresponding to the number of letters that make up the spelling. For practical purposes it may be convenient to make this assumption.[1] However, real speech is not "separated" into individual sounds within words but consists of sequences closely linked in segments (words and short phrases) of varying length, each of which is a continuous stream of sound. A common sentence, for example, such as one reads in a news story may be composed of one or several such segments, but the sounds that compose the words and short phrases flow together without a break. This commonplace and obvious fact is of the very first importance in understanding how certain kinds of sound change take place. In attempting to represent this stream of sound accurately we find that the traditional alphabet is not a sufficiently precise instrument for the purpose; hence we invent what is called a phonetic alphabet composed of some familiar letters and some strange symbols, each one defined so as to represent approximately the same sound value wherever it is used.

The Phoneme and Its Allophones

As we learn to use the phonetic symbols we soon make two important discoveries. The first of these is the ambiguity of our common alphabet. In *break*, *breathe*, and *breath*, the spelling *ea* represents three different sounds and requires three different symbols. Also some single letters stand for a group of sounds, such as the personal pronoun *I*, which in phonetic notation requires two symbols [ai]. On the other hand, two or more letters may require only one symbol. In *thing*, for example, *th* is one sound, and *ng* is one sound, so that the whole word requires only three symbols [θɪŋ].

The second important discovery has already been alluded to. Two sounds which seem at first glance to be the same will be found upon close inspection to be somewhat different because, as parts of a continuous stream of speech, they are slightly modified by their position. For example, the words *top*, *stop*, *later*, and *late* all appear to contain the same sound, [t], and for most practical purposes this is so; but a trained phonetician

---

[1] We leave out of account at this point certain gross inconsistencies in spelling such as the fact that *buff* rhymes with *rough* or that *so*, *toe*, *throw*, and *though* all rhyme.

would find that they are different and represent them differently in a detailed phonetic transcription. In general, however, we ignore such differences and regard these four sounds as one. In other words, the difference between one of these *t*'s and another will not signal a difference in meaning. In technical language they all constitute one **phoneme.** If we should want to refer to the fact that this phoneme is not always precisely the same sound, we would say, also in technical terms, that it has four **allophones.**[2]

one or 2 or more var-iants of the same phoneme

The phoneme is so important a feature of language study today that it merits a little further attention in the interest of clear understanding. Any native speaker, even a child who cannot read, will recognize the difference between *pen* and *pin* as very significant, despite the fact that the phonetic difference between the vowels is relatively slight, because he is accustomed to using this slight difference to make big differences in meaning: *bet/bit, let/lit, red/rid, slept/slipped,* etc. The difference then is phonemic. On the other hand, the vowel in a word like *bad* will vary in different regions of the English-speaking world, and the difference will be phonetically as great as that between *pen* and *pin;* but this difference will not matter to any native speaker, because it doesn't *mean* anything different; in other words, it is not a phonemic difference.

What is para's point - getting at what?

BUT?

Making the Sounds of Speech

phoneme - smallest units of sp. that disting. one utterance from another.

Speech, as everyone knows, is produced in the mouth by the activity of the tongue as it controls the flow of sound made by the breath and the voice. Hence we sometimes speak of the parts of the mouth as speech organs. Actually we have no organs which have been adapted by nature for speech in the same sense in which the eye has been adapted as the organ of vision. Man has invented speech and trained himself to use for this purpose organs already part of his physical structure.

This distinction is important because, at the time in our young lives when we began to respond to speech stimuli, we could have learned to use a theoretically infinite number of different sounds. By constant and repeated practice, however, we fitted ourselves to use expertly a relatively small

---

[2] In some treatises phonemic transcription is enclosed in slant lines and distinguished throughout from phonetic transcription, which is enclosed in brackets. In this text we will generally disregard this distinction and use brackets throughout except in the summaries of changes of phonemic structure, where the distinction between phoneme and allophone is essential.

number of these possibilities, and at the same time we unfitted ourselves to use all the other possibilities. In another speech culture, however, we would as easily have learned a completely different set of muscular habits. A child born of Chinese parents and separated from them immediately after birth to be raised in an English-speaking society would speak English with the same precision as his English foster brothers, and would no doubt experience the same difficulties they would experience in learning to speak Chinese in maturer years. Since, then, there is nothing "natural" or "essentially right" in any language system, there is no violation of natural or moral law involved in any purely linguistic change.

Classification of Sounds

The parts of the oral passage which are used in the making of speech sounds—speech organs, if you will—are the tongue, the vocal cords, the uvula, the nasal cavity, the roof of the mouth, the teeth, and the lips. (See the illustration opposite.) Sounds are therefore partly classified and named accordingly.

CONSONANTS

The classification of **consonants** is as follows:

Labial or **bilabial,** when the lips form the point of articulation, as in *pull, bill, will, mill.*

Labiodental, by interaction of lip and tooth, as in *fear* and *veer.*

Dental, when the tongue rests against the teeth, as in *thin* and *then.* The first of these two sounds is represented by the Greek letter theta [θ] and the latter by a symbol from the old English alphabet, the "crossed *d*" [ð], called also *eth.*

The roof of the mouth is divided into three areas. Immediately behind the teeth is a convex ridge called the alveolus. Behind that is the hard palate and still further back, the soft area called the velum. Hence we have sounds classified as:

Alveolar, like the initial sounds of *tin, din,* and *sin.*

Palatal, like the initial sound of *shin.* This is represented by the long or "straight *s*" [ʃ] or by the "checked *s*" [š]. Corresponding to this sound is another which never occurs initially or finally in native English words

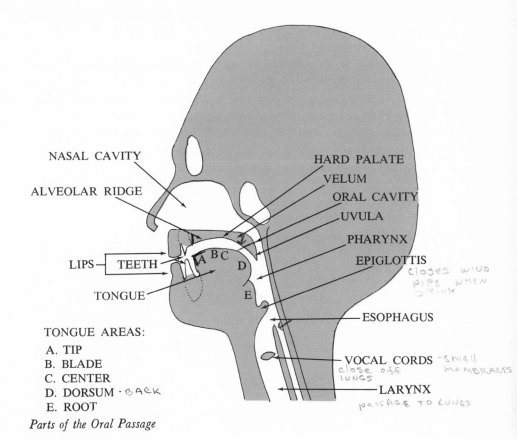

NASAL CAVITY

ALVEOLAR RIDGE

LIPS — TEETH

TONGUE

HARD PALATE

VELUM

ORAL CAVITY

UVULA

PHARYNX

EPIGLOTTIS *closes wind pipe when drink*

ESOPHAGUS

VOCAL CORDS *-small membranes close off lungs*

LARYNX *passage to lungs*

A B C

D

E

TONGUE AREAS:

A. TIP
B. BLADE
C. CENTER
D. DORSUM *·BACK*
E. ROOT

Parts of the Oral Passage

but is found as the medial consonant in *pleasure*. Its symbol is the "tailed *z*" [ʒ] or the "checked *z*" [ž].

   Velar, like the initial sounds of *cull* and *gull*. Some varieties of [k] and [g] as in *kit* and *give* are articulated far enough forward in the mouth to be called palatal, but the difference is ignored here because it is not phonemic. Another important velar consonant is the final sound of *sing*, corresponding to the spelling *ng*, which never occurs in English initially. It is represented by a "tailed *n*" [ŋ].

   In the rear of the velum is a small visible projection called the uvula; behind this a passage connects the throat with the nasal cavity. When the uvular part of the velum, which is of course movable, closes off this passage, as it does in most of the sounds of English, the nasal cavity does not function. But when the passage is left open, part of the voice stream enters and vibrates in the nasal cavity, producing the sounds called

Nasal: [m], [n], [ŋ].

Below the uvula is the larynx, visible from the outside as the "Adam's apple." If you place your fingertips here and make a buzzing sound, you will feel a vibration which is set up in the larynx by the vocal cords. Despite their name these vocal cords are not cords like the strings of a violin, but consist of two folds of tissue which can be drawn together and closed at the middle like a pair of tiny curtains. The opening between is called the glottis, from which issue sounds called

Glottal, the most important of which in English is that found as the initial sound in *house*, [h].

When the vocal cords are closed, the breath sets them in vibration, as mentioned above, and the resulting type of sound is what we call "voice." Not all sounds, however, are accompanied by this vibration. Hence it is possible to divide sounds into

Voiceless, such as [p], [t], [k], [s], and the corresponding

Voiced: [b], [d], [g], [z].

If you have been attempting to reproduce the sounds so far referred to, you will notice that they are produced by a narrowing of the mouth passage so that the breath or voice is pressed through with a frictional noise. This is accomplished in several ways. The voice stream may be stopped altogether and then released, giving us the sounds called **stops,** which may be either voiceless or voiced: bilabial, [p] and [b]; alveolar, [t] and [d]; velar, [k] and [g], to which may be added the voiced glottal stop [ʔ].

In other sounds the breath or voice is not interrupted completely as in the stops, but is continued through a narrowed passage with frictional noise. Such sounds are therefore called

Fricatives, also occurring as voiceless and voiced pairs: labiodental, [f] and [v]; dental, [θ] and [ð]; alveolar, [s] and [z]; palatal, [ʃ] and [ʒ]; and the voiceless glottal [h]. Somewhat similar to these are the

Affricates,[3] each composed of two sounds in very close succession: the voiceless, [tʃ] as in the initial sound of *chew*, and the voiced, [dʒ], as in *jaw*. In a third group almost no frictional sound is heard. These are the

Laterals, the initial sound of *low*, [l]; nasals, as already explained, [m], [n], [ŋ]; **semivowels,** as in the initial sounds of *run*, [r]; *we*, [w];

---

[3] The affricates are sometimes classified as single sounds, and represented by [č] and [ǰ].

year, [j]. These are all generally voiced, but there is some difference of practice in regard to [w]. Some speakers make a distinction between the initial sounds of *where* and *wear*, *which* and *witch*, *whether* and *weather*. [w̥] (or even [hw]) is preserved in Scotland and Ireland, and in some parts of the United States, especially when it is supported by the influence of the schools. In other parts of this country, notably in the East, [w] is used rather generally, even among educated speakers. The same is true for the educated speech of Southern England.

CONSONANTS OF PRESENT ENGLISH *(FRENCH HARD FOR FOREIGNERS TONGUE BET. TEETH)*

	LA-BIAL	LABIO-DENTAL	DEN-TAL *(INTER)*	ALVE-OLAR	PAL-ATO-ALVE-OLAR	PALA-TAL	VELAR	GLOT-TAL
Stops:								
Voiceless	p			t		k	k	ʔ
Voiced	b			d		g	g	ʔ
Fricatives:								
Voiceless		f	θ	s	ʃ (š)	[ç]*	[x]*	h
Voiced		v	ð	z	ʒ (ž)		[ɤ]*	
Affricates:								
Voiceless					tʃ (č)			
Voiced					dʒ (ǰ)			
Nasals	m			n		ŋ		
Laterals:								
Voiceless								
Voiced				l			l	
Semivowels:								
Voiceless	w̥ (ʍ)							
Voiced	w			r		j†		

* The voiceless palatal and velar fricatives [ç] and [x] and the voiced velar fricative [ɤ] do not occur in Modern English, but will be referred to in reviewing the sounds of Early English.

† The symbol [y] is commonly used today for the palatal semivowel, but since we must reserve the [y] for the Old English high front rounded vowel, the use of [j] is more convenient for the semivowel.

S, ʃ long s, š - carrot

Before going on, test your understanding of the nature of the consonant phonemes by working out the following exercise. Each of the pairs below is a minimal pair. (What does this mean?) Select the contrasting elements in each pair and name the significant feature or features of enunciation in which they differ. For example:

bill–pill	b–p	voiced–voiceless
pill–kill	p–k	labial–palatal
bill–till	b–t	voiced, labial–voiceless, alveolar
bill–sill	b–s	voiced, labial, stop–voiceless, alveolar, fricative
night–knight	none	

kit–pit, mitt–nit, tug–tuck, mutt–mush, sip–lip, ship–rip, tip–whip, shove–dove, seem–seen, run–rung, sum–sung, ridge–rich, chuck–tuck, chuck–shuck, measure–mesher, edge–etch, writ–mitt, knit–nip, sat–gnat, nature–neighbor, fissure–fisher, leisure–leecher, lesion–legion.

VOWELS

All of the sounds so far described are called consonants. The remaining sounds are **vowels.** It will be noticed, however, that as we describe the consonants we progress from narrow opening to wide opening. When we come to the [w] and [j] the dividing line between consonant and vowel becomes quite vague.

In fact, the main difference between the consonants and vowels is the degree of mouth opening. The vowels are voiced and are produced with a wider mouth opening than the consonants. The degree of opening is determined by the position of the tongue. When it is elevated toward the roof of the mouth, the passage becomes narrower, as in the vowel of *me,* and as the tongue is lowered the passage becomes wider, as in the sound *ah.* According to the height of the tongue, then, vowels are classified as **high, middle** (or **mid**), and **low.**

However, low or high elevation does not take place uniformly along the entire length of the tongue. The vowel in *me* is pronounced by high arching of the front of the tongue toward the forward part of the palate. On the other hand, *ah* is pronounced with relatively little arching of the tongue, and that little is farther back in the mouth. Hence we classify vowels as **front, central,** or **back** according to the position at which the greatest elevation takes place.

Compare also *tea* and *too*. The second of these vowels is accompanied by a puckering or forward rounding of the lips, which enables us to distinguish **unrounded** and **rounded** vowels.

Finally, since the tongue is a muscle, it may be tensed as in the vowel of *heat*, or it may be more relaxed, as in *hit*. Hence a vowel may be **tense** or **lax.**

In the initial attempt to analyze speech sounds, the student will find the consonants fairly easy to classify, first, because the point of articulation varies over the entire area from the lips to the glottis, and second, because the closure is nearly complete and therefore quite perceptible. With the vowels, however, the closure is never complete and the distance between front and back articulation is very much shorter. It is advisable, therefore, to memorize the position of the vowel symbols with the illustrative words on the vowel chart on page 44.[4] Also, in using the chart it is necessary to keep in mind the following:

1. The positions on the chart correspond roughly to positions in the mouth. It is assumed that the speaker is facing to the left; hence, front refers to the front of the mouth.

2. All of the back vowels except [ɑ] are rounded, i.e., produced with some degree of rounding of the lips.

3. If two vowels occupy one square, the upper is tense and the lower is lax.

4. The high and mid tense vowels, both front and back, usually occur, as in the key words, with length, and therefore are shown with the colon following: [iː], [eː], [uː], and [oː]. In descriptions of Present English

---

[4] For more detailed accounts of the exact character of American English vowels see Arthur J. Bronstein, *The Pronunciation of American English* (New York, 1960) and Charles K. Thomas, *An Introduction to the Phonetics of American English*, 2d ed. (New York, 1958). For the Received Pronunciation (RP) in England see A. C. Gimson, *An Introduction to the Pronunciation of English* (London, 1962). On the pronunciation of individual words the well-informed student will not be able to dispense with John S. Kenyon and Thomas A. Knott, *A Pronouncing Dictionary of American English* (Springfield, Mass., 1953) and Daniel Jones, *English Pronouncing Dictionary*, 11th ed. (London, 1956).

THE VOWELS IN PRESENT ENGLISH

	FRONT	CENTRAL	BACK
HIGH	i (*seat*) ɪ(*sit*)	(y) ɪ (*just*, adv.)	(*pool*) u (*pull*) ʊ
MID	e (*sate*) ɛ (*set*)	ɝ (*fur*) * ɜ (*fur*) † ɚ (*over*) * ə (*over*) † ʌ (*blood*)	(*pole*) o
LOW	æ (*sat*)	a (*card*, N. Eng.)	ɔ (*pall*) ɒ (*wash*) ɑ (*palm*)

r-colored.   † *r*-less.

these vowels would usually, and more accurately, be transcribed as diphthongs: [ɪi], [eɪ], [ʊu], and [oʊ]. It is more convenient, however, in elementary historical accounts to continue to refer to them as "long vowels." Since the difference in these instances between the long vowel and the diphthong is not phonemic, no confusion should result.

╳ 5. In the simplest phonemic notation [ə] or [ər] may be used for all mid central nuclei.

VOWEL LENGTH

Most of the vowels may occur as **short** or **long**. As we use these terms, they actually designate length. It has been common practice in American schools to call the vowel of *mat*, [æ], "short *a*," and that of *mate*, [e:], "long *a*." For our purposes these are not the same vowel at all even though they are represented in the common spelling by the same letter. The difference between short and long might be seen in *at* and *add*. The first of these vowels would be [æ], the long variety being indicated by a colon placed immediately after the vowel symbol. In general, difference in length is not phonemic, but it may be so in some regional forms. For example in the Middle Atlantic states and most of the country to the west *fought* and *fort* are distinguished by the number of phonemes, [fɔt] and [fɔrt]; but in many parts of New England and the South, where [r] in this position is not heard, its loss results in lengthening the vowel [fɔ:t].[5] In such cases the long and short vowels are in phonemic contrast.

As a simple vowel, [a], front or front central, is not heard in many parts of the United States, though it is common in some parts of New England, where it replaces [æ] in words like *half*, *pass*, and *path*. When lengthened by loss of *r* it becomes [a:] as in *park*.

The vowels that recur with greatest frequency in English are not accurately distinguished at all in the conventional alphabet. One of these is commonly called "short *u*," as in *cut*, but it occurs under other spellings as in *come*, *blood*, and *tough*. Its symbol is [ʌ], unless it occurs in nonstressed syllables, when it is designated [ə] as in *about* [əˈbaʊt],[6] *edify* [ˈɛdəfaɪ], *commit* [kəˈmɪt], *column* [ˈkɑləm]. This sound also occurs at the end of many words in those parts of the English-speaking world called the "*r*-less regions,"[7] where *r* is vocalized (i.e., becomes a vowel) before consonants and in final position. In these areas the second syllable of *over* (unless followed by a vowel) would be [ə], whereas in other areas, where the *r* coloring is preserved, the symbol is [ɚ]. The corresponding sounds in stressed position, as in *fur*, are indicated by [ɜ] and [ɝ]. In the *r*-less regions, therefore, *further* is represented [fɜðə] but elsewhere [fɝðɚ].

In those areas where final *r* has been lost it is often restored as a linking *r* before a word that begins with a vowel; thus [faːðə wʌz], but [faːðər ɪz]. By analogy a linking *r* is sometimes inserted after final [ə] in

---

[5] Or [fɔət].

[6] A superior stroke before a syllable is used in phonetic transcription to indicate primary syllabic stress; an inferior stroke indicates secondary stress. See below, p. 68.

[7] In the United States these regions include parts of New England, the South, and the metropolitan area of New York.

words which never ended in *r*, as in *sofa;* for example [so:fər iz]. Such an *r* is called intrusive.[8]

The high central vowel, conveniently referred to as the "barred *i*," is illustrated in the difference between the adjective *just*, as in "he has a just claim [dʒʌst], and the adverb, as in "he just came in" [dʒɪst]. The latter vowel is the subject of a difference of opinion. Some linguists claim that the examples we have just cited are the only minimal pair that can be shown to be in general distribution, and therefore the barred *i* does not have sufficient contrast to support phonemic status. However, there is good reason to believe that phonemic contrast for this sound is more solidly established, at least in some regions. Since this is the majority opinion, we prefer to accept [ɪ] here as a phoneme.

The [ɪ] pronunciations have also been stigmatized as slovenly by those who are much given to spelling pronunciations. For this reason many educated people would probably deny that they use the sound at all, but the truth is that in the daily habits of even the most cultivated speakers [ə] and [ɪ] are the most frequently recurring sounds in English. For example, in the unstressed pronouns *his, her, your, their*, the [ə] or [ɪ] is the usual sound: "Watch your step" [wɒtʃ jɪr stɛp], "Send her home" [sɛnd ər ho:m].

Both of these central vowels are also found in the inflectional syllables *-ed* and *-es: wretched* [rɛtʃɪd], *passes* [pæsɪz], and *churches* [tʃɜ·tʃɪz].

The low back slightly rounded vowel, represented by [ɒ], occurs after *w*, but it varies from one speaker or region to another. Thus in *water*, three different vowels may occur in the stressed syllable: [ɑ], [ɒ], or [ɔ]. The last may be lengthened with partial voicing of [t].

In addition to the simple vowels there are the complex units called **diphthongs.** These are two vowel elements in close succession in one syllable. More accurately, they may be described as a glide from one vowel position to another. Neighboring vowels in different syllables, as in *reality*, are not diphthongs. Also, since diphthongs are sounds they should not be confused with **digraphs,** or two letters representing one sound, as in *head;* or with **ligatures,** two joined letters like *æ.* Many vowels, formerly long, have developed in Present English off-glides sufficient to give them diphthongal character. This is especially noticeable in terminal position and

---

[8] The intrusive *r* should not be dismissed as vulgar. It is common in the speech of educated people in *r*-less regions, in both the United States and England. See below, p. 174.

before voiced consonants. Apart from these, the diphthongs having the widest distribution in American English are the following:

[aɪ] (*my, ice*)   [aʊ] (*how, out*)
[ɔɪ] (*toy, oil*)   [oʊ] (*hoe, moan*)
[ɛɪ] (*hay, main*)   [ɪə] (*idea*)   *diff. from reality*

To these we should have to add as being very common in the *r*-less regions:

[ɪə] (*dear*)   [ʊə] (*moor*)
[ɛə] (*air*)   [oə] (*more*)
[ɑə] (*bar*)   [ɔə] (*war*)
[ɝɪ] (*earl*, metropolitan New York)

All of these are called **falling diphthongs** because the second element of each "falls" from strong stress to weak. In contrast we have also the **rising diphthong,** which "rises" from weak stress to strong [iu], for example, as in *few* or *mute.* In Present English this diphthong is commonly realized as [ju].

Exercises

Test your understanding of the new alphabet.

1. Write the standard spelling for each of the following pairs. For example:

si:p–sɪp   *seep–sip*
brɔ:d–dʒɔ:d   *broad–jawed*
baɪt–bi:t   *bite–beet (beat)*

wæks–tæks, skaɪ–ski:, dʌsk–dʌks, nɔ:d–mɔ:d, næt–mæt, fe:n– *jane*
ve:n, fe:n–fɛ:r, fu:l–fo:l, wu:nd–waʊnd, po:l–pɔ:l, *pale paul* cɑ:m– *calm*
co:m, bu:ti–bɪuti, kʌt–kɪut, pɪur–pu:r, hæt–he:t, mɛt–me:t, *cond*
ru:fɚ–rʌfɚ, pʊl–pu:l, bʌt–bu:t, o:vɚ–o:və, si:r–si:ə, ʃu:r–ʃu:ə,
mɔ:r–mo:ə, pɝt–pɛt, pe:r–pe:ə, ɔɪl–ɝl, tɔɪl–taɪl, kɔ:l–kaʊl,
fɔɪl–faɪl, kwaɪt–kwaɪət, ru:n–ru:ɪn, fʊl–fu:l, rɔ:t–ro:t, *ruin ruin wrought wrote* u:z–ʌs, *ooze us*
ju:z–ju:s, dʒʊz–dʒu:s, jet–dʒet, ji:r–dʒi:r.

use use   year jeer   ?
          Jews juice

ə – schwa

2.   Rewrite the following pairs in phonemic notation:

feel–fill, pate–pet, pair–fair, cane–care, better–butter, can–cane, ran–run, shun–sun, cadge–catch, ketch–catch, car–core, wear–wore, far–four, poor–pour, full–fool, food–feud, puling–pooling, shore–sure, much–match, food–flood, top–tap, rob–cob, rob–robe, robin–robbing, sunk–sung, wind(v.)–wind(n.), fine–fin, lout–loot, file–foil, alms–aims, lounge–lunge, whit–wit, wander–wonder.

feel - fill   [fil   fɪl]

pate - pet   [pet   pɛt]

pair - fair   [pɛər - fɛər].

cane - care   [ken - kɛər]

Chapter 5

HISTORICAL PHONOLOGY

Sound Change

The enumeration of the phonemes that we have just worked out is valid for the state of American English today. There are, of course, other ways of representing these phonemes. One very popular system is that proposed by Trager and Smith,[1] in which the vowels we have classified as long are described on good phonetic grounds as diphthongs, since the length actually produces a glide. Thus *fate*, which we would transcribe here as [fe:t], becomes in the Trager-Smith analysis [feyt] or [feɪt]. Also all of the mid central vowels are classified as one phoneme [ə]. But whatever the system, the analysis is restricted to the present state of the language. All descriptions that eliminate considerations of historical change are, as we have seen, synchronic; but, since we are interested in the history of the language, our point of view must be mainly diachronic. Let us, then, go on to learn something about sound change.

Formerly historical linguists assumed that most sound changes resulted from a process of evolution. Today the precise nature of this process is the subject of some difference of opinion, but controversy can be avoided by simply stating that a sound in one historical period is **replaced** by a different sound in a later period. Despite some uncertainty of the exact nature of the change, it is still possible to speak of various types of sound change and their effects.

---

[1] George L. Trager and Henry L. Smith, *An Outline of English Structure* (Norman, Okla., 1951.)

For example, we say that Old English long *a* (OE *ā* [ɑː]) became Middle English long open *o* (ME *ǭ* [ɔː]) or that ME *ǭ* replaced OE *ā*. It is of capital importance to keep in mind that this change is not primarily a change in written symbols. In fact, spelling changes do not invariably follow sound changes. What we are really saying is that a slight modification of a muscular habit took place. In this instance we would call the change **raising** and **rounding**: raising, because the arching of the tongue became slightly higher; and rounding, because the lips were slightly protruded. The difference between the two sounds is similar to that between the two sounds in American English heard in the pronunciation of *water:* [wɔtɚ] and [wɑtɚ]. This difference is regional, as in the earlier period, but it is not reflected in different spellings.

As we shall see later, extensive raising produced one of the most important series of changes in our language. The opposite tendency, called **lowering,** is well illustrated in the two pronunciations of *creek*. The standard or at least the spelling pronunciation has a very high tense vowel [kriːk], but in a more popular but still respectable variant the vowel is lowered and more lax, [krɪk], rhyming with *pick*. The lowered vowel, also commonly heard in *eagle*, [ɪgəl], is usually rejected as substandard, although in the noun *breeches* the same modification is never questioned.

Change of tongue position can also produce **fronting** and **retracting** in both vowels and consonants. Readers of English poetry have encountered the noun *kirk*, preserved in Northern England and Scotland for *church*. *Kirk* is an older pronunciation whose continuance in England was probably due to Scandinavian influence. The standard form developed from it by fronting of both the initial and final consonants. In this case, since the fronting resulted in a palatal consonant, it is also **palatalization.**

Retraction is illustrated in *handkerchief*. Here the alveolar nasal [n] of *hand* has been retracted to the velar position [ŋ], giving us [hæŋkɚtʃɪf]. A particularly interesting illustration of these two processes is the history of the suffix *-ing*, which in its earliest form was [ɪŋg]. This was Chaucer's pronunciation, but the velar stop [g] was eventually lost. Then in the Early Modern period the velar nasal [ŋ] was fronted to [n], at first in vulgar speech but in the eighteenth and nineteenth centuries in cultivated speech as well (*shillin'*, *puddin'*, *farthin'*, etc.). More recently, however, the spelling has been influential enough to retract this sound again to the velar position, [ŋ]. In the standard speech of the United States, however, [ɪn] is more common among educated people than most of them care to admit.

ROUNDING AND UNROUNDING

Rounding has reference to the position of the lips and is found in all the back vowels except [ɑ]. It consists of a forward movement of the lips such as one experiences in shifting from [iː] to [uː]. Progressive rounding is illustrated in the history of the numeral *one*. In its earliest historical form the word was *ān* [ɑːn], which by Chaucer's time had, in the standard speech, been raised and rounded to [ɔːn], spelled *on, oon, one*. At this stage it entered into the compounds which are preserved as *only, alone,* and *atone*. The rounding process, however, continued so far that the initial sound became a labial consonant, and we now have [wʌn]. Here *w* is the result of progressive rounding, but in other instances *w* itself can be the cause of rounding, particularly in a following *a*, which explains the contrasting pronunciation of such pairs as *war* and *car, quart* and *cart, ward* and *bard*.

The opposite tendency, **unrounding,** is also possible. Thus the vowels of *blood* and *flood*, which according to their early history should rhyme with those of *mood* and *food*, are found today as unrounded vowels. The earlier short [a] before [l] in such words as *all, ball, call, bald,* has become a low rounded vowel, [ɔ], in Modern English, but in a few areas of American English it is unrounded to [ɑ].

VOICING AND DEVOICING

The classification **voiced** and **voiceless** sounds has already been explained (p. 40). When a change occurs in the phonetic environment of a given sound, **voicing** or **devoicing** may take place. The plural *-s*, originally voiceless, becomes voiced after vowels and voiced consonants (*birds, pins, hoes,* etc.). On the other hand, the past tense suffix *-ed*, originally voiced, is devoiced after voiceless consonants so that *massed* and *passed* are indistinguishable from *mast* and *past*. Voicing and devoicing are very common in standard speech. Notice, for example, that the final voiceless consonant [θ] of *north* and *south* is voiced to [ð] before the suffix *-ern*, and conversely the final voiced consonant of *broad* and *wide* is devoiced before the voiceless suffix *-th* of *breadth* and *width*.

Independent and Dependent Change

Sound changes may also be classified as **independent (isolative)** and **dependent (combinative)**. The former take place without the influence of neighboring sounds, usually without explanation, and sometimes not in all dialects. We do not know why Chaucer's first person possessive *mine*, which he would probably have rhymed with *machine*, evolved into, or was replaced by, the modern pronunciation [maɪn]. We know that this change was one of a system of far-reaching changes in all of the long vowels. But the same pattern of change did not generally occur in related languages, and, for that matter, not all of the changes were fully carried out in all the English dialects. In Scottish English words like *house* and *mouse* preserve the original sound [u:] and rhyme with the present sound of *loose;* and in Ireland many of the *ea* words like *sea* and *tea* have preserved an older sound [e:] and rhyme with *may*.

Moreover, this state of flux in the long vowels shows some evidence of continuing. The mid back rounded vowel, formerly heard as [o:] or [ou] in *boat*, *home*, and *holy* is now heard as the diphthong [əu] in cultivated British speech generally, and there are signs of a like development in the United States. Nothing is more indicative of the inherent tendency of the living language to change than the persistence of independent sound shifts.

Dependent or combinative changes result from the influence of neighboring sounds. To some extent they may be due to the intuitive search for economy of effort. For example, when the prefix *in* is placed before a word like *plant* the tendency to modify it to *im* is almost irresistible. This pronunciation, of course, is well established in reputable usage and is reflected in the spelling, but when very similar changes occur in popular speech in violation of the spelling, they are generally condemned as "slovenly" pronunciation. A good example is the word *pumpkin*, of which Kenyon and Knott record the observation, "We were drilled in school not to say [pʌŋkɪn]" and add, "eloquent testimony to its prevalence."[2] Here the loss of [p] and the retraction of [m] to [ŋ] are quite similar to the processes that give the current and reputable pronunciation of *handkerchief*, but the parallel is ignored by those who insist upon spelling pronunciations and who are generally ignorant of the fact that changes such as

---

[2] *Pronouncing Dictionary*, s.v. "pumpkin."

these have been in operation throughout the history of the language and have given us many word forms which are never questioned.

ASSIMILATION

The examples cited above illustrate **assimilation;** that is, the modification of a sound to make it more like, or identical with, a neighboring sound. In *implant* the alveolar nasal [n] has become a labial to share in the labial quality of [p], which follows it. Here the assimilation is only **partial,** because the two phonemes remain distinct. In *immobile (in-mobilis),* however, the two neighboring sounds have become identical phonemes; hence the assimilation is **complete.**

These examples of assimilation find ready acceptance because they have parallels in Latin. Also respectable because of their long-standing use are pronunciations such as [blægəd] for *blackguard,* [kʌbəd] for *cupboard,* [justə] for *used to,* and [hæftə] for *have to.* In popular speech, however, educated people, somewhat inconsistently, often condemn [rɛkənaɪz] for *recognize* and [strɛnθ] for *strength,* though these pronunciations result from the same tendencies as the former and may eventually become as well established.

We have also a type of assimilation which does not permanently modify the phonemic structure of a word, but affects enunciation in particular contexts. For example, in the sentences "We will miss you," or "Won't you stay awhile," *miss you* would be realized as [miʃuː] and *won't you* as [woːntʃuː], though the same modification would not take place in *miss them* or *won't they.* Assimilation of this kind was a recognized feature of Sanskrit and is still called by the name the Hindu scholars gave it, **sandhi.**

DISSIMILATION

On the other hand there occurs, but much less frequently, an opposite tendency in sound change called **dissimilation.** By this process one of two identical phonemes (usually *r*) near each other, but not necessarily side by side, may be made unlike. This also has very ancient precedents which have been taken into English. The first *r* of Latin *peregrinus* became dissimilated in Old French and eventually became English *pilgrim.* In Latin *turtur,* it was the second *r* which became dissimilated to give us English *turtle.* The process is still alive, though its results in the current popular speech are not all fully established. The dissimilation of the first *r* in *stenographer* [stɛ'nɑgəfɚ] and *February* [fɛbjuəri] are nonstandard, though a similar change in *governor* [gʌvənɚ] and *surprise* [səpraɪz] is in much more general use among educated people.

METATHESIS

A quite different kind of development consists in a reversal of position. It is called **metathesis** and was fairly common in the older states of the language. In Chaucer *asked* appears as *aksede* (sometimes spelled *axede*). *Wrought*, which survives in a specialized meaning but was originally the common past tense of *work*, shows metathesis of *o* and *r*. Some other examples occurring in modern use are dialectal or nonstandard.

Metathesis sometimes escapes notice in unstressed position, as in the second syllable of *apron* [epərn], *children* [tʃɪldərn], and *hundred* [hʌndərd], but in stressed positions it is generally avoided by conservative speakers, as, for example, in *perspiration* or *pretty*.

LOSS AND GAIN

Loss occurs when sounds or whole syllables disappear. An obvious example is the loss of final *b* in *bomb, lamb*, and *tomb*. Loss of final elements has been so extensive as to modify the whole grammatical structure of English. More will be said of this effect later. It can be noted here that many words which were polysyllables in the language of King Alfred have in the succeeding centuries suffered loss of one kind or another: *hláforde* has become *lord, hlǽfdiga* has become *lady, náhwæðer* has become *neither; néahgebūr* has become *neighbor*, and so on. Today widespread familiarity with the printed word as well as emphasis upon spelling make such changes unwelcome among the educated, but the tendency is persistent, as is seen in the standard pronunciation of *factory* [fæktrɪ]. Emphasis upon the preservation of all syllables has had an ironic effect on the word *literature*, where efforts to preserve the second syllable have resulted in the growing (though still nonstandard) pronunciation [lɪtətʃɚ]. In cultivated British speech there is less resistance to the elision of the unstressed vowel before *r* in such words as *anniversary, camera, comparable. secretary, suffering*.[3]

---

[3] See Gimson, p. 231.

The opposite tendency, **gain,** is also familiar but less common. This leads some speakers to insert an unstressed linking vowel between two consonants. It is heard in the nonstandard pronunciation of *athletics* [ˌæθəˈlɛtɪks] and *film* [fɪləm]. Readers of Shakespeare, however, will remember this phenomenon in *alarums,* and if we go back farther still, we find that it has produced such standard forms as *blossom, bottom, borough, hollow,* and *sorrow.*

SUBSTITUTION

We have also a type of modification which consists of **displacement,** or the substitution of one sound for another from a different phonological tradition. A good example of this took place in the fifteenth century, when, in words like *bern, derk, fer, smert,* and *ster,* [ɛr] was replaced by [ar], most probably introduced from a different regional dialect. These particular words, and many others as well, adopted a new spelling to agree with the pronunciation, and both remain in Present English: *barn, dark, far, smart,* and *star.*[4]

ANALOGY

The most fruitful source of substitution, however, is **analogy,** which affects both sounds and word forms. The past tense of *bear,* for example, is now *bore,* which does not derive from its Old English predecessor, *bær* or *bæron,* but results from analogy either with its own past participle or with the proper past tense of *swear.* Analogy is familiar to everyone in the early habits of children, who, accustomed to the common pattern *help-helped, kick-kicked, push-pushed,* extend their experience to include *throw-throwed.* The influence of books and schooling will eventually bring them to terms with tradition, but in earlier times when these advantages were the privileges of the few, the force of analogy had a more permanent effect on the language. In Old English there were many more strong verbs than we have today; that is, verbs whose past tense and past participle were formed by a change of stem vowel, as in *sing-sang-sung.* But the ever-increasing number of weak verbs, which added the dental suffix *-d/-ed,* established a prevailing pattern which attracted so many strong verbs to the weak conjugation that today the strong verbs are a dwindling minority.

---

[4] On this development see further, p. 179.

Similarly many older noun declensions have been lost. In King Alfred's time the addition of -*s* to form the plural (and possessive) was only one of several ways to decline a noun, but this numerically superior declension eventually attracted many nouns from the other declensions. As a result we have now only a handful of the older plurals without -*s*, such as *deer/deer*, *ox/oxen*, and *man/men*.

Enough has now been said about lexical and sound change to show that our language is a living process. We can see that the changes still at work are evidence of its vitality and are not different in kind from the changes which, operating for hundreds of years, have fitted our speech and writing to all our needs from the most commonplace uses to the most exalted literary expression. Recognition of these processes, it is hoped, will provide a more intelligent understanding of the history of the English language.

Chapter 6

MORPHOLOGY AND SYNTAX

Word Forms

In our discussion of words and the formation of new words by compounding and affixing, we have already ventured into the field of **morphology,** thus illustrating the fact that the various levels of language have important bearing one upon the other. The word *morphology*, as its derivation from the Greek *morphē* indicates, refers to forms of words or units of form that make them up. These consist of stems (including roots) and affixes. According to their position affixes may be classified as prefixes and suffixes. In some languages there are also infixes, which perform the same function as prefixes and suffixes but are inserted within a stem. However, since they retain only a shadowy existence in English (like the *n* in *stand* as compared to the past *stood*), we may ignore them.

AFFIXES

Affixes may also be divided in another way. Most of those to which we referred earlier are derivational. Their usual effect is to indicate functional or semantic shift, as for example in the addition of *-ness* to an adjective or *super-* to a verb. But there is another important type, which to some extent everyone has confronted who has learned one of the foreign or classical languages usually studied in school. The student of Latin, to choose the most striking example, has mastered an imposing set of word endings

57

which signal grammatical relations and which he calls declensions and conjugations, or, in general, inflections. Suffixes of this kind are therefore called **inflectional.**

STEM

That part of a word which remains when the affix is removed is called the **stem.** Thus in *weaknesses*, with reference to the suffix *-es* the stem is *weakness;* but in *weakness* itself the suffix *-ness* has been added to the stem *weak*, which if further divided can produce only units of sound but not a smaller familiar group of sounds. Hence it is also a **root.**

This example shows that more than one affix may be added to a root, but if an inflectional suffix is among them it must come last. Another way of saying this is that a derivational suffix may be stem-forming, but an inflectional suffix may not. Two exceptions to this rule may be noted. First, a few words like *oxen* and *children* may add the possessive to the plural ending, but these are few and constitute hardy survivors of an older state of the language. Second, we may speak of "having the *makings*" or "seeing many *openings*." In these instances, however, the exception is only apparent, for here *-ing* is really a derivational suffix which forms a verbal noun and resembles the participial ending *-ing* because in the course of history two different suffixes, one derivational and one inflectional, have fallen together.

Obviously, word analysis suggested by these considerations is not identical with that given in a dictionary when a word is divided into syllables. *Webster's Collegiate Dictionary* supplies us with an analysis of *similarity* consisting of five syllabic units, and for some practical purposes this is a useful guide. However, we cannot relate these units to the type of morphological analysis referred to here, though, of course, since the word has been borrowed from Latin, its syllabication has an explanation in the history of Latin forms. But considering only its English environment, we observe a minimal base *simil*, to which we may add the derivational suffixes *-ar*, *-e*, *-itude*, and *-arity*. Apparently *simil* functions as a root stem. Comparison of *similitude* with *magnitude*, *fortitude*, and *plenitude* and each of these with related words suggests that *-i-* functions as a stem-forming suffix, but from the historical point of view we should refer these words to their Latin background, since they came into English ready-made.

In *weaknesses*, however, we have a word completely formed of native elements, *weak* constituting both root and stem to *weakness*, and the latter the stem to *weaknesses*. Each of these, *weak*, *-ness*, and *-es*, is a unit of form to which we give the name **morph**. The last of these is an inflectional morph which expresses plural meaning.

Morpheme and Allomorph

By comparing *weaknesses* with *breakfasts* and *postcards* we discover that the same grammatical meaning is expressed graphically by *-s* and *-es* but that these refer to three phonologically different items [s], [z], and [ɪz]. We count all three together as one significant unit of form, designated a **morpheme**. The three variants are **allomorphs** of the same morpheme; all have the same meaning value and similar though not identical sound. The morpheme may be written {Z}. If we wish to distinguish this morpheme from the phonemically similar morphemes of the possessive singular of nouns and the third person singular of verbs, we may designate them respectively {Z₁}, {Z₂}, and {Z₃}.[1]

Most of the nouns of the language take one or another of the three common plural allomorphs, but any one noun will always take the same allomorph.[2] *Cap*, *mark*, and *mat* always take [s]; *bud*, *bug*, and *tab* always take [z]; *church*, *bush*, and *edge* always take [ɪz]. In other words, their distribution among the nouns of the language is such that one does not replace the other in the same phonetic environment, but together they make up the complement of plural allomorphs; that is, they are in **complementary distribution**.

For the moment we have oversimplified the facts. While it is true that this inflection is found in the majority of the nouns of English (except such as have retained foreign plurals like *alumnae*, *radii*, and *axes*), a few nouns survive from an older system and disturb the simple regularity of inflection toward which English has been moving for centuries. In fact, similar exceptions are to be found in every part of Modern English gram-

---

[1] Notice that the braces mean that the segment included between them is viewed in its morphological value; that is, as a morpheme even though it is composed of only one phoneme.

[2] There are a few nouns which have two plurals. *Hoof*, for example, has *hoofs* [hʊfs] and *hooves* [huːvz], the first of these being regular and the second a still optional older form. However, the second of the two inflectional allomorphs requires a second allomorph of the stem.

mar. Thus *sheep* and *deer* never take any plural ending (in technical terms, they take a **zero** ending [∅]). *Ox*, unlike *fox* and *box*, always takes *-en*. A few nouns like *man, tooth,* and *mouse* have no endings but do take a change of stem vowel. In these words we could say that the stem morpheme has two allomorphs except that the two forms are in grammatical contrast. More accurately, the plural signal is stem change plus zero, for which the symbol [∴∅] will suffice. *Fish* has two possible plurals, [∅] and [ɪz]. If both of these plural forms are used interchangeably by the same speakers they are said to be in **free variation,** but usually they are in semantic contrast, the first referring to the number of individual fish and the second to the number of species. Some noun stems have positional allomorphs; for example *leaf* has [liːf] and [liːv], *shelf* has [ʃelf] and [ʃelv]. These are in complementary distribution.

Two other survivals fit rather badly: *brethren* and *children*. One explanation of these is that the stem has two allomorphs: [brʌðɚ], [breðr] and [tʃaɪld], [tʃɪldr], but the presence of *r* in [tʃɪldr] is disturbing. Moreover, in neither noun can the *r* be confidently left in the stem, for the common pronunciation of the suffix, [ɚn], suggests that [rɪn] and [ɚn] are inflectional allomorphs in free variation.[3]

In a similar way we can discover the allomorphs of the verb inflection for tense: [t], [d], [ɪd], [∅], and [∴∅], as in *passed, rubbed, patted, set,* and *sat;* but again a small number of irregularities surviving as vestiges of an earlier state of the language would have to be accounted for.

Older Inflection

The inflection of the vast majority of English nouns today is very simple—simpler, in fact, than appears in traditional school grammars, where three cases, nominative, possessive, and objective, are usually provided for. For most nouns, however, only two forms occur, a singular base form and a plural form with an inflectional suffix which serves also for the possessive singular. Formerly inflection was more abundant in the English noun and pronoun. The personal pronoun in Old English had four different case

---

[3] The OE plural was *cildru* (later *childer*); thus [r] is one of three redundant plural signals: change of stem vowel, the original *r*-plural, and *-en* borrowed from the OE weak declension. The metathesized suffix *-ern* is at least as old as the sixteenth century, when Richard Mulcaster, who wrote in 1582 on English sounds, implied that it was the more common pronunciation.

forms, and then it was justifiable to speak of the nominative case for the subject, the accusative for the direct object, the dative for the indirect object, and the genitive for possession and other relations as well. The dative and accusative were also used after prepositions.

Thus the masculine pronoun had the forms *he* [he:] in the nominative, *hine* [hi:nə] in the accusative, *him* in the dative, and *his* in the genitive. In Modern English, of course only *him* has survived for the two object cases. In the Old English noun the nominative and accusative had already fallen together. *Eorl* 'nobleman,' for example, was the same in both nominative and accusative singular, as *eorlas* was the same in nominative and accusative plural. But the dative case in both numbers had a characteristic form, *eorle* and *eorlum*, as was also true of the genitive, *eorles* and *eorla*. Obviously, this system is now very much reduced, but the older case names are still sometimes used with the meaning explained here, even when they have no distinctive case forms. Inflectional suffixes have dwindled in importance over the centuries in all the other parts of speech except the personal pronouns.

Free and Bound Morphs

It is apparent that some forms which we have referred to as morphs (*man, child, leaf*) are completely meaningful in themselves and occur as "words." These are **free morphs.** Others, like the inflectional suffixes and positional allomorphs of stems, occur only in combination with other morphs. These are **bound morphs.** Thus, while *roof* is used as a "word," the stem that would remain after removing the plural suffix of *rooves*, that is, [ru:v], cannot be so used and is therefore a bound morph. Usually a compound word is a combination of free morphs: *barroom, lighthouse, outboard*. The meaning of the free morphs in each of these compounds is easy to determine, but occasionally the operations of folk etymology present us with forms analogous to free morphs but with no apparent semantic relation to the compound. For example *cranberry, gooseberry,* and *raspberry*[4] seem to be analogous to *blackberry, blueberry, elderberry,* and *strawberry*, but they do not lend themselves to the same kind of analysis.

As in the new word formations explained earlier, some morphemic features arise from analogy. At one time the standard form of the singular

[4] See *OED*.

possessive pronoun in the first person ended in -*n* (OE *min*). When used as a possessive adjective, this later lost the -*n* before nouns beginning with a consonant. Compare Middle English (ME) *mi fader* with *mine uncle*. Still later -*n* fell out before all nouns. In the predicate position, however, the original ending is preserved. Compare "It is my fault" with "The fault is mine." The complementary pair *my–mine* suggested new formations to complement *his* and *your;* that is, *hisn* and *yourn*, which are sometimes heard in uneducated speech but, of course, never in the language of the educated, whether colloquial or written. Somewhat similar analogies, however, have turned out to be both useful and respectable. Thus *criticism* and *Catholicism* have provided a suffix which gives us the indispensable *witticism; Platonist* seems to justify a suffix -*nist* for *tobacconist;* and *politician* must have produced -*cian* for *mortician* and *beautician*. We seem, indeed, to be living in a period of continuing fertility in words and word forms.

Some interesting problems in the analysis of forms spring from the mixed origin of the English vocabulary, especially from the fact that, while Germanic roots are for the most part monosyllabic, base forms derived from Latin and French are not so limited. True, it is easy to resolve the set *adduce, conduce, induce, produce,* and *reduce* into the irreducible stem morpheme {dju:s}, each word containing also a prefix familiar from its use in numerous other words. Compare, however, *brownish* and *burnish*. At first glance, both words seem to have the familiar suffix -*ish*, but further observation reveals that *brown-* and *burn-* are not comparable items, since the latter has no semantic value in itself.[5] Similar to *burnish* we can discover *abolish, astonish, lavish, perish,* and *relish*, which also appear to be root stems in which we must reject -*ish* as suffix. A still further search, however, brings to light *admonish, famish, finish, polish,* and *publish*, with which we may contrast respectively *admonitory, famine, final, polite,* and *public,* thus demonstrating the function of {ɪʃ} as a verb-forming suffix. In the former set, therefore, we would say that the suffix is appended to a **unique morph.**

Syntax refers to groups of words rather than to single words. Although morphologic and syntactic considerations often overlap,[6] as when

---

[5] This root *burn-* has no relation to the verb *burn*. Etymologically it is a cognate of *brown*, but this fact is inadmissible in synchronic analysis.

[6] De Saussure was more peremptory: "Forms and functions are interdependent, and it is difficult if not impossible to separate them. Linguistically, morphology has no real autonomous object. It cannot form a discipline distinct from syntax." (Ferdinand de Saussure, *Course in General Linguistics*, trans. Wade Baskin [New York, 1966], p. 135.)

we consider the tenses of the verb in Present English, syntax has its own distinctive features. In this area **government, agreement,** and **word order** are important concepts. In its earliest period the grammatical structure of English more closely resembled that of Latin. Then government and agreement functioned more extensively, and word order was correspondingly less definitive. Today government survives only with the case forms of the pronoun. Agreement remains only in pronoun reference, between the subject and the -*s* ending of the verb in the present tense, and between demonstrative and noun.

Word Order

Word order, however, is of the first importance. Compare the following two sentences in English and Latin:

> *Caesar oppugnavit hostem.*
> Caesar attacked the enemy.

Here the order of the words in Latin does not matter. *Caesar*, because of its form, must be the subject, whether it is at the beginning or end of the sentence, and for the same reason *hostem* must remain the object. In English, however, if the positions are reversed the meaning is reversed. Thus we rely upon an established order, actor-action-goal or subject-verb-object (SVO), as a syntactic feature which determines meaning.

Normal word order may, within limits, be altered. In **transposed order** part of the verb phrase occupies the final position after the object. This is an important feature of modern German syntax, as in

> *Er hat die Zeitung nicht gelesen.*
> He has the newspaper not read.

Formerly transposition occurred in English, but it is seldom encountered today except in an archaic style. The difficulty in using transposition today can be demonstrated by comparison between the two sentences following:

> He had painted the house.
> He had the house painted.

Inverted order, however, is common and functionally important. It is the normal mode of forming questions:

> He is famous.
> Is he famous?

When negative adverbs precede SV, inversion is the rule:

> I have never heard the like.
> Never have I heard the like.

For emphasis we may also invert the order to OSV:

> This I will not endure.

The position of the adjective is usually before the noun, but post-position occurs in some established forms like *all things human,* or with adjectival groups like *a man without a country* or *a place in the sun.* Adverbs are more freely placed. In initial position they frequently become sentence adverbs:

> Finally he went home.

In this position the adverb sometimes undergoes an interesting shift in meaning. Compare

> He went away, but he did not go happily.
> He was dangerous, but happily he went away.

Detailed analysis of English syntactic structure may be carried out in different ways. Two are now well known in American English. The first is **immediate constituent analysis.** This does not differ from traditional sentence analysis in its essential nature, but, of course, its technique is much more sophisticated, giving more detailed and more accurate results. The other, not yet fully explored, is newer and more radical. Since it undertakes to describe every possible type of sentence in the language as a **transform** evolved by an elaborate series of steps from a small number of basic sentences, it is called **transformational grammar.** In the more recent developments of transformational (or **generative**) grammar, attention has been centered on sentences as they occur in intuitive speech responses (**surface structures**) and the underlying basics (**deep structures**). Specifically, it hopes to formulate the "rules" that describe the generation of all possible English sentences from deep structures. Generative terms and concepts are also being applied to areas of linguistic analysis other than syntax. These fields, however, are too extensive and the results too tentative to permit a useful summary here.[7]

Morphophonemic Change

As remarked at the beginning of this section, one of the important phenomena in the development of Modern English is the extent to which various kinds of changes affect others. Sound changes lead to changes in form, and morphologic changes lead to changes in syntax. The noun plural suffix in Old English and Early Middle English was composed of a vowel plus [s]; but later, when the vowel was lost in the suffix, as when *bokes* > *books* and *floures* > *flowers*, the final [s] became subject to combinative change conditioned by the final sound of the stem. As a result we now have three allomorphs of $\{Z_1\}$. When phonological changes in this way produce morphological changes, the resulting variations are called **morphophonemic.** Such modifications have been at work in the language for a long time.

A good example is the history of the declension of the noun *man*, whose prehistoric plural was **manniz*. The vowel [i] in the plural suffix [iz] led to the fronting of the stem vowel to [e] by a process called **umlaut** or **mutation** (pp. 91–92), and thus the Old English historic spelling of the plural stem was *menn*. Since this stem modification came to be characteristic of the plural, the suffix was dropped before the earliest English written records, and the Old English nominative and accusative plural stood as *menn* or *men*.

After the Old English period a different but related change modified

---

[7] Immediate constituent analysis is explained in W. Nelson Francis, *The Structure of American English* (New York, 1958) and Eugene A. Nida, *A Synopsis of English Syntax* (The Hague, 1966). For transformational grammar see H. A. Gleason, Jr., *An Introduction to Descriptive Linguistics* (New York, 1961), ch. 12; also, *Linguistics and Grammar* (New York, 1965), chs. 10–12. A much simplified statement is available in R. A. Jacobs and P. S. Rosenbaum, *Grammar 1* and *Grammar 2* (New York, 1967). A more advanced treatment is supplied by the same authors in *English Transformational Grammar* (Waltham, Mass., 1968). For the application of generative methods to phonology see Noam Chomsky and Morris Halle, *The Sound Pattern of English* (New York, 1968).

the declension of this noun still further. The dative plural had not undergone mutation and therefore remained in Old English as *mannum*. In the course of time, however, the *-um* suffix of this dative plural underwent **phonetic reduction** (pp. 143–45) and was finally lost altogether in Middle English. Since *man* was a characteristically singular form, the dative plural could now retain its plural significance only by imitating the nominative and accusative plural *men*. By analogy, then, all the forms of the plural except the genitive became identical.

When analogical change leads in this way to the reduction of the number of forms in a paradigm, the process is called **leveling**. Similar phonetic reduction and leveling have led to the general loss of case endings in the noun except for the possessive *-s*. The grammatical relationship formerly signaled by the dative case is now expressed by word order alone, as in

Science has given *man* countless improvements.

or by phrase construction with greater freedom of position, as in

Science has given countless improvements *to man*
Science has given *to man* countless improvements.
To man science has given countless improvements.

These examples illustrate phonological change which leads to a change in the morphological system and this in turn to syntactic adjustment.

Suprasegmental Features

One level at which phonology and syntax are interrelated is in a set of features not well represented, or not represented at all, in conventional spelling: **pitch, juncture,** and **stress.** Stress is indicated by marks or **superfixes** above the literal symbols. Pitch and juncture contribute to the **intonation pattern.** Superfix and intonation symbols may be referred to as **suprasegmental** to distinguish them from the **segments** or phonemes represented by the usual phonetic letter symbols.

PITCH

Pitch, or rather, variation in pitch, is that which enables us to distinguish between command and question in the utterance "You must go." Here falling pitch indicates one meaning; rising pitch, another. Or again, in the utterance "Do not go," high pitch on *do* and rising pitch on *go* express a polite entreaty rather than a command.

JUNCTURE

Juncture is that feature of enunciation which enables the hearer to recognize significant boundaries between sounds, words, and groups. **Close juncture** occurs between the sounds of a syllabic unit and need not often be referred to. **Open juncture** is more important. In most of our speech we are aware of word divisions only because we remember the printed spelling. Thus in normal speech, "What do you think?" becomes [wadɪjə + θɪŋk], in which the first three words of the conventional spelling are not separated. At times, however, word separation is essential to meaning, and this separation is achieved by open juncture, sometimes called **plus juncture** because of the symbol used to express it. It is exemplified in the kind of distinction we make in the following contrasting pairs:

how scare [haʊ + skɛ:r]   house care [haus + kɛ:r]
I scream [aɪ + skri:m]   ice cream [aɪs + kri:m]
why choose [waɪ + tʃu:z]   white shoes [waɪt + ʃu:z]

Open juncture has played a minor historical role in the modification of a few words by what may be called "metathesis of juncture." Thus *an ewt > a newt, a napron > an apron, a nadder > an adder*. Though it is never acknowledged in contemporary spelling, the same shift is often heard in sequences like *an apple* and *at all*.

Terminal juncture, as the name indicates, occurs at the end of word groups. It somewhat corresponds, though very imperfectly, to the comma, the period (or semicolon), and the question mark. The shortest is **level juncture,** called also **single-bar juncture** [/]; this is a perceptible pause, but without rise or fall of pitch, as after the first word in "Yes, I think so" [jes/aɪ + θɪŋk + so:]. In uninhibited speech the same juncture may occur at places where the conventional writing system would not encourage the use of the comma, as in "I can't see. Can you?"

Other terminal junctures are **rising juncture** or **double-bar juncture** [//], which is the characteristic terminal mark for questions, and

falling juncture, or **double-cross juncture** [#], which occurs commonly at the end of a statement:

> I can't see. Can you? [aɪ + kænt si:/kɛn + ju//]
> No, but I can hear. [no:/bət aɪ kɪn + hi:r #]

Falling juncture may also occur in questions that begin with an interrogative word, as in

> What was his purpose?
> Who are his sponsors?

STRESS

Syllabic stress and word stress have functioned much more extensively in historical change than pitch or juncture. If the English verb *love* has three inflectional morphemes in contrast to a very much larger set for the corresponding verb in other languages, such as *amare* in Italian, the difference is due to the fact that the English inflectional suffixes, having occurred in the early periods of the language always under weak stress, were gradually reduced in sound until only a few remain. Syllabic stress occurs in words of more than one syllable. In transcription it is marked by a small stroke in superior position *before* the syllable, as in ['æksɛnt]. With more than two syllables an intermediate or secondary stress also occurs and is marked by a similar stroke in inferior position [ˌkwɑdrə'lætərəl]. Unstressed or weakly stressed syllables are unmarked.

In groups of words, however, we must go further. Like syllabic stress, word stress may be strong or weak, but we distinguish two intermediate stages. In the phrase "at the next crossroad" three stress levels would be sufficient: [æt ðə nɛkst krɔ́:srò:d]. But a different stress pattern occurs in "at the next paved road," where two intermediate levels must be distinguished, necessitating four levels in all: [æt ðə nɛkst pê:vd ró:d]. Here *next* is under tertiary stress, *paved* under secondary stress, and *road* under primary stress. It is by recognition of the difference between tertiary and secondary levels of stress that we distinguish between *a blackbird* and *a black bird, a greenhouse* and *a green house,* and *the White House* and *the white house.*

Contemporary Trends

Almost any expert analysis of the language would strike the usual educated person, accustomed as he is to conventional school grammar, as strange if not repellent. The linguist may assume for purposes of analysis that the language is, for the moment, fixed, but the general public makes this assumption in a different way and with different results. It is habituated to thinking of an abstract ideal of correctness which retains authority whether obeyed or not, and it especially bows to the authority of established spelling. The feeling is rather common, then, that the characteristics of the spoken language are inferior to those of the written language, and that when the two differ, one must apologize for the colloquial.

This attitude helps to conceal the nature of important developments in contemporary English. For example, in the expressions "I have to run along now" and "I used to go there," the verbs are enunciated very commonly in the English-speaking world as [hæftə rʌn] and [ju: stə go:]. The spellings *have to* and *used to* preserve the memory of the original forms and contribute to the stability and universal familiarity of the written medium, but they conceal the emergence of two new auxiliaries, one expressing necessity and the other customary past action.

Also unrecognized is a set of modal auxiliaries in common colloquial use with what now amounts to an inflectional ending for a perfect tense. It has two allomorphs in complementary distribution, one, [ə], occurring before a following consonant, and the other, [əv], occurring before a vowel. Both are phonetic reductions from *have*, which is preserved in the spelling and in certain emphatic uses under primary stress: *could have* [kʊdə], [kʊdəv], *would have* [wʊdə], [wʊdəv], and so on, for *should, must, may*, and *might*. The semiliterate public expresses its recognition of this development by writing *could of* for *could have.*

Or again, the future is usually thought to consist of *shall* or *will* with the complementary infinitive (main verb). The fact is, however, that future meaning is more often conveyed in the spoken language by forms traditionally classified as present:

I fly to London tomorrow.
I am flying to London next month.
I am going to fly to London next month.

In colloquial use the last of these is frequently heard in its phonologically modified forms, [gɔntə], [gɔ:nə], or [gʌnə], and functions in popular speech as a new future auxiliary, but, of course, it is never so represented in standard spelling.

The use of *going to* as future auxiliary raises the question of its significance in certain expressions like "He was going to fly there for Easter." Here, apparently, *was going to* refers to a future event from a past point of view, thus suggesting comparison with the traditional future perfect, which refers to a past event from a future point of view. Obviously the syntactic verb structures allow us greater range for fine distinctions in grammatical meaning than the older morphological structures. Compare also:

(a) I was going to give up my advantage.
(b) I was not going to give up my advantage.
(c) I was about to give up my advantage.
(d) I was not about to give up my advantage.

Sentences (a) and (c) express somewhat different shades of temporal meaning, but (b) and (d) express about the same shade of negative determination, though in recent American English (d) seems to be growing in favor.

The use of *get* as an auxiliary has also some remarkably varied use. In I *Henry VI* (I.iv.25) Shakespeare wrote

Or by what means got'st thou to be released?

This illustrates the custom, much in use since the sixteenth century, of using *get* with an infinitive. In its early use the infinitive must have been felt to be the object, as in "He did not get to go." Today, however, Shakespeare's words would be rendered "How did you get released?" where *get released* is clearly a passive. Curiously enough, this idiom is one of the few in English that admit of transposed word order. Compare the following:

He got wounded.
He got himself wounded.

In the second sentence *wounded* may be construed as an objective complement, but it is an interesting historical coincidence that when transposed order was a feature of English, the participle often agreed with the object. History is apparently repeating itself.

A quite different meaning and use for *get* appear in the sentence "We got started," structurally passive but suggesting an active meaning. This is even more clearly expressed in "We got fooling around," which seems to be a later stage of "We got to fooling around."

From this last example we assume not only that *get* is a passive auxiliary and a word of many meanings, but that it provides for a new form, or "aspect" as it is sometimes called, paralleling the simple and progressive forms. Compare the following:

> They moved at last.
> They were moving at last.
> They got moving at last ($<$ They got to moving at last).

If it is true, as some authorities believe, that the progressive form developed when the preposition (*on* $>$ *a*; see p. 208) was lost before the gerund, we are witnessing a similar process repeated in Modern English.

We may conclude, then, that our language, however much we may be attached to its present state, is by no means an "end product" but an entity which is always to some degree becoming something else.

Exercises

1. In the following list some words are old forms with newly acquired meanings, in more or less cultivated usage; some are relatively new words, also more or less respectable, which have been formed in different ways. What can you find out about the meaning and status of each? How many can be called "neologisms"? By what type of word formation have they been put together? Is there any printed information about the date and circumstances of their first appearance? Check the words in this list in Howard Wentworth and Stuart B. Flexner, *Dictionary of American Slang* (New York, 1967), and in John S. Farmer and W. E. Henley, *Dictionary of Slang and Its Analogues, Past and Present* (New Hyde Park, N.Y., 1966).

> *beat, beatnik, blitz, bookmobile, brainwash, chintzy, chow, con, corny,*
> *crocked, crumb, crummy, dig, duds, egghead, finalize, fink, frisk,*
> *gobbledegook, goof, gunsel, heist, high, highbrow, hipster, hood, irre-*

gardless, jalopy, jazz, joe, liberate, liquidate, lowdown, medicare, megaton, minicam, oddball, pad, pinched, plastered, razz, rod, roll (v.), scab, scads, schlemiel, schmo, scram, screwball, shindig, sleazy, snide, square, squeal, stash, stewed, stinko, tight, wacky, whizz, wise, wisecrack

2.   Among the words above many are clearly unusable for formal written use. Can any be distinguished as cant (belonging to the speech of a particular class or occupation)? Of those which you classify as slang, can you identify any that might be heard in the informal or familiar speech of educated adults?

3.   What process of word formation is illustrated in each of the following groups?
    (a)   *acorn, crayfish (or crawfish), mushroom, causeway*
    (b)   *beg, rove, drowse, diagnose, donate*
    (c)   *chuckle, screech, slam, sniff, sob, yawn*
    (d)   *smog, brunch, bash, chortle*
    (e)   *ad, bus, chap, hoax, mob*

4.   What process of semantic change is illustrated in each of the following groups?
    (a)   *grand, cute, marvelous, splendid, fabulous*
    (b)   *miser, poison, eaves, ferry, stool*
    (c)   *butler, citizen, cupboard, front*
    (d)   *busybody, counterfeit, doom, outlandish, vulgar*
    (e)   *alderman, cavalier, courteous, pastor*

5.   Many popular words and phrases originate as figures of speech with vivid, forceful meaning. Often they become tiresome clichés and are happily forgotten, but a number retain a permanent place in the language, such as *lion's share, crow over, shark* (referring to a person), *greenhorn*, etc. Duplicate these in contemporary popular speech.

6.   Study the earlier meanings of *crazy, idiot,* and *insane*. What tendency in word use accounts for the semantic change?

7.   One of the most productive tendencies in the popular use of English has been, and still is, the formation of verb-adverb combinations. They offer abundant material for the study of the processes of word making and

word meanings. Distinguish first between verb-adverb combinations and verbs followed by prepositional phrases:

He's breaking *in* his new pipe.
He put tobacco *in* his new pipe.
We tried to head *off* their flight.
We pried the head *off* the jar.
She turned *on* the water and filled the jug.
She turned *on* the water and sailed back.

8.   In each pair above, how would you describe the difference between the italicized words in terms other than meaning? Test them as to stress, juncture, and freedom of position. Of these three elements, which seems to be the most constant feature of verb-adverb combinations? Before making a decision, consider other sentences, for example:

He knocked on the door.
He walked out the door.
He looked out the window.
He waited out his time.
He dealt out the cards.
He drove in the sweepstakes.
He drove in the winning run.
He drove in the garage.
He drove in the nail.

9.   When an adverbial particle is used as a prefix, how is the meaning or function of the word affected? Compare the following groups:

(a)   *undergo–go under*
overlook–look over
outweigh–weigh out

(b)   *offset–set off*
downgrade–grade down
overturn–turn over

(c)   *outbreak–break out*
intake–take in
upturn–turn up

10.   Some verb-adverb combinations can be used as verbs or nouns; for example toss + up, pick + up, push + over. How is the difference indicated in conventional orthography? in phonemic notation?

11. When verb-adverb combinations are followed by an object, is there any difference between the position of a pronoun object and that of a noun or clause? Compare:

> We paid off all the employees.
> We paid them all off.
> Hal never found out what he wanted.
> He never found it out.
> He turned the car in.

Collect a number of such examples and try to determine whether it is possible to form a syntactic rule which will describe the variations that a native speaker would be likely to use.

12. Can the following Latin (or Greek) derivatives be replaced by native synonyms? To what extent are these replacements likely to be verb-adverb combinations? Is there anything to choose between the two synonyms?

> *inflate, collect, illuminate, extinguish, eliminate, demolish, exhaust, obliterate, analyze, review, erase*

13. Some combinations are ambiguous:

> *bear out* 'carry away,' 'corroborate'
> *put out* 'publish,' 'expel,' 'extinguish'
> *take off* 'remove,' 'depart'
> *back up* 'support,' 'retreat'

Do these instances and some observations you must have made above suggest the value of cultivating the less popular but more precise synonyms?

14. Some combinations are open to the criticism that the adverb is redundant. Is this criticism valid? Consider such expressions as *connect up, meet with, count up*. How many such expressions can you find in which the adverb adds little if any meaning? Do you find these objectionable? Examine each on its own merits before drawing a general conclusion.

15. Contemporary speech is full of verb-adverb combinations used as nouns (*blowout, breakdown, drawback*) or adjectives (*leadoff, drive-in, give-*

away). On this subject consult the article by E. R. Hunter in *American Speech* (22 [1947]: 115–19). Can you add more recent acquisitions to this list?

16.   The interrelation of syntax and word meaning can be illustrated in this pair of sentences:

(a)   He will not be able to speak hopefully on that subject.
(b)   Hopefully he will not be able to speak on that subject.

As used in sentence (b), *hopefully* has recently achieved a kind of popularity which makes it a "vogue word" and arouses a certain amount of adverse criticism. What grammatical term would you apply to its use in this sentence? How many parallels can you find for it in established usage? Is this usage defensible?

17.   Simeon Potter (*Modern Linguistics* [New York, 1964], pp. 90–93) classifies English compounds in seven groups:

(1)   *bookcase, aircraft, beehive*
(2)   *icebreaker, dressmaker, screwdriver*
(3)   *breakwater, cut-throat, spoilsport*
(4)   *blackbird, redwood, shorthand*
(5)   *peaceloving, life-giving, breath-taking*
(6)   *old-fashioned, broad-shouldered, narrow-minded*
(7)   *blue-black, light-red, red-hot*

(a)   Can you discern the basis of this classification? In each word what is the relation of one free form to the other and to the whole compound? In this classification where would you place *underdog, long-winded, easygoing, makeshift, bittersweet, bridgehead, hairdresser?* Would you put *hammerhead* in the first or third group? Find other examples for each group.

(b)   In groups 1, 4, and 7 all the examples given are composed each of two monosyllables. Is this an essential characteristic? Do they all have the same stress pattern?

(c)   All the examples given in groups 2, 5, and 6 have suffixes. Are these suffixes added to the compound or to the second free form? To find an answer to this question, try removing the suffix. Is the resulting compound stem a usable item in the English vocabulary?

18.   Compare the phonetic symbols used in Kenyon and Knott's *Pronouncing Dictionary* (p. xvii) with those in Daniel Jones's *English Pronouncing Dictionary* (p. xlii). The two systems are not identical in all respects. The following words would be pronounced alike in England and America, but observe the different methods of notation: *nation, get, see, sit, go, put, too.*

19.   What interesting facts, perhaps unknown to you, can be learned from studying the pronunciations recorded in both of these works for the following words: *absorb, ate, appreciate, diversion, dog, falcon, fertile, forest, garage, governor, hog, literature, ration, schedule, tissue?*

20.   A popular quasi-speech noise is sometimes represented in print as "tsk-tsk." What is unusual about the mode of articulation of this sound so far as English speech habits go? Is the spelling adequate? Could it be more accurately represented by the phonetic symbols that you are acquainted with?

21.   Consider two contrasting quasi-speech expressions, both of which are (a) guttural or glottal, (b) reduplicated. One has affirmative meaning; the other, negative. Can you indicate these sounds in phonetic spelling? What part does stress play in the contrast?

22.   Transcribe the following piece of dialogue in phonetic notation as you think it would sound among friends of yours in moments when they are not particularly conscious of language as such:

> You ought to be on your way.
> No, I don't have to leave till ten.
> But you used to start earlier.
> I know, but I'm going to take my time now.

What analysis would you make of the verb phrases as they appear in this transcription?

23.   What types of sound change are illustrated in popular pronunciations of each of the following groups?

   (a)   *rented, let me see, give me one, grandpa, horseshoe*
   (b)   *corner, orderly, ordinary, quarter*
   (c)   *family, aspirin, different, Catherine*

Part II

THE EARLY HISTORY OF ENGLISH

Chapter 7

LANGUAGE AND PREHISTORY

Cognate Languages

One of the important concepts in linguistic history is that of related languages, or, as they are sometimes called, **cognate** languages. These have evolved as different languages from what at a much earlier time was one language, which may be referred to as the parent or ancestral language. For example, French, Spanish, Italian, and Portuguese are modern evolutions of ancient Latin. We know this because we have preserved the knowledge of the history of the people who speak these languages as well as an abundance of texts in the parent language. If, however, we did not have the visible evidence of the parent tongue, it would still be possible to draw conclusions about it from a study of the similarities and differences in the descendant languages. This kind of study is called comparative grammar,[1] and it is one of the achievements bequeathed to us by the great linguistic scholars of the nineteenth century. Of course, since the conclusions of comparative study on the state of a prehistoric language are to some extent hypothetical, they are less certain and less detailed than the surviving evidence of a parent language and therefore subject to revision as our knowledge of history and prehistory expands.

---

[1] In the sense in which it is used here, grammar includes not only an account of conjugations, declensions, and rules of propriety, but the complete study of a language, including its sounds, inflections, lexicon, and syntax, as well as their changes with the passage of time.

Language Descent

The kind of relationship that exists between a language and its ancestor as well as its cognates is illustrated in the following table:

LATIN		ITALIAN	SPANISH	FRENCH
pater	'father'	padre	padre	père
mater	'mother'	madre	madre	mère
unus	'one'	uno	uno	un
duo	'two'	due	dos	deux
tres	'three'	tre	tres	trois
tu	'thou'	tu	tu	tu
venire	'come'	venire	venir	venir
cantare	'sing'	cantare	cantar	chanter
habere	'have'	avere	haber	avoir

Since we know that the similarities in the three modern languages are derived from a common ancestor, the records of which have been preserved, we may assume that similar likenesses in other languages point to an ancestral tongue which has not been preserved in writing. Compare, for example, the following:

GERMAN	ENGLISH
Mann	man
Vater	father
Mutter	mother
Bruder	brother
Schwester	sister
Hand	hand
Finger	finger
Fuss	foot
singen	sing
ich	I
du	thou
haben	have

Three possibilities can be adduced to explain these similarities between English and German. First, the words were borrowed from one language to the other; second, one of these languages was derived from the other; third, both languages were derived from a common source now lost. The first explanation is improbable because general observation of language behavior does not support the theory that words of such common and essential use are usually borrowed in great numbers. The second possibility is more plausible, but, when we include the evidence from still other languages like Dutch, Swedish, Danish, Norwegian, and ancient Gothic (now extinct as a living language, but surviving in writing), we are led to the third possibility, the common ancestor, as the most convincing explanation of the three. This hypothetical ancestor is called **Proto-Germanic**, or **Primitive Germanic.**

Proto-Germanic

It is even possible, by patient and detailed examination of all the extant data, to reconstruct by the comparative method the approximate form of prehistoric words. Take, for example, the English *finger*, to which the German *Finger* is so close. Among the earliest written records of the Germanic peoples we find Old English *finger*, Old Saxon and Old High German *fingar*, Old Norse *fingr*, Gothic *figgrs;* from all of these we assume the existence in Proto-Germanic of a form **fingro-z*.

In Proto-Germanic, however, we have not reached the end of the comparative process, because we can discover additional likenesses between English and other languages which are not Germanic. Consider the following:

GREEK	LATIN	ENGLISH
agros	*ager*	acre
phratēr	*frater*	brother
deka	*decem*	ten
duo	*duo*	two
gonu	*genu*	knee
pous, podos	*pes, pedis*	foot
treis	*tres*	three

Obviously the resemblances between English on the one hand and Latin and Greek on the other are not so close as those between English and German, but extended observation of all the relevant facts from these and a number of other languages proves that these languages are indeed related. The prehistoric mother tongue, the basic forms of which are deduced by the comparative method, is called **Proto-Indo-European.**[2] It is assumed, then, that at a very early period, not subject to precise definition but certainly several thousand years before Christ, a language spoken by a relatively small number of people, most probably in Eastern Europe,[3] began to split into dialects. Groups of these early people separated by migration from other groups, and during a time when distance or other geographical barriers made social intercourse impossible, minor differences in language became greater and greater, and eventually dialects evolved into languages. Within each of these several groups, the process of splitting was repeated in later times to such an extent that today this one ancient language has by different evolutionary routes developed into many important languages spread over Europe and Western Asia.

It is fairly easy to comprehend such a process from what we can see of the English language in the modern world. In the sixteenth century, the relatively small number of people speaking English lived in one small island. During the succeeding centuries, their language was carried by migrating groups to different parts of the world, where in the course of time the speech of these separated colonies developed special dialect features. An American, for example, though he understands his transatlantic neighbor in Britain, is aware of very prominent differences. Were it not for the fact that in modern times these differences are counteracted by a common written convention and other means of intercommunication, they would quite probably continue to grow until they made mutual understanding impossible. At that point American and British would be different languages. Moreover, within the American speech community

---

[2] Formerly called also **Indo-Germanic** by the German scholars, and earlier **Aryan.** The latter term is now old-fashioned, and has also been degraded by unpopular political uses.

[3] The first home of the Indo-Europeans was once thought to have been in Asia. A recent theory places it in Northern Europe, between the Elbe and the Vistula. See Paul Thieme, "The Indo-European Language," *Scientific American*, October 1958, pp. 63–74. A standard work on this subject is Harold Bender, *The Home of the Indo-Europeans* (Princeton, 1922).

itself we are aware of regional differences, which, under the proper conditions of time and isolation, could conceivably result in a subgroup of languages.

The Indo-European Family

In some such way, then, Indo-European has in the course of thousands of years developed in different branches, some of which are further divisible into groups and subgroups, as follows.

I. *Indo-Iranian* consists of two divisions.

    A. *Indic* includes a number of languages spoken in India, the most ancient form of which is *Sanskrit*, of inestimable importance to our knowledge of Proto-Indo-European. Sanskrit was revered and preserved for religious and literary purposes, but the more popular dialects, called the *Prakrits*, are the ancestors of the modern Indic languages. One of these, *Hindi*, is now the official language of India. Another language, *Urdu*, is spoken in Pakistan. Related to them also is the language of the Gypsies, known as *Romany*.

    B. *Iranian* is preserved in two ancient forms: *Avestan*, named from the sacred book of the Zoroastrian religion, and *Old Persian*. The latter is preserved only in inscriptions, but a later form of it is the language of the *Shah Nameh*, which contains the story of Sohrab and Rustum, known to readers of English literature from Matthew Arnold's poem. From this language we have the modern forms spoken in Iran, Afghanistan, Baluchistan, and Kurdistan.

II. *Armenian* in its earliest recorded form is called *Old Armenian*, but the written remains do not go back earlier than the fifth century of the Christian era. Today it is divided into an eastern branch, found in the Soviet Union, and a western branch, in Turkey.

III. *Albanian* records from earlier times are even scantier and more recent than Armenian, the earliest dating from the fourteenth century. In both of these languages the lexicon is very heavily influenced by other languages.

IV. *Balto-Slavic*, like Indo-Iranian, has two important subdivisions.

    A. Some earlier written materials of the *Baltic* group are in a language now extinct, called *Old Prussian*.[4] The modern forms are *Lettish*, the language of Latvia, and *Lithuanian*. The latter has a special interest because of the number of primitive features it has preserved.

B.   The *Slavic* languages are the better known of the two divisions. An early form of Slavic, known as *Old Bulgarian* or *Old Church Slavic* has been preserved from the ninth century and has been the liturgical language of the Orthodox Church. The modern Slavic languages are divided geographically. The southern group comprises *Bulgarian* and three languages spoken in Yugoslavia: *Macedonian*, *Slovenian*, and *Serbo-Croatian*. The western branch includes *Polish*, *Czechoslovakian*, and *Wendish*. In the eastern group are *Great Russian*, *White Russian*, and *Ukrainian*. It is Great Russian that is usually meant by the term *Russian*.

V.   *Hellenic, or Greek*, is well known in its older forms because of the antiquity of its written records. The Indo-European Greeks moved into the Greek peninsula as early as 2000 B.C., supplanting a more ancient culture. Their civilization, and with it their language, spread into adjoining areas. The most important of the ancient Greek dialects, that of Athens, called *Attic*, became known and was extensively used throughout the Mediterranean world as a consequence of the victories of Alexander the Great. The importance of its literature has also given it an extensive influence in the growth of Western civilization. From the common Attic speech most of the dialects of modern Greece are descended.

VI.   The *Italic* languages appeared in the Mediterranean world somewhat later than Greek. Like Hellenic, Italic existed in several dialects, one of which, *Latin*, supplanted the others in importance, became the dominant language of the ancient world, and produced the great literature which has come down to our time. The popular Latin speech, however, was carried in the days of the Roman Empire to various parts of Europe, where it became the basis of what we call today the Romance languages: *Italian, French, Spanish, Portuguese,* and *Rumanian,* as well as some others which do not now have national status, mainly *Provençal, Catalan, Sardinian,* and Romance dialects in Switzerland.

---

[4] The term *Prussian* did not originally refer to the Germans, but was applied to them when they supplanted the original inhabitants of the area known as Prussia.

VII. *Celtic* is now of relatively minor economic and political importance. It was, however, the language of those intrepid warriors known to the Romans as Gauls. At the height of their power they spread to Spain, Italy, and even Asia Minor, where they established a colony known as the Galatians, to whom St. Paul wrote his well-known epistle. As many schoolchildren know, they were subdued on the continent by Julius Caesar, and their language was eventually replaced by Latin. In Britain, however, which was also occupied at that time by Celts, the Celtic language survived. It has come down to us in two varieties: *Goidelic*, represented by *Irish Gaelic*, *Scotch Gaelic*, and *Manx* (of the Isle of Man); and *Brythonic* or *Cymric*, represented by *Welsh*, *Cornish*, which has recently died out, and *Breton*, spoken in Brittany (France).

VIII. *Germanic* is for our purposes the most interesting, for it is the branch to which English belongs. The earliest evidences of Germanic come from the fourth century, the most important being a number of Old Norse runic inscriptions and a translation of part of the Bible by Ulfilas into *Gothic*. This ancient work has been preserved, but as a spoken language Gothic is now extinct. In the seventh century Germanic written records became more abundant. From these early writings as well as from the later surviving literature of the daughter languages we construct the parent language, *Proto-Germanic*. Like the Proto-Indo-European, of which it is a branch, Proto-Germanic has evolved into subgroups. These are usually classified as *North Germanic*, which includes the Scandinavian languages: *Danish*, *Swedish*, *Norse*, and *Icelandic*; *East Germanic*, all of whose members, including Gothic, are now extinct; and *West Germanic*. This last may again be subdivided into *Low* and *High West Germanic*. In this context the words "low" and "high" have no reference to social or literary prestige. They are purely geographical terms: "low" refers to the lowlands along the coast; "high" to the more elevated inland regions. High German has become what we today call simply "German"; it is the standard language of Berlin and Vienna. Low West Germanic was divided in early times into *Old Saxon*, which has come down as a regional dialect of Germany called *Plattdeutsch; Old Franconian*, which has become *Dutch* and *Flemish;* Old Frisian, which has become the *Frisian* of the Netherlands province of Friesland; and *Old English* (formerly called Anglo-Saxon), which, with important changes, has become the language of the modern English-speaking world.

It must be emphasized that the classification of these languages and the reconstruction of their prehistoric forms, Proto-Germanic and Proto-Indo-European, are based upon incomplete data from which conclusions are made by human ingenuity. As new evidence comes to light and old theories are reconsidered, important revisions of the scheme become necessary.

One such possible revision affects the position of English. It has been pointed out that there are resemblances that would warrant grouping together the Scandinavian languages and the now extinct eastern group (Gothic). All the other Germanic languages would in this scheme compose a second group, and among them Anglo-Frisian would be a subgroup linking the northern and southern groups. This theory has not been universally accepted.

Another theory familiar to students of historical linguistics has to do with a proposed classification of the Indo-European family. In the first four branches listed above a sound change occurred which is not to be found in the other related languages: the original Proto-Indo-European (PIE) palatal [k] was modified to [s]. This change is illustrated in the contrast *satem*, Avestan for 'hundred,' and *centum*, its Latin cognate. Using these words as labels, we may refer to Indo-Iranian, Armenian, Albanian, and Balto-Slavic as *satem* languages and to Greek, Italic, Germanic, and Celtic as *centum* languages.[5] Formerly it was believed that this difference supplied a sufficient basis upon which to assume an original split in Indo-European into an Eastern and a Western branch, but this hypothesis has now lost favor. Some time before the first World War, Western scholars became aware of the records of a language, since called *Tocharian*, which existed for an indeterminate period of time as a small enclave in Central Asia. If the *satem* group is essentially Eastern, Tocharian should be a *satem* language, but it has turned out to be a *centum* language.

In another important advance, not, however, related to this theory, archaeologists turned up in Crete and Greece a number of ancient tablets which can be dated from 1200 B.C. and earlier. These contained inscriptions in two mysterious languages, designated rather vaguely Linear A and Linear B. The latter has been deciphered in recent years and is now

---

[5] The initial sound of *centum* in ancient times was [k], which, before [e] and [i], developed into [s] or [tʃ] in the early Middle Ages. In Proto-Germanic this [k] became aspirated to [x], spelled *h*. Hence English *hundred*.

known to be a variety of early Greek, called Mycenaean. As a result we now have Greek records rivaling in age the Vedic Sanskrit and therefore bearing upon the dating of the evolution of the Indo-European system.

The most exciting of all recent finds, however, has been the unearthing of the remains of the ancient Hittite Empire. The term "Hittite" is familiar to readers of the Bible, but very little information about the Hittite people was available before archaeologists began to uncover in 1907 in Asia Minor the site of their empire, which was once powerful enough to challenge the supremacy of the Egyptians. The newly deciphered Hittite language is generally thought to constitute a separate branch of Indo-European, though some scholars go so far as to suppose that it is not a descendant of Proto-Indo-European but cognate to it, and so points to a state of language, Indo-Hittite, from which both Hittite and Proto-Indo-European descended. This question, however, remains unsettled.

English and Prehistory

The "family tree" of English, therefore, follows these stages: Proto-Indo-European, Proto- or Primitive Germanic, West Germanic, Low West Germanic (all of these undated), Old English (formerly called Anglo-Saxon), Middle English, Modern English.

The earliest historic records in English date from about the late seventh century; hence we may use this point in time as the beginning of the Old English period, though the language represented in the earliest texts had surely been the spoken language of England for a century before that. The Middle English period extends from about 1100 to about 1500. Some scholars prefer to put the beginning of the Modern period earlier, but as stated by Wyld, who chooses a date as early as 1400, "such divisions as these are necessarily arbitrary and largely depend upon what features are selected as distinguishing tests."[6]

A detailed account of the changes through which our language evolved in the prehistoric period lies outside of our domain, but a few significant events ought to be explained because they are often mentioned in linguistic discussions and are of far-reaching consequence.

---

[6] Henry C. Wyld, *A Short History of English*, 3d ed. (New York, 1927), p. 27.

ABLAUT OR GRADATION

The first of these was a feature of the Proto-Indo-European period. It is called **ablaut** or **gradation**. Because of the extensive system of conjugations and declensions in this primitive language many native words were polysyllabic, and word stress shifted from one syllable to another in such a way as to modify the vowel of a given syllable in tone, length, and quality. Tone does not function significantly in modern English, but changes in length and quality due to shifting accent can be illustrated. What happens to the vowel in the final syllable of *qualify* when we add further suffixes to make it *qualification?* Or to the vowel in the second syllable of *history* when it becomes *historic* or *historian?* Among various speakers four varieties of pronunciation may be heard in the vowel of the second syllable: [ə], [ɑ], [ɔ:], and [Ø]. In ablaut, variations similar to these are termed **grades** (hence *gradation*). These are distinguished as the **normal grade,** the **lengthened grade,** and the **weak grade,** which may vanish to the **zero grade.** In their later evolution in different languages the same root syllable in its various grades may turn up in cognates whose form and meaning have been so extensively modified that they can be traced to their origin only by extensive research. The eminent British linguist Simeon Potter[7] cites an interesting occurrence of ablaut in the root syllable which has given the Latin verb *sedēre* 'to sit' and five English cognates whose relation to the Latin word is not immediately apparent:

Normal grade	High-tone	[e]	*sed- > sit
	Low-tone	[o]	*sod- > sat
Lengthened grade	High-tone	[e:]	*se:d > seat
	Low-tone	[o:]	*so:d > soot
Weak grade		[ə]	*səd ⎫
Zero grade		[Ø]	sd ⎭ > nest (ni-sd-os)

Soot might be guessed as that which 'sits' or settles in the chimney, but few would be likely to guess that *nest* was compounded of the root syllable *sd,* in which the vowel had been reduced to zero, the adverb *ni-* 'down,' and a suffix. But by an understanding of the operations of ablaut, *nest* can be analyzed as the 'sitting-down place.'

Ablaut, then, helps to establish the original identity of many cognates in different Indo-European languages. A simpler example is the

---

[7] *Modern Linguistics,* pp. 80–84.

gradation *geneu, *goneu, *gneu, which produces respectively Latin *genu*, Greek *gonu*, and English *knee* ([g] having become [k] in all the Germanic languages).

The most prominent effect of ablaut upon Modern English is the vowel gradation in the strong verb. Although some of the older strong verbs have been modified by analogy, the seven classes remain, as illustrated by the following types:

1.	ride	rode	ridden
2.	choose	chose	chosen
3.	sing	sang	sung
4.	bear	bore	born
5.	eat	ate	eaten
6.	stand	stood	stood
7.	fall	fell	fallen

GRIMM'S LAW

Two well-known phenomena occurred in Proto-Germanic. One is sometimes called the First Sound Shift, but more often Grimm's Law, after the celebrated nineteenth-century philologist Jacob Grimm (better known to the general public for his interest in fairy lore). Grimm's Law is a description of important consonantal changes which distinguish the Germanic from the other Indo-European languages. In other words these changes occurred in all the early Germanic dialects, but not in the other languages descended from the parent tongue. Some of the shifts involved are somewhat too complex for an elementary explanation, but in condensed and simplified form they can be stated thus:

a. Voiceless stops [p, t, k] became fricatives, respectively [f, θ, x].

b. Voiced stops [b, d, g] became voiceless stops, respectively [p, t, k].

c. Voiced aspirated stops through intermediate stages became nonaspirated voiced stops [b, d, g].[8]

---

[8] The voiced aspirated stops may be represented as b^h, d^h, and g^h. However, they are unfamiliar sounds to the general public, since they are not Modern English phonemes. The same is true of the intermediate stages except the second, [β, ð, ɣ]. [β] is a voiced bilabial fricative, which in Old English either became [b] or fell in with the voiced allophone of the *f*-phoneme. PG [ɣ] was a voiced velar fricative which had a stop-allophone, [g], after nasals. On [ɣ] in Old English see below, p. 128.

Since these changes did not occur in Indo-European outside the Germanic languages, we find, for example, original *p* and *t* in Latin *pater* beside *f* and *th* in English *father*, original *t* in Latin *tres* 'three,' original *d* in Latin *decem* 'ten,' and original *g* in Latin *genu* 'knee.'

Further refinement of Grimm's Law was subsequently provided by Karl Verner (and called after him Verner's Law), who showed that the voiceless fricatives [f,] [θ], [x], and [s], when not preceded by a stressed vowel, became voiced to [β], [ð], [ɣ], and [z], the last of these being further modified to [r.] The results of this change, however, are often obscured by subsequent analogical change, though the words *sodden*, originally the past participle of *seethe* (which then meant 'to boil'), *(for)lorn*, originally the past participle of *lose*, and the plural *were* still testify to its operation.

GERMANIC ACCENT

Verner's Law, however, forcefully brought to the attention of scholars the importance of accent in linguistic history, and it was soon realized that in addition to the effects described by Grimm's Law and Verner's Law, a tendency developed in Proto-Germanic of the very greatest consequence to the subsequent history of English. This consisted of the fixing of the stress or accent on the first syllable of all words except verbs, the exception being "due to the fact that in Germanic a syntactic combination of prepositional adverb with verb was not yet a single word at the time when the main stress of words was fixed on the first syllable, and such combinations ultimately developed into compound words stressed on the second element."[9]

This tendency has continued into Modern English and accounts for such contrasting stress patterns as the noun *conduct* ['kandʌkt] and the verb *conduct* [kən'dʌkt], or the adjective *perfect* ['pɚfɪkt] and the verb *perfect* [pɚ'fɛkt].[10] More important, however, is the fact that the fixing of the accent on the first syllable, followed by permanent weakened stress and

---

[9] Alistair Campbell, *Old English Grammar* (Oxford, 1959), p. 30.

[10] The principle, however, is not a rigid one. So long as a prefix remains "alive" to make new compositions, it will take weak stress in some positions. Thus we customarily stress the second syllable in *unsure*, *untaxed*, and *unwed*, but phrasal rhythms may induce a shift. Notice the effect of contrast in *clean and únclean*, or compare *a child unbórn* with *an únborn child*.

reduced length in other syllables, contributed to the withering away of the old Germanic inflectional system.

VERBS

Two other important features of our language structure were introduced in Proto-Germanic. The first was the loss of all tense forms except the present and the past. As a consequence we have had to adopt a new mode of expressing multiple tense distinctions, one consisting of phrase structure rather than stem and inflectional ending. Compare, for example, Latin and English in *audivi* 'I have heard,' *audiam* 'I shall hear,' *audivero* 'I shall have heard,' *audiebar* 'I was heard.'

The second was the introduction of a new class of verbs which formed the past tense and past participle with the addition of the dental suffix; that is, with the suffix which corresponds to *d/ed* in Present English. Although these **weak** verbs, as they are called, were additions to the original stock of verbs, they have become so numerous as to establish the pattern which we now call "regular." Many older strong verbs, such as *drip*, *help*, *lock*, *lose*, *mourn*, and *starve*, which originally formed the past tense by change of stem vowel, have been altered to follow this "regular" pattern.

UMLAUT OR MUTATION

Finally, an important set of changes took place in Old English, but earlier than the date of the first extant texts; hence, in prehistoric or primitive Old English. The process is called **i-umlaut** or **i-mutation**, so named because the presence of [i] or [j] in a syllable following a back vowel caused the vowel to become fronted. When the fronting was complete the *i* or *j* usually disappeared, leaving the historic form of the word without evidence of the conditions which produced the change. By the processes of umlaut,

a and $æ > e$	$\bar{a} > \bar{æ}$	$ea > ie > i/y$
$o > e$	$\bar{o} > \bar{e}$	$io > ie > i/y$
$u > y$	$\bar{u} > \bar{y}$	$\bar{e}a > \bar{i}e > \bar{i}/\bar{y}$
		$\bar{i}o > \bar{i}e > \bar{i}/\bar{y}$

In the following examples the prehistoric form shows the conditions which produced umlaut and the disappearance of the *i* or *j* in the historic form: **bankiz > bench*, **bandjan > bend*, **brugja > bridge*, **dōmjan > deem*, **fōdjan >*

feed. It is this process that also explains the different vowels in *long* and *length, strong* and *strength, old* and *elder,* and accounts for the plural forms *mice, lice, feet, teeth, geese, men,* not to mention the earlier plural forms of *book, cow, nut,* and others, which have since been replaced by the common plural in *-s.*

Exercises

1. From the point of view of etymology, what do the members of each of the following groups have in common? In one respect two of these groups are unlike all the others. Can you discover what this difference is?

    (a) *brat, plaid, javelin, vassal, flannel, clan, bog*

    (b) *spaniel, meander, parchment, millinery, surrey, worsted*

    (c) *dunce, panic, tantalize, lynch, tawdry, boycott*

    (d) *bishop, church, priest, school, climax, crisis*

    (e) *beet, plant, mile, street, cheese, dish, pound*

    (f) *beef, faith, saint, duke, court, judge, armor, chair*

    (g) *ballot, bulletin, ruffian, umbrella, piano, balcony, comrade*

    (h) *alcohol, alcove, zero, cotton, magazine, sofa*

    (i) *call, bind, give, gate, sky, die, ill, ugly*

2. In what way do the stress patterns of the following two groups differ? What is the historical explanation for this contrast?

    (a) *outdwelling, outpatient, outlander*

    (b) *outguess, outrun, outsmart*

3. The difference between *bind* and *bound* is said to be due to ablaut or gradation. What does this mean, and where did the difference originate?

4. A number of related words have differences in form due to umlaut or mutation; for example *fall–fell* (a tree), *knot–knit, doom–deem.* If the prehistoric forms of the second member of each of these pairs were respectively **falljan, *knuttjan,* and **domjan,* how would you explain their present forms?

5. If the Old English nouns *bōc* 'book,' *gāt* 'goat,' *hnutu* 'nut' had the plurals *bēc*, *gēt*, and *hnytte*, by what process would they have acquired their present plurals?

6. In the differentiation of some pairs both ablaut and umlaut have played a role. Can you prove this statement from the etymons (that is, earlier forms) given in *OED* for *cool–chill, drink–drench?*

7. On an outline map of Europe and Asia mark off the areas in which Indo-European languages are the native languages.

Chapter 8

EARLY ENGLISH

External History

By Early English we mean English in the medieval period, which includes both Old English and Middle English. Its external history consists of those events and conditions in the general history of England which influenced the development of the language.

THE OLD ENGLISH PERIOD

Celtic Predecessors

The home of the English language, the land which we now call England, could not have borne that name before the fifth century of the Christian era, when inroads of Germanic tribes from the mainland of Europe drove off the earlier inhabitants. These earlier natives were Celtic and had themselves in prehistoric times invaded the British Isles, replacing a still earlier non-Indo-European race. They had come in two waves. One branch, called Goidelic Celts, eventually occupied what are now Scotland, Ireland, and the Isle of Man. The Brythonic Celts occupied Britain, that is, the area that was in time to become England.

As pointed out earlier, during the period when the land was inhabited by the Celts, whom we shall call Britons, the Romans took possession, and, though they did not displace the Britons, established over them a Roman rule administered by Latin-speaking Roman officials. In the course

94

of events the native Britons became to some extent Romanized in language and customs; and when the Roman Empire adopted Christianity, Britain became Christian with it.

Eventually, however, Roman power declined, and about the beginning of the fifth century the Romans left the island altogether. The native Britons now found themselves in the position in which we see today many former colonial peoples in Asia and Africa. Subjected for centuries to foreign rule, they had not developed for themselves a ruling tradition or a ruling class, nor experienced native armed services. Among the most dangerous weaknesses of such a period of adjustment are internal division, resulting from rivalry for power, and vulnerability to attack from without.

The Coming of the English

Under conditions of this kind the invasion of Britain by hostile tribes from the continent began about the middle of the fifth century. The traditional date is 449. The newcomers came from the coastal lowlands along the North Sea between the peninsula now called Denmark and the River Rhine. They are often referred to as Anglo-Saxons, though the first to come were actually Jutes, who may have been accompanied by some Franks and Frisians. These invaders took permanent possession of the southeast peninsula of Kent. The Saxons came later and occupied much of the remainder of the more southerly part of the island. Their settlements are reflected in the geographical names Essex (East Saxon), Sussex (South Saxon), Middlesex, and Wessex (West Saxon). Of these the West Saxons were destined to become the most influential in English literary history.[1] The Angles appear to have been the latest arrivals, but they came in such large numbers and occupied so large an area in the Midlands and the North that they gave their name to the whole land, *England* being a modification of *Angle-land*.

What happened to the Britons? Many were killed defending their homes and Christian civilization against the overpowering heathen barbarians. Some remained to live among their conquerors, but they were eventually absorbed. Others fled across the channel to form the settlement

---

[1] Wessex was the center of government in the late Old English period, but the name is not used officially for any part of England today. Thomas Hardy revived it for the scenes of his novels.

named after them, Brittany, which is now part of France. The greatest number, however, retreated westward to take refuge in Wales and Cornwall (formerly known also as West Wales). The modern Welsh, then, are the descendants of this ancient conquered people.[2]

The Language of the Invaders

At the time of the invasions the new masters of the land did not form one homogeneous group, politically or linguistically. From the beginning several kingdoms maintained a separate existence. The most northerly of these, because it lay north of the Humber River, was named Northumbria, but it included not only the northern counties of modern England but also Scotland as far as the Firth of Forth. The two middle kingdoms were Mercia and East Anglia, the latter comprising Norfolk and Suffolk. The more southerly kingdoms included, in addition to Kent, the Saxon kingdoms of Essex, Sussex, and Wessex. These seven are sometimes referred to collectively as the Heptarchy, although they were not united in a formal confederacy. In different periods one or the other of them maintained a supremacy of power. In the earliest period this lay with Northumbria, later with Mercia, and finally, for more than two hundred years before the passing of the Anglo-Saxon kings, with Wessex.

The languages of the several tribes were very closely related but not completely identical. In fact, the subsequent dialect divisions of Old English have often been attributed to the original tribal differences. It seems equally probable, however, that these dialects developed after the settlement and were due rather to geographical separation. Whatever their origin, regional differences were to be maintained for hundreds of years and have survived to this day. The extensive Anglian area included two important dialect regions, Northumbria and Mercia. Kent and its adjacent southeastern areas retained a distinctive linguistic character, as did the more extensive section, the Southwest, lying between the Thames and the southern coast, which constituted the kingdom of Wessex. Most of our knowledge of Old English literature is dependent upon texts composed or rewritten in the West Saxon literary language of this region.

---

[2] At that time they would not have called themselves "Welsh." The word is the English form of a term used in various Germanic languages to refer to the Celts or the Romans.

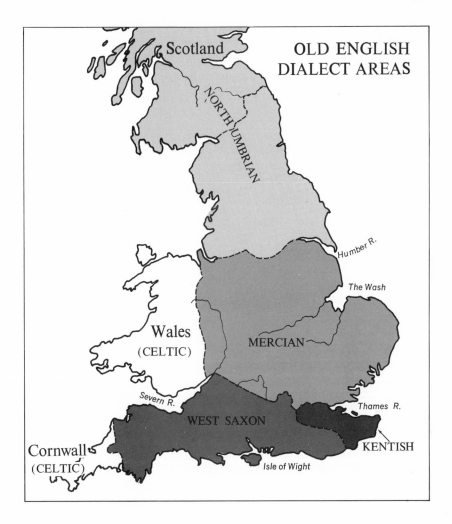

OLD ENGLISH DIALECT AREAS

Scotland

NORTHUMBRIAN

Humber R.

The Wash

Wales
(CELTIC)

MERCIAN

Severn R.

WEST SAXON

Thames R.

KENTISH

Cornwall
(CELTIC)

Isle of Wight

Earliest Borrowing

Despite their differences, the dialects were sufficiently alike to constitute one language, a branch of Low West Germanic, and therefore belonging to an Indo-European family different from that of either Celtic or Latin, which had prevailed in Britain before the coming of the Anglo-Saxons. The history of England and of the English language, in the strictest meaning of the terms, may then be said to begin with the first Germanic settlements.

The language, however, had had an earlier life upon the continent, where the tribes had experienced some effect of the advancing Latin culture, which had spread over a large part of Western Europe. From the Latin names for ideas and conveniences new to them, the Anglo-Saxons had already taken such words as *camp, wall, street, mile,* and *pound*.[3] Intercourse with the Celts in Britain was slight or at least unfavorable to the exchange of ideas. Consequently borrowing of Celtic words or of Latin words which the Celts had learned from the Romans was confined very largely to place names. One of the commonest of these is the Latin *castra* 'camp,' which came to mean 'a walled town' and appears in English place names in the form *caster* (Lancaster, Doncaster), *cester* (Gloucester, Leicester, Worcester), and *chester* (Chester, Manchester, Winchester). Aside from such loan words, the English language in its earliest state was purely Germanic in its lexicon and its grammatical structure. Later we shall see how these have changed with time as a result of both external influence and internal evolution.

Beginnings of English Christianity

ROMAN INFLUENCE

The first of the external influences, which came almost as soon as the period of invasion and occupation was completed, was destined to modify English culture profoundly and for all time. In 597 Augustine[4] and a group of fellow monks, sent by Pope Gregory the Great, arrived in England to call the Anglo-Saxon worshipers of Odin and Thor to the following of Christ. Fortunately for the missionaries, their first serious confrontation was with Æthelberht, king of Kent, whose wife was already a Christian. The newcomers were hospitably received and established a church and

---

[3] Albert C. Baugh (*A History of the English Language,* 2d ed. [New York, 1957], pp. 91–92) estimates the total number of these words to be about fifty. In addition to the above and to those which have not survived in Modern English he lists as certain or probable borrowings from this early period the Old English forms of *bishop, chalk, cheap, cheese, church, copper, cup, dish, flask, kettle, kitchen, peas, pit, tile,* and *wine.*

[4] Not to be confused with St. Augustine, bishop of Hippo, one of the most celebrated of the Fathers of the Church. Both, however, were later venerated in England under the name of St. Austin.

monastery in Kent. By the time of Augustine's death, about 614, the new religion was firmly established there.

Later, in 627, Paulinus, assistant to Augustine, carried the Christian message to Edwin, king of Northumbria, whose conversion also was assisted by a Christian wife. The story which the Venerable Bede,[5] author of *The Ecclesiastical History of the English People*, tells of the acceptance of the new religion by Edwin's thanes is worth repeating. When the proposal to accept Christianity was put to the assembly of King Edwin's nobles, one of them spoke as follows:

> It seems to me, O King, that this present life of man upon earth in comparison to the time that is unknown to us is as if you are sitting at food with your aldermen and thanes in the winter time; and the fire is kindled and the hall is warmed, and it rains and snows and storms outside. A sparrow enters and flies quickly through the house, coming in through one door and out through another. Behold! in the time when he is inside, he is not touched by the winter's storm, but that is the twinkling of an eye, the smallest portion of time, and he goes quickly from winter into winter again. So small a thing, then, this life of man appears. Therefore, if this teaching brings us anything more certain or proper, it is worthy to be followed.

If we have here a fair example of the Anglo-Saxon mind and temper, it is not to be wondered at that England soon became one of the most enlightened centers in Europe. Paulinus' work, subsequently interrupted by wars between the kings of Mercia and Northumbria, was taken up and continued in a way that must now be mentioned.

IRISH INFLUENCE

During the period of the invasions, while religion and learning were in eclipse in Britain, they flourished among the monks of Ireland. Fired by enthusiasm for Christian thought and learning, these missionary-minded monks carried their fervor across the water to Britain. One of the most famous of them, St. Columba, established a monastery on Iona, off the west coast of Scotland, which served as a power center to radiate religion

---

[5] Still commonly referred to by this title, though he is now honored in the Roman liturgical calendar as St. Bede, the Venerable, Doctor of the Church.

and learning through Scotland. From there St. Aidan moved on to found an establishment at Melrose in Scotland and a more famous one on Lindisfarne, or Holy Island, off the coast of Northumbria. In 635, at the invitation of King Oswald, Aidan came to Northumbria where he and his monks took up the work which Paulinus had left unfinished. "The ascetic yet cheerful life," wrote Trevelyan, "of these ardent, lovable, unworldly apostles of the moorland, who tramped the heather all day to preach by the burnside at evening, won the hearts of the men of the North. Indeed, Christianity had never, since its earliest years, appeared in more attractive guise."[6]

For our purpose the importance of these activities has less to do with the spread of religion than with the dissemination of learning, but in these times the two went together. The Irish influence in the North was fated to recede before the more highly organized Latin system from the South, but its contribution to English culture in the meantime would be hard to overestimate. To quote again:

> To this form of monasticism we owe not only the Book of Kells but the manuscript art of Lindisfarne, wherein Celtic and Saxon native ornamentation were blended in perfect harmony with Christian traditions from southern lands. The Irish monks also revived a knowledge of classical secular literature, which had almost died out in Western Europe. While Pope Gregory the Great was reproving a Gallic Bishop for studying Latin grammar and poetry, the Irish Christians were busy saving it for the world in their remote corner where the Papal censure was unheard. Thence, they carried it to the England of Benedict Biscop and Bede, where it greatly fructified; finally, in the days of Charlemagne, it was taken back across the sea by Alcuin to begin its reconquest of the illiterate continent.[7]

Early Scholarship and the Latin Language

The period of evangelization was followed by one in which a succession of scholarly men stimulated the development of learning in so high a level as to be without equal in Europe. Theodore of Tarsus and his assistant Hadrian brought to England the study of Greek as well as of Latin. The native Englishman Benedict Biscop, who made five journeys to the conti-

---

[6] G. M. Trevelyan, *History of England* (London, 1945), p. 60.

[7] *Ibid.*, p. 55.

nent, brought back treasures of books to enrich the libraries of the great monasteries which he had founded at Wearmouth and Jarrow. In the latter of these lived and died the Venerable Bede, perhaps the most respected of all early Christian historians. A pupil of Bede's, Egbert, became archbishop of York and established there a school, one of whose products was the celebrated Alcuin, to whom Charlemagne turned for help to revive learning in his empire.

True, education and learning in Anglo-Saxon England were confined for the most part to the clergy; but, in fact, the educated classes in all ages, at least until recent times, have consisted of a small minority. Not until the later Middle Ages did this minority begin to include laymen in large numbers. It is of the first importance, then, to notice that from the beginnings of English civilization literacy was closely associated with the Latin language. It was the language not only of the church liturgy, but of all serious writing—philosophy, theology, history, geography—whatever, in fact, an educated person turned his attention to. Moreover, large numbers of the educated not only read, but spoke Latin as a second language in all professional activities. And we shall see that in the course of time the preeminent position of Latin was even further strengthened.

The effect of this preeminence on the vocabulary of English obviously must have been extensive. A language which has served the needs of a barbarian people may exploit its own internal powers of growth to keep pace with a moderate rate of cultural progress. But faced with immediate and rapidly expanding needs it will make use of external support if available. The educated men who read extensively in Latin must sometimes have had need of its resources when they spoke and wrote their native language. It would be strange indeed if they did not find it necessary to introduce a Latin word into an English context.

Decline in the Viking Period

The auspicious beginning that we have just described was, however, destined for a violent interruption. During the eighth century, the Scandinavians, who were still pagans, became aggressive, and began to mount hostile attacks in various directions over Europe. One wing, composed largely of Swedes, moved eastward toward Russia and reached Constantinople. An outer line, followed mostly by Norwegians, struck at northern England and Scotland, Ireland, the smaller islands, and Spain, and penetrated the Mediterranean. Part of this movement also reached the shores of North America. A third line of invading forces moved between the other two and, composed largely of Danes, fell on the coast of France and on eastern and southern England. These hostile forces are sometimes referred to as Vikings or Norsemen, but in England at that time they were often referred to as the Danes.

In the early period the attacks consisted of raids for plunder. By the middle of the ninth century, however, they assumed the proportions of invasion. Large armies appeared on the coast and soon overran most of the land. Only the kings of Wessex were able to make a stand against them. The most celebrated of these, King Alfred the Great, imposed a stunning defeat upon the Danes in 878 and forced upon them a treaty of peace. By the terms of the treaty large numbers of Danes were allowed to settle peacefully in the Midlands and North of England, where they followed their own mode of life in such numbers that that part of England became known as the Danelaw.

The peace, unfortunately, did not forever end the Danish threat. At the end of the tenth century, the invasions were renewed, but this time, as no king of Alfred's capacity was on hand to stop them, they culminated in the accession of the Dane, King Canute, who ruled all of England from 1017 to 1035.

Revival of Learning

One result of the Viking movement in England was the complete destruction of the cultural achievement of the North, and indeed an almost total interruption of learning in all parts of England. One of Alfred's claims to greatness consisted of his efforts to revive learning and reestablish the traditions of civilized life. In this he was only partially successful, but later a genuine revival did succeed. As a result an extensive literature has come down to us in the English of Wessex, which became for a time the standard literary language.

This standard language did not, however, reflect the actual state of the spoken language throughout the kingdom. Large parts of the population in the central and northern parts of the island who lacked the influence of books and education were of mixed English and Scandinavian stock. At that time the Scandinavian tongues were more similar to English than they are today. In fact the Danes could learn English with relative ease. Nonetheless, a widespread bilingualism in this part of the land led to two important results: first, many words of Norse origin came into use among English speakers; and second, the use of the English language by many unlettered foreign folk supported a tendency toward the gradual disappearance of many features of the English grammatical system.

These effects are not, of course, fully apparent in the recorded literature of Old English, which, as stated above, continued to be written in the West Saxon literary tradition familiar to the scholars and scribes of the late Old English period. It is this literary language that is known to us today as *Old English*.[8]

In summary, then, the events before the twelfth century most important to the history of the English language were:

1. The settlement of the Anglo-Saxon tribes in England in the fifth and sixth centuries, with the establishment there of a Low West Germanic tongue, the basic features of which have been permanent.

2. The rapid spread of Christian Latin learning in the seventh and eighth centuries.

3. The Scandinavian invasions and settlements in the ninth century, which affected the grammar and lexicon of spoken English, though these effects were not visible in the literary language until later times.

4. The reestablishment of Latin learning and the maintenance of a written literature in English between King Alfred's time and the coming of the Normans.

THE MIDDLE ENGLISH PERIOD

Coming of the Norman French

The last of the Anglo-Saxon kings of England was Edward the Confessor, who had spent a part of his early life as an exile in Normandy. He retained

---

[8] A word of caution is in order. The term *Old English* is sometimes used by the general public to refer to any English which is antiquated. Thus the language of Shakespeare or of Chaucer is sometimes called Old English. Technically Shakespeare's language is Early Modern English and Chaucer's is Late Middle English. Old English refers to English before the twelfth century.

an affection for things French and, as king of England, accepted the help of foreign favorites in his administration. Among his friends was William, duke of Normandy, who visited England in 1051 and supposedly received from Edward the promise of succession to the throne. On this and other equally dubious claims, William took the kingship of England by force upon the death of Edward in 1066, setting aside the rights of the native claimant, Harold of Wessex. By 1070 William had subdued all of England to his rule. The immediate and obvious effects of the Conquest were political. William finally established such complete control of the island that the old independence of the Anglo-Saxon earls was destroyed. Their possessions passed into the hands of Norman or other French adherents of the Conqueror so completely that by the end of the century the upper nobility was completely French and more closely bound to the crown than the nobility had ever been in Anglo-Saxon England. The new masters in turn bestowed lands upon French followers whom they could trust. In this way the aristocracy, both nobles and gentry, became predominantly French in language.

Also, since bishops and abbots of great monasteries were recognized as lords of the realm, the native hierarchy was eventually replaced by one pleasing to William and his successors. Some of the individuals involved were indeed men of great ability, such as Lanfranc and St. Anselm, both of whom had come, one to succeed the other, from the great Abbey of Bec to the archbishopric of Canterbury. Many, however, were mere political appointees of very dubious competence to administer a monastery on monastic, or even elementary Christian, principles. The following report from the contemporary Anglo-Saxon Chronicle testifies vividly to this state of affairs.

> In this year [1083] a disagreement arose at Glastonbury between the Abbot Thurstan and his monks. The monks complained to him in friendly fashion and begged that he govern them according to the rule, and they would be loyal and obedient to him. The abbot, however, would have none of this but did them evil and promised them worse. One day the abbot entered the chapter-room, spoke against the monks and threatened to mistreat them. He sent for laymen, who invaded the chapter-room, fully armed against the monks. Then the monks were terrified. Not knowing what to do except to scatter, some ran into the church and locked the doors against the soldiers, who followed them to the church, intending to drag them out since the monks dared not leave. And that day a terrible thing occurred there. The Frenchmen broke into the choir, hurling missiles toward the altar

where the monks were. Some of the soldiers went to an upper floor and shot arrows down into the sanctuary so that many of the arrows stuck in the crucifix above the altar. The wretched monks lay about the altar; some crept underneath it, earnestly begging mercy of God since none might be expected of men. What more can we say except that the soldiers poured down arrows while others broke open the doors and surged in. They slew some of the monks, and so many others were so badly wounded that the blood flowed from the altar, down the steps, and onto the floor. Three monks were murdered and eighteen wounded.[9]

Such and so tender was the Christian hand of the French in England. The changes, however, were more than merely administrative or political. Five centuries earlier, when Christianity had first spread in Anglo-Saxon England, the native monastic scholars included among their interests a concern for the preservation in writing of the cultural inheritance of the past, even though it had been pagan. To this concern we owe the present existence of such literary treasures as *Beowulf*. No such tolerance was to be expected of the Norman spoiler, lay or religious, for his fellow Christians, his fellow monks, or the illiterate peasants who could turn only to them for light and comfort.

The English Language in Decline

It is no wonder, then, that literature in the native language ceased to be officially encouraged on any large scale in the cloisters, where alone it could possibly have survived in that era. For a long period of time such writing as would appeal to the leisure classes of court and manor would be in French, or in that variety of it which we call Anglo-Norman. Serious writing in general, such as would appeal to the learned clergy, was in Latin. In the twelfth and thirteenth centuries, a considerable body of writing flowed forth in Anglo-Norman and Anglo-Latin, but in English, with a few striking exceptions, there was only a thin trickle of religious writing such as might be preserved by the lower clergy of English descent for the lower classes of native laymen, or by a rare native bishop like St. Wulfstan, bishop of Worcester, whose peace and influence not even William dared violate.

---

[9] From the original text in Charles Plummer, ed., *Two of the Saxon Chronicles*, 2 vols. (Oxford, 1892–99), 1: 214–15. An excellent complete translation is also available: G. N. Garmonsway, ed., *The Anglo-Saxon Chronicle* (London, 1953), pp. 214–15. In this translation see also the account of Henry of Poitou (pp. 257–58).

So far as the spoken language was concerned, English continued to be used by the numerical majority, but after a generation or two there was no longer recognized a single standard form of English with the prestige of upper-class speech or literary preference. The results of this condition were principally two: first, the spoken language continued in use for a long period of time without the conservative influence of a written literature, and therefore inherent tendencies to change were unchecked and progressed rapidly; second, the differences between regional forms, or dialects, were more firmly established than ever.

These results were, in turn, to have far-reaching consequences on the state of the language and the literature. First, however, let us see how English at last recovered its status as the language of the whole people and of its literature.

Recovery

In the course of time intermarriages between native English and Anglo-Normans increased, and, in the normal processes of family life, many children of these marriages learned to speak English as well as French. Many other native English put themselves to the trouble of learning French because of its social or other practical values. In this way, a part of the population came by degrees to form a bilingual "middle" between the highest and the lowest social orders. Undoubtedly this middle would have continued to grow in any case, but political events in the thirteenth century favored such growth in a special way.

So long as important families of Norman descent continued to hold feudal estates in both England and Normandy, as was common from the Conquest through the twelfth and into the thirteenth century, simple necessity and convenience required the preservation of French among the upper classes. In such cases, however, the feudal landowner in theory owed a double allegiance, one to the king of England and the other to the king of France. Allegiance to the king of France was not at first a matter of concern, for the simple reason that his power was relatively weak. Henry II of England, for example, who held the throne from 1154 to 1189, ruled with great power and prestige over a far larger part of France than the king of France himself. This imbalance was, however, soon to be redressed by a decline in the power of the king of England and a rise in the power of the king of France.

In 1204 King Philip II of France took control of Normandy, which was then lost to the English crown. Thereafter, as hostility between the kings grew more intense, feudal loyalty made it more and more necessary for Anglo-Norman nobles to choose one overlord, the king of England or the king of France, and to relinquish the estates held under the other. Forty years later this necessity became legally binding by joint proclamations of King Henry III of England and King Louis IX of France.

At the same time active hostility developed in England against things French, even among the descendants of the old Anglo-Norman families. When Henry III, already in trouble because of his unpopular foreign entanglements, married a French wife (1236) and introduced many new French favorites into positions of power in England, the older families nursed a strong resentment against the new French. Finally, in 1337, active war broke out between France and England and was renewed intermittently for so long that it is known to historians as the Hundred Years' War.

Despite its declining position, French did not lose all of its prestige, but continued to be cultivated, with two important differences: first, the old Norman dialect was now considered to be provincial, and Central or Parisian French became the fashion; second, in the course of time nearly all Englishmen, even those who learned and used French skillfully, like Geoffrey Chaucer and John Gower, learned it as a second language, a part of their education rather than of their birth and early speech.

Thus, by the time of Chaucer's birth, about 1340, English was again the native language of all classes of people in England. This is made quite explicit in the words of William of Nassyngton, who, about this time, was translating from Latin and French sources a book of religious instruction, near the beginning of which he wrote:

Na latyne wil I speke ne wast,
Bot Inglische þat men vses mast,
ffor þat es yhour kynde langage
Þat yhe haf mast here of vsage.
Þat can ilke man vnderstande
Þat es borne in Ingelande,
ffor þat langage es mast shewed
Als wele amonge lered als lewed.
Latyne, als I trowe, can nane
Bot þa þat has it of skole tane.
Summe can frankische and na Latyne

Þat vsed has court and dwelled þar-jn,
And some can of latyne a party
Þat can frankys bot febilly,
And som vnderstandes Inglische
Þat nouthir can latyn na frankische;
Bot lered and lawed, alde and yhunge,
Alle vnderstandes Inglische tunge.[10]

The extent to which this development was completed before Chaucer's death in 1400 is shown by two other pieces of evidence. In this period, as in all periods, old methods and customs were more jealously preserved in courts and schools than in other parts of society, except perhaps the church. In the courts of England from the time of the Conquest, cases had been pleaded in the Anglo-Norman tongue even though the parties concerned might know nothing of the language. However, by mid-fourteenth century the general ignorance of French became such an inconvenience that the Sheriff's Court of London (1356) began to conduct its proceedings in English. Six years later (1362) Parliament legislated in the famous Statute of Pleading that henceforth court trials must be conducted in English. Official recognition was thus expressed that the practical use of French as a living language anywhere in England was a thing of the past—a state of affairs accepted at the end of the century even by the royal family, for in addressing to Parliament his claim to the throne (1399), the usurper King Henry IV spoke in English.

Also, by long-established custom the education of the young had been carried on in French. Since only children of the upper class received an education, and since their first step in learning was to read Latin, the procedure was to translate from Latin into French. This method was so tenaciously preserved that as late as the time of Chaucer's birth, a child who spoke English as his native tongue had first to know French before he could learn Latin. Conservative though teachers usually are, this prac-

---

[10] *Speculum Vitae*, British Museum Add. MS. 33995, f. 1: 'I will not write in Latin but in English, which people use most, because that is your natural language, which you most commonly use and which every man can understand who is born in England, for it is most in use among learned and uneducated. None know Latin except those who have learned it in school. Some, who frequent the court and live there, know French but no Latin. And some know Latin but little French, and some understand English that know neither Latin nor French. But all, learned and unlearned, old and young, understand the English tongue.'

tice had to be given up by the middle of the fourteenth century, partly
perhaps because of the unsettled conditions that resulted from the Black
Death, for, as one chronicler tells us, after that time John Cornwall and
Richard Pencrich, two masters of Latin grammar, changed the custom
"so þat now, þe ȝere of oure Lorde a þowsand þre hundred and foure
score and fyue . . . children leueþ Frensche and construeþ and lerneþ
in Englische."[11]

Regional Dialect

As English became more generally used by literate folk, conditions were
established favorable to the appearance of a substantial literary output in
English, and such indeed did appear, though there was no consensus on
the particular regional variety of English that was proper to literature.
As a consequence, the student today who wishes to read Middle English
literature extensively in its original form must be familiar with several
important dialects. First, there was Northern English, which included not
only the shires north of the Humber River, but Lowland Scotland as well.
Because of the influence of Scottish national feeling this dialect continued
to be used for serious literary purposes longer than any other purely
regional variety. Its most familiar example is perhaps the poetry of Robert
Burns, but from the fourteenth to the sixteenth centuries it supported a
rich literary tradition.

   The southern area included the language of Kent and that of the
Southwest, the latter being the lineal descendant of the speech of the Old
English kingdom of Wessex. Between these two extremes lay the broad
Midland area, which must be divided in two, for the speech of the West
Midlands was quite different from that of the East and enjoyed in the
fourteenth century a truly astonishing literary renaissance, leaving to us,
among other things, both *Piers Plowman* and *Sir Gawayne and the Green
Knight.*

   This type of English was not, however, destined to prevail. More
important were the varieties of speech and writing of the eastern half of
the Midland area. There are strong reasons for locating the center of the

---

[11] Cited at length in Baugh, pp. 178–79. It must not be supposed from this passage
that English became the subject of instruction. Only Latin was considered suitable
for scholastic attention, and the child's first effort in formal education was to read the
Lord's Prayer in Latin.

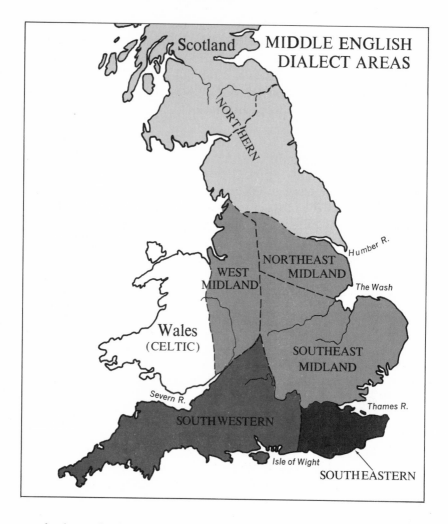

standard speech of the late fourteenth century in the Southeast Midlands. Here was located the city of London, the most populous city in England, and at that time its chief seaport. Here also were to be found the great centers of legal training, the Inns of Court, to which young men of birth and position came from all over England. Though Oxford and Cambridge were at no great distance from London, their influence on the course of the language has not been established, but the influence of Westminster, at that time outside the city, center of all the activities of the royal government, was of the first importance. The speech of the courtiers who frequented London and its environs and of the small army of civil servants who conducted the king's business became the mark of the sophisticated gentleman.

The literary standard, however, need not always in this period have coincided with the prestige speech. Chaucer's English was certainly the literary English acceptable at the court. His poetry was also read, admired, and even imitated by succeeding generations, but it has been shown that a Midland variety, in some respects not identical with Chaucer's language and owing more to the Central Midlands than the Southeast, was extensively cultivated in this period, especially, though not exclusively, in religious prose, Wyclifite as well as orthodox. Later, in the second quarter of the fifteenth century, as English became more generally used in official documents, the "Chancery" standard was adopted, with some minor characteristics different from either.[12] All three have their place in the history of the emerging standard language. It is, of course, a fortunate accident of history that Chaucer used the East Midland English for the greatest poetry that had been written in England up to that time. It has sometimes been said that our standard language was determined by Chaucer's decision to use it. We know now that the truth is the other way around. Chaucer used it because it was native to him and, in its most important features, that best known to men of the court and men of affairs in and about London.

Before the end of the fifteenth century, then, we come to the close of the Middle English period and of the Middle Ages in general, and to the threshold of the English Renaissance. By this time English has recovered a single language standard for cultivated society and literary expression, one which was to give voice in the sixteenth century to one of the richest epochs in the literary history of the world.

---

[12] M. L. Samuels, *English Studies* 44 (1963): 81–94.

Chapter 9

EARLY ENGLISH

Middle English and Old English

The English language of the Middle Ages is divided into two phases: Old English, extending to 1100 or 1150, when the social effect of the Norman Conquest was complete; and Middle English, which lasted to the fifteenth century, when a standard language had emerged with characteristics sufficiently like our own to be called Modern. If a date is needed to fix the maturity of this growth, we might, somewhat arbitrarily, select the beginning of the Tudor period in 1485, though there are reasons for selecting a date earlier than that but certainly not much later.

Some knowledge of the character of the language in the two early periods is useful, both to explain the features of Modern English, which often seem puzzling if not altogether whimsical, and to provide access to early literature of permanent artistic worth. The further back in time one proceeds, of course, the more unfamiliar the language appears, until in its earliest preserved form it looks like a foreign language altogether. For convenience, then, let us look first at the medieval states of the language in reverse order.

ENGLISH IN THE AGE OF CHAUCER

The language of Chaucer is usually classed as Middle English and that of Shakespeare as Modern. Actually, the sound of Shakespeare's language differed somewhat more from our own than is commonly supposed, but these differences as well as differences in other aspects of the language, grammar, and vocabulary, were not so great as to put the modern reader to the need of a translation or of special language study.

In Chaucer's language, however, the contrasts with Present English are more numerous, including differences in sound which the student of literature cannot safely ignore. In the two hundred years that separated these two great poets, extensive and rapid changes took place in the vowels of English, especially the long vowels, and there occurred other important changes in the form and meaning of words.

Wyclif's Bible

The characteristics of English in Chaucer's age may be seen in the Nativity story from the Gospel of St. Luke as given in a translation of the Latin Vulgate (sometimes called the Wyclif translation) made by John Purvey just about the time when Chaucer was composing the Canterbury Tales.

And it was don in tho daies, a maundement wente out fro the emperour August, that al the world schulde be discryued. This firste discryuyng was maad of Cyryn, iustice of Sirie. And alle men wenten to make professioun, ech in to his owne citee. And Joseph wente vp from Galilee, fro the citee Nazareth, in to Judee, in to a citee of Dauid, that 5 is clepid Bethleem, for that he was of the hous and of the meyne of Dauid, that he schulde knouleche with Marie, his wijf, that was weddid to hym, and was greet with child. And it was don, while thei weren there, the daies weren fulfillid, that sche schulde bere child. And sche bare hir first borun sone, and wlappide hym in clothis, and 10 leide hym in a cratche, for ther was no place to hym in no chaumbir. And scheepherdis weren in the same cuntre, wakynge and kepynge the watchis of the ny3t on her flok. And lo! the aungel of the Lord stood bisidis hem, and the cleernesse of God schinede aboute hem; and thei dreden with greet drede. And the aungel seide to hem, 15 Nyle 3e drede; for lo! Y preche to 3ou a greet ioye, that schal be to al puple. For a sauyoure is borun to dai to 3ou, that is Crist the Lord, in the citee of Dauid. And this is a tokene to 3ou; 3e schulen fynde a 3ong child wlappid in clothis, and leid in a cratche. And sudenli ther was maad with the aungel a multitude of heuenli kny3thod, heriynge 20 God, and seiynge, Glorie be in the hi3este thingis to God, and in erthe pees be to men of good wille. And it was don, as the aungelis passiden awei fro hem in to heuene, the scheephirdis spaken togider, and seiden, Go we ouer to Bethleem, and se we this word that is maad, which the

Lord hath maad, and schewide to vs. And thei hiȝynge camen, and   25
founden Marie and Joseph, and the ȝong child leid in a cratche. And
thei seynge, knewen of the word that was seid to hem of this child.
And alle men that herden wondriden, and of these thingis that weren
seid to hem of the scheephirdis. But Marie kepte alle these wordis,
berynge togider in hir herte. And the scheepherdis turneden aȝen,   30
glorifyinge and heriynge God in alle thingis that thei hadden herd
and seyn, as it was seid to hem.

GRAPHIC FEATURES

Now while it is certainly true that this English is noticeably different from
ours, it is also true that the likenesses are greater than the differences. Of
the latter some are merely in the conventions of writing (**graphics**). At the
time of which we are speaking and indeed until well into the modern
period, *u* and *v* were regarded as variations of the same letter, and therefore each of these might be found where today we would expect use of the
other: *descryued* (l. 2), *Dauid* (l. 5), *sauyoure* (l. 17), *vp* (l. 4), *vs* (l. 25). The
same was true of *i* and *j*: *iustice* (l. 3), *ioye* (l. 16). Again, *i* and *y* were used
for the same vowel, but the present custom of always using *y* in final position had not yet been established: *sudenli* (l. 19), *heuenli* (l. 20), *awei* (l. 23),
thei (l. 25). More noticeable is the survival in the fourteenth century of the
old letter ȝ (called "yogh"), which in initial position was equivalent to
consonantal *y* as in *ȝe* 'ye' (l. 16), or, in medial and final position, was a
voiceless fricative [x] or [ç], retained now only in the spelling *gh*: *nyȝt*
'night' (l. 13), *hiȝeste* 'highest' (l. 21). Another graphic difference is the
doubling of letters for vowel length, similar to the doubling of *e* and *o* in
modern usage: *wijf* (l. 7), *maad* (l. 3). Finally, it appears that spelling was
much less consistent than it is today, when we are expected to spell the
same word always in the same way: *scheepherdis* (ll. 12, 30), *-hirdis* (l. 29).

LEXICAL FEATURES

Considering the fact that this language is now close to six hundred years
old the number of obsolete words is not strikingly large: *tho* (l. 1), *clepid*
(l. 6), *meyne* (l. 6), *wlappide*[1] (l. 10), *cratche*[2] (l. 19), *heriynge* (l. 20), *hiȝynge*

---

[1] The phonological history of *wlap* is not certain.

[2] Introduced as early as the thirteenth century, but reintroduced in the nineteenth
in its French form, *crèche*.

(l. 25). Other items not altogether strange show some variation in form, or a semantic difference, or both: *maundement* (l. 1), *discryued*[3] (l. 2), *knouleche* (l. 7), *for that* 'because' (l. 6), *wakynge* (l. 12), *maad* (l. 3), *kny3thod* (l. 20). Obvious variations appear also in the form or meaning of prepositions: *fro* (l. 1), *to* (l. 11), *on* (l. 13), *bisidis* (l. 14) and especially *of* (l. 3), which with the same spelling did double duty for both 'of' and 'off.'

FORM

Differences in form (morphological), consisting of the retention of inflectional endings now obsolete, are not more numerous. Some are merely spelling variants, such as *-id* for *-ed*, but others are somewhat more substantial. Old noun plurals in *-n* such as *ien* 'eyes,' or plurals with no suffix, such as *hors* 'horses' might have been expected, though in fact none do occur in this passage. Verbs with plural subjects regularly have *-en* suffixes, and a few show other minor variations from current use: *bare* (l. 10), *schinede* (l. 14), *schewide* (l. 25). Among the pronouns *3e* (l. 16) is the regular nominative plural of the second person, *hem* (l. 14) the objective plural of the third, and *her* (l. 13) the possessive plural.

SYNTAX

In the larger matters of syntax and style there is very little if any difference sufficient to create an obstacle to understanding. The participial modifier following the pronoun (l. 27) would not be usual today, and two other features are altogether discontinued: the negative imperative *Nyle 3e drede* (l. 16) lit. 'not-will ye dread,' for 'do not be afraid,' and the inversion of the simple verb as in *go we* 'let us go' (l. 24) and *se we* (l. 24) 'let us see.' Also an article or a preposition may be used or omitted (ll. 5, 9) contrary to current use. Perhaps the most striking syntactic feature is the double negative (l. 11), now frowned upon but until the sixteenth century quite acceptable.

    In general, however, the sentences follow a recognizable pattern. They sometimes allow a slightly looser structure with more loose coordination than a modern stylist would recommend, but the arrangement of

---

[3] Notice that, although Modern English has restored the Latin spelling *b* for the French *v*, this word is used here in a meaning closer to its Latin source.

subjects, verbs, modifiers, phrases, and clauses is that which we all know. An intelligent modern reader, even though historically unsophisticated, might well judge Purvey's language "quaint," but hardly "different."

Phonology

So far, then, as form and syntax are concerned, English had become "modern" by the fourteenth century. However, many of the familiar forms conceal extensive differences in sound, not immediately apparent because our English spelling convention has not evolved in harmony with the changes, especially those affecting the long vowels, which took place between Chaucer and Shakespeare.

VOWELS

The phonetic values of the written vowel symbols in fourteenth-century English are somewhat like those encountered by the student who is beginning the study of Spanish or Italian.

The following table gives the generic name for each of the long vowels, its variant spellings in Middle English texts, and its approximate phonetic value.

ME SOUND	ME SPELLING	PHONETIC SYMBOL	PRONUNCIATION
$\bar{\imath}$	i,y	[i:]	as in PE *seed*
$\bar{e}$[4]	e,ee	[e:]	as in PE *mate*
$\bar{\varepsilon}$[4]	e,ee	[ɛ:]	as in PE *bear*
$\bar{a}$	a,aa	[a:][5]	as in PE *car*
$\bar{u}$	ou,ow	[u:]	as in PE *rude*
$\bar{o}$[4]	o,oo	[o:]	as in PE *coat*
$\bar{\varrho}$[4]	o,oo	[ɔ:]	as in PE *cause*

The Middle English $\bar{u}$ was commonly spelled *ou*, to help distinguish it from the *u* in words borrowed from French, in which *u* first had the value of [y:]. Since this latter sound was probably not in wide use in East

---

[4] Some editors of ME texts call $\bar{e}$ and $\bar{o}$ "close" vowels, and $\bar{\varepsilon}$ and $\bar{\varrho}$ "open" vowels, referring to the greater degree of opening between tongue and palate in the second pair.

[5] ME $\bar{a}$ has often been equated to [ɑ:]; but see E. J. Dobson, *English Pronunciation, 1500–1700*, 2 vols. (Oxford, 1957), 2: 594–606.

Midland speech (from which the standard language has been derived), it was modified to the rising diphthong [ɪu] and remains approximately the same today in many words of French origin: *use, music, cure,* etc. Thus it fell together with the same sound in words of native origin in which the spelling was *eu/ew* and *iu/iw* such as *knew, new.* Thus *hue* (OF *hu* 'cry') and *hue* 'color' became homonyms.[6] Other diphthongs are indicated by the spellings *au (aw), ei/ai (ey/ay), iu (iw), oi (oy), ou (ow).* The spelling *oi* stood for two sounds [ɔɪ] and [ʊɪ], but in Modern English these have been leveled by spelling influence to [ɔɪ].[7]

Chaucer's short vowels were not as significantly different from ours as his long vowels, but a few differences are important enough to notice.

1. Short *a* was not [æ], but a sound further back, sometimes said to be [ɑ], but more probably [a].

2. Short *u* was rounded like the vowel of *pull,* not unrounded as in *dull.* Short *u,* however, was sometimes concealed under the spelling *o,* especially before and after *n* or *m.* This practice is retained in the modern spelling of *son* and *ton.*

3. Short *o* was rounded as in the present standard speech of England, not as in the common American pronunciation of *hot* and *lot.*

4. Short vowels in unstressed syllables may have been reduced to [ə], especially in prefixes and inflectional endings. Final unstressed *-e,* when preserved, had this sound.

CONSONANTS

Most consonants have not changed; for most the values attached to letters in Modern English may be applied, but a few differences are to be noted.

1. Consonants now silent were sounded in such words as *knight, know, folk, half, gnaw, write.*

2. Spellings of *ng* indicated two sounds as in *finger,* not one as in *singer.* In fact, [ŋ] was not a Middle English phoneme, but an allophone of [n] when it occurred before *g* or *k.*

---

[6] Actually there was a third Middle English diphthong. It was spelled *eu/ew* and was pronounced [ɛu] rather than [iu], but ultimately it fell together with the other two, thus adding the third homonym *hew* (OE *hēawian* 'cut').

[7] On the importance of recognizing the preservation of these two diphthongs, see p. 183.

3. The spelling *gh* was not yet silent but had the value of [x] or [ç] as in German *nach* or Spanish *hijo*.

4. *r* was trilled, at least slightly.

5. Initial *h* was silent in words of French origin, as it still is in *honor* and *hour*. This practice was sometimes extended to native words, especially if they occurred under weak stress, as in *he*, *him*, *hem* 'them,' *had*.

STRESS AND SYLLABICATION

Words from French also preserved for a time their original stress pattern, as reflected in such spellings as *citee* and *contree*. This fact is of particular importance in reading verse. For example, in Chaucer's lines

> *And bathëd every veyne in swich licour*
> *Of which vertu engendred is the flour*

the metrical pattern indicates stress on the second syllable of *licour* and of *vertu*. These were not for Chaucer artificial pronunciations.[8]

Also important in the reading of verse is the fact that the inflectional ending *-ed* was frequently syllabic. Thus *bathed* in the above couplet had two syllables. Final unstressed *-e*, vestige of an older inflectional ending, was certainly dying out in general speech by the end of the fourteenth century, but the conservative tradition was utilized by Chaucer in his poetry to suit the needs of meter. Consequently, in reading his lines we find it necessary at some points to pronounce *-e* [ə] and at others to pass it by as simply an orthographical relic. At the end of a line *-e* was certainly pronounced at some points, as we conclude from the rhymes in the first stanza of *The Book of Troilus*:

> *The double sorwe of Troilus to tellen*
> *That was the kyng Priamus sone of Troye,*
> *In lovynge how his aventurës fellen*
> *Fro wo to wele and after out of joie*
> *My purpos is, er that I partë fro ye.*[9]

---

[8] Variation in stress continued to be common until the sixteenth century, as readers of Shakespeare know who have encountered such pronunciations as *cómplete, perséver,* and *envý.*

[9] This is a weakened or unstressed form of the objective case of the pronoun and has the short vowel [ə]. It is not to be mistaken for the nominative plural *ye*, which has a long vowel. See pp. 141, 193.

In line 5, *fro ye* must be two words [frɔ jə], and therefore the rhyming words are dissyllabic. Some readers prefer always to sound *-e* at the end of a line, thus imparting a more fluid quality to the reading. These points are illustrated fairly well in the opening lines of "The Knight's Tale":

> *Whilom, as olde stories tellen us,*
> *Ther was a duc that highte Theseus.*
> *Of Atthenes he was lord and governour,*
> *And in his tyme swich a conquerour*
> *That gretter was ther noon under the sonne.*
> *Ful many a riche contree hadde he wonne;*
> *What with his wysdom and his chivalrie,*
> *He conquered al the regne of Femenye,*
> *That whilom was ycleped Scithia,*
> *And weddede the queene Ypolita,*
> *And broghte hire hoom with hym in his contrée*
> *With muchel glorie and greet solempnytee,*
> *And eek hir yonge suster Emelýe.*

Notice that the endings in roman type must be pronounced to fill out the ten-syllable, five-stress line. Compare, however, *regne* (l. 8), *queene* (l. 10), and *broghte* (l. 11). Notice the varying stress on *contrée* in lines 6 and 11.

Summary

The most important considerations, then, for reading the language of Chaucer's time refer to: (1) major differences in the sounds of the long vowels and the diphthongs; (2) fewer, but still important differences in the short vowels and consonants; (3) still fewer important differences in word order and word forms; (4) important differences in vocabulary which will be noticed later.

ENGLISH BEFORE THE NORMAN CONQUEST

Looking back from Chaucer to Old English we encounter very remarkable changes. About the same interval of time elapsed between the writing of the extant copy of *Beowulf* and the birth of Chaucer as has elapsed between the birth of Shakespeare and the writing of these lines. And yet, while we can read Shakespeare with relative convenience, Chaucer would have found *Beowulf* as strange as a foreign language. In other words, so far as the written records bear witness, the changes that occurred after the Norman Conquest were more radical than in any other period of which we have historical knowledge.

The most important of these changes in the language were of two kinds: those that affected its lexicon or its total word resources, and those that affected its grammatical structure, or more precisely its morphology. For practical purposes we may contrast Chaucer's language or that of his time with that of the late West Saxon authors, though the latter was more directly preserved in the Southwest dialect, which differed in some relatively minor respects from Chaucer's.

The same narrative that we read in the Wyclif-Purvey translation of the Bible had also been translated into Old English some time before the Norman Conquest. Both translations were made independently from the Latin, not one from the other. Nevertheless, they adhere to the original closely enough to furnish us with an excellent means of comparing Old English with Middle English.

    1. Sōþlīce on þām dagum wæs geworden gebod fram þām
     Indeed in those days (it) was commanded by the

cāsere Augusto, þæt eall ymbehwyrft wǣre tōmearcod.
Emperor Augustus that all (the) world were (to be) enrolled.

    2. Þēos tōmearcodnes wæs ǣryst geworden fram þām dēman
     This enrollment was first made by the judge

Syrige Cirino.
of Syria Cyrinus.

    3. And ealle hig ēodon, and syndrige fērdon on hyra
     And all they went, and each one traveled to his (own)

ceastre.*
city.

    4. Ðā   fērde   Iosep fram Galilea of þǣre ceastre
     Then journeyed Joseph from Galilee from the city

Nazareth on Iudeisce ceastre Dauides, sēo is genemned
(of) Nazareth to (the) Judean city of David, which is named

Bethleem, for þām þe hē wæs of Dauides hūse and hīrede;
Bethlehem, because he was of David's house and family;

5. Þæt hē fērde mid Marian þe him beweddod wæs,
That he journeyed† with Mary who to him wedded was,

and wæs geēacnod.
and was with child.

6. Sōþlīce wæs geworden þā hī þār wæron, hire dagas
Indeed, (it) happened when they there were, her days

wæron gefyllede þæt hēo cende.
were fulfilled that she give birth.

7. And hēo cende hyre frumcennedan sunu, and hine mid
And she bore her firstborn son, and him with

cildclāþum bewand, and hine on binne ālēde, for þām þe
swaddling-clothes wrapped, and him in (a) manger laid, because

hig næfdon rūm on cumena hūse.
they had not room in (the) guests' house [inn].

8. And hyrdas wæron on þām ylcan rīce waciende, and
And shepherds were in the same country watching, and

nihtwæccan healdende ofer heora heorda.
nightwatches holding over their flocks.

9. Þā stōd Drihtnes engel wiþ hig, and Godes
Then stood (the) Lord's angel before them, and God's

beorhtnes him ymbe scēan; and hī him mycelum ege ādrēdon.‡
brightness them about shone; and they with much fear feared.

10. And sē engel him tō cwæð, Nelle ge ēow ādrædan;‡
And the angel them to spoke, Do not ye fear;

sōþlīce nū ic ēow bodie mycelne gefēan, sē bið
indeed now I to you announce great joy, which shall be

eallum folce;
to all folk;

11. For þām tō dæg ēow ys Hǣlend ācenned, sē is
Because today to you is (a) Savior born, who is

Drihten Crīst, on Dauides ceastre.
(the) Lord Christ, in David's city.

12. And þis tācen ēow byð: Gē gemētað ān cild
And this (a) token to you shall be: ye shall find a child

hrǣglum bewunden, and on binne ālēd.
with swaddling clothes wrapped, and in (a) manger laid.

13. And þā wæs fǣringa geworden§ mid þām engle
And then was suddenly with the angel

mycelnes heofonlīces werydes, God heriendra and þus
(a) multitude of the heavenly host, God praising and thus

cweþendra,
saying,

14. Gode sȳ wuldor on hēahnesse, and on eorðan sybb
To God be glory on high, and on earth peace

mannum gōdes willan.
to men of good will.

15. And hit wæs geworden þā ðā englas tō heofene fērdon,
And it came to pass when the angels to heaven went,

þā hyrdas him betwȳnan sprǣcon and cwǣdon, Utun faran tō
the shepherds them between spoke and said, Let us go to

Bethleem, and gesēon þæt word þe geworden is, þæt Drihten
Bethlehem, and see the word that has happened, that (the) Lord

ūs ætȳwde.
to us revealed.

16. And hig efstende cōmon, and gemētton Marian and
And they hastening came, and found Mary and

Iosep, and þæt cild on binne ālēd.
Joseph, and the child in (a) manger laid.

17. Þā hī þæt gesāwon, þā oncnēowon hig be þām
When they that saw, then knew they by the

worde þe him gesǣd wæs be þām cilde.
word that to them spoken was of the child.

18. And ealle þā ðe gehȳrdon wundredon be
And all those that heard wondered concerning

þām þe him þā hyrdas sǣdon.
those (things) which to them the shepherds said.

19. Maria gehēold ealle þās word, on hyre heortan smēagende.
Mary   kept   all those words, in her   heart   reflecting.

20. Dā   gewendon hām þā hyrdas, God wuldriende and
Then   returned   home the shepherds, God glorifying   and

heriende on eallum   þām   ðe hī gehȳrdon and gesāwon,
praising for   all   those (things) that they   heard   and   saw,

swā tō him gecweden wæs.
as   to them   spoken   was.

---

* The plural phrase *on hyra ceastre* is here translated in the singular.
† The phrase 'that he journeyed' is a mistranslation of the Latin *ut profiteretur* 'that he might be enrolled.'
‡ The phrases *hī him . . . ādrēdon* and *ge ēow ādrǣdan* are reflexive constructions not used in Modern English.
§ The phrase *wæs geworden* is a passive construction not used in Modern English.

GRAPHIC AND PHONOLOGICAL FEATURES

On first observation one might be pardoned for doubting whether this is English at all. With some direction, however, it is possible to find familiar things behind the strange appearance. In the first place, the relation of the letters to the sounds represented is not unlike that of Middle English. The letters *i*, *e*, *u*, *o*, and *a* have approximately the same values. Here, however, *y* is not a variant spelling for *i*, but represents a rounded vowel [y], similar to French *u* or German *ü*. There is also the symbol *æ* which represents the sound of the vowel in modern *hat*, long as well as short. Two diphthongs are also present here, *ĕo* and *ĕa*. Of these the first was to be simplified in Middle English as *ĕ*; in the second, however, the short and long forms have different histories, *ea* becoming *a* (thus *eall* > *all*), but *ēa* falling together with *ǣ*, both appearing in the standard language as ME *ę̄*[10] (thus OE *strēam* > ME *streem* [strɛːm]).

---

[10] This statement is a simplification of a more complex state of affairs. This translation of the gospel was written in the West Saxon dialect, in which there were two long vowels *ǣ*[1] and *ǣ*[2]. In the Anglian dialects, however, from which the standard language is derived, *ǣ*[1] was *ē*. This became ME *ę̄*.

As to the consonants, it will be noted that the letters *v* and *k* do not appear at all. These were to be introduced later by Anglo-French scribes. Therefore *f* and *c* had to do double duty. Between vowels, *f* became [v], but otherwise was pronounced as we pronounce it. Before *a, o, u* the value of *c* was [k], but before *e, i* it was generally [tʃ].[11] An even more ambiguous letter was *g*, which had three possibilities: initially before back vowels it was a voiced stop, as we use it today in words like *go* and *gate;* before front vowels it was fronted to a sound like initial *y* in *year;* medially between back vowels it was a voiced velar fricative [ɣ], for which we have no equivalent among Modern English phonemes. When doubled before a back vowel *gg* remained a velar stop, but when palatalized before front vowels it was spelled *cg* and pronounced [dʒ] as in *sedge*. In final position after a front vowel *g* sometimes was fronted and eventually formed a diphthong with the preceding vowel; thus *dæg* > *day*, *weg* > *way*.

The letter "thorn," *þ*, and the letter *ð*, called "eth" or simply "crossed *d*," were used where we use *th*, but no consistent difference in sound seems to have distinguished them. They might both occur for the voiceless consonant (as in PE *thin*) or its voiced counterpart (as in PE *then*). Between vowels they represented voiced sounds.

Finally, but phonologically of considerable importance, consonants were distinguished as to length, a feature occurring in Modern English only in compounds like *bookkeeper*. Long consonants were indicated in the spelling by doubling.

---

[11] The word *cende* [kendə] contradicts the statement, but it was the rule that the consonant remained [k] before vowels which had been fronted by *i*-umlaut.

Chapter 10

EARLY ENGLISH

Changes in Phonemic Structure

With the information thus far supplied, it is possible to read the translations of the Gospel narrative of St. Luke approximately as they were heard,
the one in the tenth or eleventh century, the other in the fourteenth. Can
we go further, grouping and classifying in such a way as to indicate the
phonemic structure of English in each of these periods? The answer is that
we can, but with some caution and with some reservations. For example,
the initial symbol in the Old English word *for* (v. 7), and *fērdon* (v. 15)
stood for the voiceless [f], whereas in *næfdon* (v. 7) and *ofer* (v. 8) it was
voiced as [v]. In Present English the difference is phonemic, but also the
contrast is supported by a spelling or graphic contrast. Since this was not
the case in Old English writing, we might suspect that the two sounds
were merely allophones of the same phoneme. However, the example of
modern pairs like *get* and *gin*, or *sheath* and *sheathe*, shows that this conclusion cannot be too easily assumed. Therefore, although the two sounds
eventually became separate phonemes, the exact date of the split remains
a matter of speculation.

Today it is relatively easy to determine the phonemes of a living
language behind its conventional spelling, because we have, at least in the
case of English, not only rich and varied written evidence of its sounds but
the continued evidence of the spoken language as well. For Early English
the written evidence is relatively scanty and the aural evidence nonexistent. We are obliged, therefore, with great care to interpret alphabetical
symbols of a past age as they were used over a long period of time during

which the corresponding sounds were presumably in a state of change, and from them deduce the course of phonological history despite the slow and uneven way in which the written symbols were modified. For example, in Old English (ge)cynd 'kind' the vowel had the value of [y], later [y:], and in rind 'rind' the vowel had the value of [i], later [i:]. Eventually the vowel in the first word became [i:] but continued to be spelled y. When did the phoneme /y:/ merge with /i:/? The evidence appeared only after the sound change was fully established—when, for example, a poet rhymed kynd and rind, or when he used a y spelling for historic /i:/, as in rynd.[1]

From the two different translations of the Nativity story it is apparent that the state of the language was considerably altered in the course of a few hundred years. It is usual to divide this early epoch into Old and Middle English, but each of these covered several centuries, and within them variations were quite important, not only chronologically but also according to the region in which a piece of writing originated.

Moreover, the definition of epochs like Old and Middle English, though they are customary and useful in historical discussion, may suggest a relative permanence in the state of language extending over several centuries.[2] This is, of course, a misleading assumption, particularly when it includes the notion of a "transition" period as an unsettled time between more stable and more important periods. The truth is that language in all periods is transitional in the sense that change is the normal state of things. Not all aspects of a language change at the same rate of speed, but it is probable that the most constant rate of change is found in the sounds of a language.

Instead of thinking, then, of a language as changing its entire structure in a transition period, it is more realistic to think of successive changes in individual phonemes, the cumulative effect of which may be extensive in several centuries. Phonemic change follows a common pattern. In special phonetic contexts a phoneme will develop positional allophones. Later, one or more of these allophones splits away as a separate phoneme

---

[1] In this account we shall indicate phonemes by slant lines and specific phones or allophones by the usual brackets.

[2] Compare the reservation of Hans Kurath (American Speech 36 [1961]: 93): "To say that language is essentially systematic at any given time . . . is not to admit that it is ever wholly systematic. . . . Relics of older usage that no longer fit into the current system and piecemeal innovations not yet systematized are ever present."

or merges with an allophone of a different phoneme. When this process is completed an important change in the structure of the language has taken place, but the entire process may take a long time.

Splitting and merger are well illustrated in the effects of umlaut, or mutation, which were already complete when the earliest English writing was put upon parchment. The plural of Old English *mūs* 'mouse' in the prehistoric period had a regular ending *mūsiz*. Under the influence of the front vowel [i] in the inflectional syllable, the stem vowel was fronted to [y:] and thus became what at first was merely a positional allophone. For a time the difference between the original [u:] as retained in the singular and its allophone [y:] in the plural remained nonsignificant. Eventually, however, the difference led to the loss of the inflectional suffix; at that point the vowels entered into contrast, and a new phoneme entered the language. Umlaut, of course, did not always produce new phonemes. A corresponding change in the plural *manniz* resulted in the historic plural *menn*. In this instance the positional allophone of the plural simply merged with the preexisting phoneme /e/. Different but equally important developments can be expected in all periods.

Subject to some limitations, then, we may attempt an approximation of the phonemic structure of Early English in the two periods of its greatest literary importance. Of the consonant phonemes represented in Late Old English writing like that of the Nativity story, the three stops and three of the seven fricatives occur in voiced and voiceless pairs:

/p/ /t/ /k/ /f/ /s/ /θ/ /ʃ/ /x/ /h/ /tʃ/
/b/ /d/ /g/   /ɤ/ /j/ /dʒ/
/m/ /n/ /r/ /l/ /w/

Some of these, notably /p,t,b,d,m,n,r,l,w/ were relatively stable during Old and Middle English except in some combinative situations. Our understanding of others depends upon our view of certain continuing changes, the most important of which find a place among the following developments.

1. Old English retained from Proto-Germanic the phoneme /k/, which first split into two allophones, velar and palatal, both of which were spelled *c*. The second of these further split into [tʃ] and [ʃ], the latter occurring after, and fusing with, /s/. The three sounds were certainly fully

distinguished in Late Old English. At any rate [k] and [tʃ] merged with similar sounds from Old French and all three were therefore different phonemes in Early Middle English. The velar sound was heard in *cuman* 'come'; the palatal sounds occurred in *cild* 'child' and *sceadu* 'shadow' and were approximately the same as their modern reflexes, that is, the sounds which have developed from them.

2. The apparent voiced counterpart of /k/, spelled *g* in modern editions of Old English texts, was derived from a voiced fricative /ɣ/ in Proto-Germanic. The stop [g] arose as a positional allophone before back vowels, either initially (*gāst*) or after /n/ (*singan*). The original velar fricative allophone [ɣ] remained between back vowels, but a palatal allophone arose with front vowels. This last, however, split away and merged with a different phoneme, /j/, from Proto-Germanic, both spelled *ge* or *gi* in Old English writing. The merger is illustrated in the similar initial sounds of *geornian* and *gēar;* the latter originated in PG /j/.

3. Proto-Germanic /x/ produced /h/ and /x/ in Old English, both spelled *h*. The former was confined to initial positions before vowels and consonants (except *w*), where it was pronounced as it is today in *heap*, *here*, and *hilt*. The latter split again into a velar allophone [x] and a palatal allophone [ç], though they retained the *h* spelling until Early Middle English, when the symbols ʒ or *gh* began to be used for these sounds. In postvocalic positions both sounds frequently became vowels in Middle English and formed new diphthongs, but they remained fricatives before /t/ until the Early Modern English period. The vestige of their former presence remains in many current *gh* spellings, as in *night* and *thought*. In Scots English, however, the fricative is still preserved.

4. Splitting and merger occurred likewise in the voiceless consonants /f/, /s/, and /θ/. Between voiced sounds all developed voiced allophones, [v], [z], and [ð], but these were not distinguished in the spelling. The first two merged in Early Middle English with like sounds from Old French and were thus recognized as new phonemes, for which the French scribes provided the convenient letters *v* and *z*. The phoneme /θ/ in Old English was spelled with the thorn letter (*þ*) or the crossed *d* (ð), but these symbols were not used to distinguish the two allophones. The crossed *d* (ð) disappeared from written documents in the thirteenth century and was replaced by *th*. Not later than the fourteenth century, when loss of inflectional endings resulted in minimal pairs like *teeth* (n.) [te:θ] and *teethe* (v.) [te:ð], the final consonants were in contrast, and /θ/ and /ð/ were separate pho-

nemes. The thorn letter, þ, often reshaped to resemble *y*, and *th* were used interchangeably for both phonemes until well into modern times.[3]

5. As indicated earlier, a characteristic of the consonant system of Old English, unlike Modern English, was length, long consonants having been indicated by doubling. The long or doubled variety of the palatal *g* was spelled *cg* and pronounced [dʒ]. Consonant length began to disappear about the middle of the thirteenth century, though doubling remains in the spelling system.[4]

The Old English vowels and diphthongs were a completely balanced set in quantitative contrast; that is, each vowel or diphthong had a long and a short phoneme:

$$/i/ \quad /e/ \quad /æ/ \quad /y/ \quad /u/ \quad /o/ \quad /ɑ/ \quad /eɑ/ \quad /eo/ \quad /io/$$
$$/i:/ \quad /e:/ \quad /æ:/ \quad /y:/ \quad /u:/ \quad /o:/ \quad /ɑ:/ \quad /e:ɑ/ \quad /e:o/ \quad /i:o/$$

The bulk of the literary records of Old English are in West Saxon. Here the symbol *æ* represented not only the short phoneme but *two* long phonemes, designated in modern times $\bar{æ}^1$ and $\bar{æ}^2$. The first of this pair is not included here, since it became /e:/ in the regional speech from which our later standard language developed. The classification of the short diphthongs is the traditional one, though it is now subject to some dispute. It is possible that in late Old English digraph spellings did not always represent diphthongs.[5] The alternative sounds suggested, however, would fall in among the short vowel phonemes and follow their subsequent history.

---

[3] Precise dates for the phonemecization of /v/, /z/, and /ð/ are difficult to prove. The Proto-Germanic bilabial voiced fricative /β/ produced the allophone [v] in Old English, but since this was generally spelled *f*, it may be assumed to have fallen in with the voiced allophone of /f/. Despite the fact that the spelling *u* for [v] appeared in proper names in Old English texts, the phonemecization of /v/ is not clearly established until Anglo-Norman times. A somewhat similar conclusion can be accepted for /z/, although the spelling *z* was also used in the same circumstances in Old English. As to /θ/ and /ð/, though we still do not distinguish them by peculiar graphs, phonemecization of /ð/ may have been as early as the period (whenever that was) when consonantal length disappeared in Middle English. Phonemic contrast may then have been recognized, since þþ had always remained voiceless between vowels.

[4] But see below on Chaucer, pp. 130–31. Length occurs in Present English only as the result of compounding, as in *penknife*, *half full*, and *misstatement*.

[5] A valuable bibliography of recent discussions of this subject is supplied by Sherman M. Kuhn in *Language* 37 (1961): 522–38.

In Early Middle English /ɑ/, /æ/, and /eɑ/ fell together as /a/; /e/, /eo/, and /io/ fell together as /ɛ/; later /y/ and /i/ fell together as /ɪ/. The short vowels /e/ and /o/ became lax (or open) /ɛ/ and /ɔ/ and therefore corresponded to the new long vowels /ɛ:/ and /ɔ:/ (see below). The short vowel system was then reduced to /ɪ/ /ɛ/ /a/ /ʊ/ /ɔ/, to which was added /ə/ by reduction of vowels in unstressed position.

Among the long vowels new phonemes resulted when /æ:/ and /e:ɑ/ fell together as /ɛ:/ and when /ɑ:/ was rounded to /ɔ:/. These are commonly called respectively long open e (ę̄) and long open o (ǭ). The rounded /y:/ was unrounded and merged with /i:/, though a new /y:/ was introduced from French, but it soon merged with the diphthong /iu/. The long vowel system was then /i:/ /e:/ /ɛ:/ /u:/ /o:/ /ɔ:/ and a new long vowel /a:/ from lengthening of /a/ in open syllables.

New diphthongs resulted from borrowing and from the vocalization of consonants, mainly /x/, /j/, /ɣ/, and /w/. By the end of the fourteenth century these were /aɪ/, /aʊ/, /ɔʊ/, /ɛu/, /iu/, /ɔɪ/, /ʊɪ/. The last two were introduced in French borrowed words, and although they were distinguished in speech, the difference between the two is hidden behind the common spelling oi/oy. From the merger of /aɪ/ and /eɪ/ a single diphthong resulted, /aɪ/, phonetically [æɪ], but both ai and ei remained in the spelling. /ɛu/ probably remained distinct through the Middle English period, but /eu/ merged with /iu/, to which was also added the reflex of French /y:/.

Summarizing the results of the splitting of phonemes and the formation of new phonemes by borrowing and merger, we have in the language of Chaucer's time:

Consonants:

/p/	/t/	/k/	/f/	/s/	/θ/	/ʃ/	/tʃ/	/h/	/x/
/b/	/d/	/g/	/v/	/z/	/ð/		/dʒ/	/j/	
/m/	/n/	/r/	/l/	/w/					

Consonant length in phonemic contrast seems to have been given up, but it has been pointed out that Chaucer did not rhyme bidden, sitten, and sonne [sʊnnə] with words like riden, writen, and sone [sʊnə], in which the vowels had not been lengthened in open position. The implication is that if these words did not rhyme, there must have been contrast in the medial consonants.[6]

Vowels:

/i:/ /e:/ /ɛ:/ /a:/ /u:/ /o:/ /ɔ:/
/ɪ/ /ɛ/ /a/ /ʊ/ /ɔ/ /ə/
/aɪ/ /aʊ/ /ɔʊ/ /ɛu/ /iu/ /ɔɪ/ /ʊɪ/[7]

At this point it is perhaps useful to add the warning that such an analysis of the phonemic structure of an unfamiliar language as we have given here does not solve the beginner's problem of learning to read it. In the first place, there is only an imperfect and inconsistent correlation between the graphic and phonemic systems. In the second place, phonemes are abstractions or generalizations; the reader who is mainly interested in reconstructing the literary expression of a former age must realize that language in terms of all its allophones in their exact values and proper positions.

Furthermore, in the comparison of the structure of one period with that of another, the similarities are deceptively simple. The truth is that in different periods the same phonemes, especially vowels, may have vastly different distributions; that is, they are found in completely different sets of words.

---

[6] Hans Kurath, "Loss of Long Consonants . . . in Middle English," *Language* 32 (1956): 442–43.

[7] Chomsky and Halle (p. 252) doubt the effective survival of /ʊɪ/, except as occupying "a marginal position in the language."

Chapter 11

EARLY ENGLISH

The Old English Inflectional System and Its Decline

The reproduction of the sounds, however, whatever difficulties they may present, is not the most difficult obstacle to overcome in reading Old English. This is to be found in the considerable differences in the forms of words and in their syntax.

Nouns

Consider, for example, in our early Bible translation, the singular *dæg* (v. 11) and its plurals *dagum* (v. 1) and *dagas* (v. 6). Or again, notice the phrase *on cumena hūse* (v. 7), meaning literally 'in the guests' house,' though the genitive *cumena* does not end in -*s*; or again *ofer heora heorda* (14), meaning 'over their flocks,' though here the plural *heorda* does not end in -*s*. In these examples we see the working of a grammatical system more closely resembling Latin than Modern English, in which both singular and plural forms of a noun had separate case endings. Thus:

	SINGULAR	PLURAL
Nom.	dæg	dagas
Gen.	dæges	daga
Dat.	dæge	dagum
Acc.	dæg	dagas

The dative case was used for the indirect object and the accusative for the direct object, but either might occur after a preposition.

Not all nouns, however, followed the same pattern. There were, in grammatical language, several inflections. These are sometimes distinguished under the names *a*-declension, *ō*-declension, *i*-declension, etc. These letter designations, however, refer to stem-forming suffixes occurring between the root and the inflectional ending *in the prehistoric state of the language*, and since they had largely disappeared in Old English they are not very useful guides. For practical purposes, we can say that many nouns[1] followed the declension of *dæg*, so many, in fact, that it became the standard to which most nouns eventually conformed, giving us our modern system of forming the possessive singular and all the cases of the plural with -*s*. A considerable number of nouns,[2] however, had originally no -*s* in the plural, though they retained it in the genitive (possessive) singular. Thus:

	SINGULAR	PLURAL
Nom.	word	word
Gen.	wordes	worda
Dat.	worde	wordum
Acc.	word	word

Therefore in verse 19 we read *Maria gehēold ealle þās word* 'Mary held all those words.'

Still others[3] had -*s* neither in the genitive singular nor in the plural. Thus for *henn* 'hen' we have:

	SINGULAR	PLURAL
Nom.	henn	henne
Gen.	henne	henna
Dat.	henne	hennum
Acc.	henne	henne

---

[1] The masculine *a*-stems.

[2] The neuter *a*-stems.

[3] Feminine *ō*-stems as well as feminines in other declensions.

In some nouns -*n* appeared as the plural ending in nominative and accusative.[4] Thus for *ēage* 'eye' we have:

	SINGULAR	PLURAL
Nom.	ēage	ēagan
Gen.	ēagan	ēagena
Dat.	ēagan	ēagum
Acc.	ēage	ēagan

Finally, a group of nouns whose plural stems had been modified in the nominative and accusative plural by *i*-umlaut had no -*s* in the plural, but, if masculine, had -*es* in the genitive singular. Thus for *fōt* 'foot' we have:

	SINGULAR	PLURAL
Nom.	fōt	fēt
Gen.	fōtes	fōta
Dat.	fēt	fōtum
Acc.	fōt	fēt

It will be helpful to remember that many -*um* endings indicate a dative plural noun, and many -*a* endings a genitive plural. A final -*e* is found also in the dative singular, but this ending frequently has other values as well.

As we have said, nearly all nouns in Modern English have been modified to conform to the masculine *a*-declension (like *dæg*) and simply add -*s* or -*es* to form the plural and the possessive singular, but survivals of the other systems remain. Most tenacious have been the umlauted plurals: *feet, geese, lice, mice, men, teeth, women.* Vestiges of this declension are also seen in the redundant plurals *kine* (OE *cu, cy*) and *breeches* (OE *broc, brec*). We have also a few nouns like *deer* and *fish*, which like many OE neuters (though *fish* was originally masculine) have no plural ending. *Oxen* is the only survival of the weak declension; the redundant plurals *children* and *brethren* have borrowed the weak ending.

---

[4] As well as in the genitive and dative singular. These nouns belong to the consonant or weak declension.

From some of these facts it will be observed that the gender of a noun was not necessarily determined by sex. In other words, gender was "grammatical" rather than "natural," and corresponded to no logical system. For example *mearh*[5] 'horse' was masculine, though the word *hors* itself was neuter; *bearn* 'child' and *mægden* 'maiden' were also neuter. The words for *stone, day, fowl, hill,* and *doom* were masculine. The words for *gift, feather,* and *needle* were feminine, but so also were those for *strength, learning,* and *sin.*

The Adjective

DEMONSTRATIVES

The means by which this distinction in gender was most clearly expressed was in the declension of the accompanying adjective. The two demonstratives,[6] which were used both as adjectives and as pronouns, were fully inflected, having three genders in the singular but a common form for the plural. The neuter singular had also a fifth case, the instrumental. The first of these two pronouns had the force of the demonstrative *that,* but could also be used as the definite article.

| | SINGULAR | | | PLURAL |
	Masc.	*Fem.*	*Neut.*	*All genders*
Nom.	sē	sēo	þæt	þā
Gen.	þæs	þǣre	þæs	þāra, þǣra
Dat.	þǣm, þām	þǣre	þǣm, þām	þǣm, þām
Acc.	þone	þā	þæt	þā
Instr.			þȳ, þon	

These forms are illustrated abundantly in the passage from the Old

---

[5] Preserved only in the feminine *mare.*

[6] The demonstrative adjective under weak sentence stress was equivalent to the definite article in modern usage, as the numeral *ān* 'one,' in similar weakened emphasis, became the indefinite article.

English gospel, used with the value of the definite article (or demonstrative adjective):

> *fram þām cāsere* 'by the emperor' (v. 1)
> *fram þām dēman* 'by the judge' (v. 2)
> *of þǣre ceastre* 'from the city' (v. 5)
> *on þām ylcan rīce* 'in the same country' (v. 4)
> *sē engel* 'the angel' (v. 10)
> *mid þām engle* 'with the angel' (v. 13)
> *ðā englas* 'the angels' (v. 15)

and as pronouns:

> *for þām* 'because'; lit. 'for that' (v. 4)
> *sēo is genemned* 'which is named' (v. 4)
> *sē is Drihten Crīst* 'who is the Lord Christ' (v. 11)
> *ealle þā ðe gehȳrdon* 'all those that heard' (v. 18)
> *be þām þe him þā hyrdas sǣdon* 'concerning those (things)
> which to them the shepherds said' (v. 18)

The second demonstrative had the force of *this;* its declension paralleled that of *sē, sēo, þæt*:

	SINGULAR			PLURAL
	Masc.	*Fem.*	*Neut.*	*All genders*
Nom.	þēs	þēos	þis	þās
Gen.	þisses	þisse	þisses	þissa
Dat.	þissum	þisse	þissum	þissum
Acc.	þisne	þās	þis	þās
Instr.			þȳs	

This pronoun is less frequent in the gospel passage, but observe:

> *þēos tōmearcodnes* 'this enrollment' (v. 2)
> *þis tācen* 'this token' (v. 12)

Only a very small part of this system remains. *Sē* was modified by leveling to *þe* and survives as the definite article. Perhaps also *sēo* is the ancestor of the feminine personal pronoun *she*. The neuter *þæt* became the standard demonstrative *that*, but incongruously was paired with the plural þas of the second demonstrative which became *those*. The neuter form þis of the second demonstrative was standardized as *this* but was paired with a new plural þise, þese 'these,' which arose in the Late Middle English period.

STRONG AND WEAK DECLENSIONS

Like the demonstratives, the common adjective was fully inflected but included also distinction in gender in the plural forms, its number and gender being of course the same as that of the noun to which it referred. However, while in general use the adjective took a strong declension, which had some features like those of the strong noun declension and some like those of the pronoun declension, it took a weak declension if it followed a demonstrative or a possessive adjective. Thus 'good men' would appear as *gōd menn* but 'the good men' as *þā gōdan menn*, or, in the genitive case, 'of good men' was *godra manna*, but 'of the good men' was *þāra godena manna*.

Some idea of the contrast between the strong and weak inflections of the adjective can be gained from the masculine forms of *glæd* 'glad':

		STRONG	WEAK
Sing.:	*Nom.*	glæd	glada
	Gen.	glades	gladan
	Dat.	gladum	gladan
	Acc.	glædne	gladan
	Instr.	glade	
Pl.:	*Nom.*	glade	gladan
	Gen.	glædra	glædra, -ena
	Dat.	gladum	gladum
	Acc.	glade	gladan

A few examples of inflected adjectives, both weak and strong, are found in the Nativity passage; for example:

hyre frumcennedan sunu 'her firstborn son' (weak) (v. 7)
on þām ylcan rīce 'in the same country' (weak) (v. 8)
mycelum ege 'with much fear' (strong) (v. 9)
mycelne gefēan 'great joy' (strong) (v. 10)
eallum folce 'to all folk' (strong) (v. 10)

It is obvious that when the inflectional system of the adjective and the article was simplified, gender as a grammatical element disappeared in nouns, remaining only in the third person singular of the personal pronoun.

Verbs

Like the noun and the adjective the Old English verb was inflected differently from ours. In the first place, the simple form (*he speaks*) was the standard type. The use of emphatic and progressive forms (*he does speak, he is speaking*) was quite limited, and, however much or little used, did not replace the simple form. The interrogative form was an inversion of the simple affirmative (*speaks he*), which is never used now except with the verbs *be, do, have*, or with the modal auxiliaries in elliptical constructions (*must you?*).

TENSE

There were, moreover, only two inflections for tense, the present and the past, a feature which distinguished the Germanic from other Indo-European languages. More elaborate tense meanings had to be expressed by phrasal verbs, sometimes called **periphrastic** tenses, from which we have derived the modern perfect and future tenses. A frequently used periphrastic verb in Old English was the passive, for which the auxiliary *weorðan* could be used in addition to *beon/wesan* 'be,' as in *wæs geworden gebod* '(it) was commanded' (v. 1), *gesæd wæs* 'was spoken' (v. 17).

An inflection for the subjunctive mood was also well preserved, though today it has almost disappeared except in the most careful formal use and in a few common expressions like "if I were you." In the older states of the language it expressed notions of wish, command, exhortation, or simple probability as distinct from a statement of fact. This is illustrated in the first verse of the Nativity story, in which the second verb, expressing the substance of the emperor's command, is in the subjunctive mood, *wære tōmearcod*.

STRONG AND WEAK VERBS

Finally the current classification of verbs into regular and irregular, according to which all verbs that do not use the past tense -*d* or -*ed* are classed as irregular, will not hold for Old English. Verbs like *drive, choose, find, steal, give, swear,* and *fall* belonged to the seven classes of **strong** verbs, which indicated change of tense by a change of stem vowel (a system originating in ablaut; see pp. 88–89) but they were quite as regular as the weak verbs which used the dental suffix. In Old English there were not only more strong verbs in use than in Modern English but there were also more of them in relation to the weak verbs. Most of the latter were derivative verbs; that is, they became verbs by functional shift, or, especially in Middle English, by foreign borrowing. It is obvious, then, that as time went on the number of weak verbs must continually increase and eventually become influential enough to attract many strong verbs into the weak conjugation by the force of analogy.

Occasionally a verb which by origin we should expect to be weak is inflected like a similar form among the strong verbs. One example of this is *strive,* which comes from Old French *estriver* but is inflected *strive, strove, striven.* Another is *ring* from Old English *hringan,* a weak verb which was modified in Middle English by analogy with *sing.* Also we find a few verbs like *dive* and *hang* which maintain both weak and strong features. This is especially true in Early Modern English, where we are likely to encounter such variations as *abided/abode, chided/chid, shined/shone,* and *thrived/throve.*

In a few instances, though a verb has become weak, its old strong past participle survives as an adjective, such as *molten, sodden,* and *swollen.*

By far, however, the greatest number of changes have been from the strong to the weak conjugation. A partial list of weak verbs whose Old English counterparts were strong includes *ache, bake, bark, brew, carve, chew, climb, dread,*[7] *fare, flow, gnaw, help, laugh, load, lock, melt, mourn, seethe, shape, shave, shove, slip, sow, spurn, starve, step, suck, swallow, wade, walk, wash, wax, weigh, wield,* and *yield.* In addition to these, *creep, flee, lose, read, shoot, sleep, sweep,* and *weep* have now a short vowel in the past; not, however, by ablaut gradation, but by combinative change resulting from the addition of the dental suffix.

Of the strong verbs which have survived as such, one feature remains to be mentioned. In Old English four principal parts of the verb were to be distinguished: the infinitive, which had a suffix *-an* and supplied the stem

---

[7] Some strong verbs such as *dread, read,* and *sleep,* had already developed weak past tenses in Old English.

for the present tense; two past forms, one characteristic of the first person singular, the other of the first person plural; and the past participle. The following are interesting examples:

wrītan 'to write'; *wrāt, writon; writen*
slīdan 'to slide'; *slād, slidon; sliden*
sincan 'to sink'; *sānc, suncon; suncen*
singan 'to sing'; *sāng, sungon; sungen*
stingan 'to sting'; *stāng, stungon; stungen*
swingan 'to swing'; *swāng, swungon; swungen*

Since we do not in Modern English inflect the past tense for number, only one of the Old English past forms was destined to survive, but there seems to have been no logic in the selection beyond the accidents of history and public taste. The first two, *write* and *slide*, belonged to the same class, but in the past *write* has kept the singular form[8] and *slide* the plural. Similarly all of the last four belonged to the same class, but though the past singular has disappeared from general usage in *sting* and *swing*, it has remained in *sing* and *sink* as an alternate form to the plural.[9]

CONJUGATION

All verbs whether weak or strong were more elaborately inflected for person and number (conjugated) than is now the case. Today we have in the present tense of the verb *hear*, for example, even if we admit the use of the subjunctive, only two forms: the general or base form, *hear*, and the single inflection for the third person singular indicative, *hears*. Old English had:

	INDICATIVE	SUBJUNCTIVE
Sing.	1. hīere	1. hīere
	2. hīerest	2. hīere
	3. hīereþ	3. hīere
Pl. (ALL PERSONS)	hīeraþ	hīeren

---

[8] Since OE *ā* became *ō* in standard Modern English, we have *wrote*.

[9] There is some tendency to regard *rang, sang,* and *sank* as superior to *rung, sung,* and *sunk* as past tense forms, but this view is not supported by history or public consent.

The past tense consists today of one form, *heard*, to which we may compare Old English:

	INDICATIVE	SUBJUNCTIVE
Sing.	1. hīerde	1. hīerde
	2. hīerdest	2. hīerde
	3. hīerde	3. hīerde
Pl. (ALL PERSONS)	hīerdon	hīerden

In current English we have also an infinitive without distinctive ending; no inflection for the imperative, compared to an Old English singular *hīer* and a plural *hieraþ;* and a simple form in *-ing* for both verbal noun and present participle compared to the Old English verbal noun in *-ung* and a present participle in *-ende*.

Pronouns

The one part of speech sufficiently inflected in Present English to bear comparison with Old English is the personal pronoun. However, Old English had three numbers in the first and second person and four cases throughout. The dual number indicated *two*. Thus *wit* meant 'we two.'

FIRST PERSON

	SINGULAR	DUAL	PLURAL
Nom.	ic	wit	wē
Gen.	mīn	uncer	ūser, ūre
Dat.	mē	unc	ūs
Acc.	mec, mē	unc, uncit	ūsic, ūs

SECOND PERSON

	SINGULAR	DUAL	PLURAL
Nom.	þū	git	gē
Gen.	þīn	incer	ēower
Dat.	þē	inc	ēow
Acc.	þec, þē	inc, incit	ēowic, ēow

THIRD PERSON

| | SINGULAR | | | PLURAL |
	Masculine	*Feminine*	*Neuter*	
Nom.	hē	hēo	hit	hīe, hī
Gen.	his	hire	his	hiera, hira, hiora, heora
Dat.	him	hire	him	him
Acc.	hine	hīe	hit	hīe, hī

All of these forms have undergone some phonological change, though most are recognizable. In the second person plural, *ēower* and *ēow* became Middle English *your* and *you*, when, by shift of accent the diphthongs became rising diphthongs, and the first element closed from palatal vowel to palatal consonant [j]. The third person neuter simply lost its initial *h*.

NEW PRONOUN FORMS

The dual forms in the first and second person plural, meaning 'we two' and 'you two' had disappeared by the thirteenth century. In the third person feminine, *hēo* was replaced by a new form, possibly a substitution of the feminine demonstrative *sēo*, though a number of explanations, more or less plausible, have been offered to support a theory of the direct phonological descent of Middle English *she/sho* from Old English forms of the feminine personal pronoun.[10] In any case, from the thirteenth century on, *sche* was the usual Midland form, while *scho* was the common Northern form. In all persons and numbers, the two objective cases were leveled under the dative, except in the neuter, which took the accusative form, since the dative *him* was not distinctively neuter.

As a result of phonological change and leveling, the third person plural forms became more difficult to distinguish from the singular forms and were eventually displaced by corresponding forms from Norse as used by Englishmen of Scandinavian descent. These appeared first in the North but were gradually adopted in the Midlands. In Chaucer's language, *thei/they* is the nominative plural form but *hire* and *hem* are retained for genitive and objective. During the fifteenth century, however, *their* and

---

[10] See in particular Robert D. Stevick, *English Studies*, 45 (1964): 381–88.

them gradually replaced *hire* and *hem* in the standard language, though the older forms had a longer life in colloquial and regional speech.

The possessive *his* continued to be used for the neuter pronoun until the sixteenth century, when *its* began to appear, though *its* is not common in Shakespeare and was not used at all in the original King James Bible. By the end of the seventeenth century, however, it was fully established.

The forms of *hwā* 'who,' which was always in Old English an interrogative, paralleled those of the personal pronoun:

	MASCULINE	NEUTER
Nom.	hwā	hwæt
Gen.	hwæs	hwæs
Dat.	hwǣm	hwǣm, hwām
Acc.	hwone	hwæt
Instr.		hwȳ, hwī

The early use of this pronoun was restricted to interrogative meanings, the relative use having developed from it in Late Middle and Early Modern English. The common genitive from which we derive *whose* is no longer used interrogatively as a neuter but still occurs as the neuter possessive of the relative *which* in such phrases as " a hill, whose peak was buried in the fog." The neuter instrumental survives as the conjunction or interrogative adverb *why*, in Middle English often in the phrase *for why*.

OE *hwilc* 'which' and *hwæðer* 'which of two' were also used both as interrogative adjectives and as interrogative pronouns, but were declined according to the strong declension of adjectives.

Loss of Inflection

This extensive inflectional apparatus had largely disappeared by the end of the Middle English period. Though its loss has sometimes been attributed to the discontinuance of the Old English literary tradition after the Norman Conquest, this cannot have been the sole or even the principal cause, since grammatical systems do not in general depend upon the existence of a written tradition.[11] The process of simplification must have begun before the appearance of the earliest written literature in Old

---

[11] Cf. de Saussure, p. 24.

English, to judge from the fact that historic Old English had fewer forms than Proto-Germanic. The "law of Germanic accent" had much to do with this trend. As the accent was never shifted to the inflectional syllables, their reduction increased with time. This in turn is assumed to have led to the establishment of word order as the basic syntactic feature of Modern English. It is possible, however, to see a different order of cause and effect, namely, that the word-order pattern had begun to take shape very early and that the later syntactic order as well as phonological changes led to the reduction of the inflectional system. Whatever the primary cause, the vowels in unstressed inflectional syllables became less clearly distinguished until by the Early Middle English period they were reduced to [ə],[12] spelled *e*. Other than -*s* the final consonants in inflectional syllables were reduced to -*n*, which later was dropped, except in some past participial suffixes. In the last stage Old English endings like -*an* and -*um* were represented by -*e*. By the end of the fourteenth century in the Midlands and much earlier in the North, this also was lost in the spoken language, though it continued to be written, and it accounts for the extensive use of silent final -*e* in modern spelling.

The final -*e*, then, which remained from an older inflectional ending, was by the end of the fourteenth century no longer remembered as such. Consequently it was often added by analogy to words which historically had no title to an inflectional syllable at all. Such an -*e* is called **inorganic**.[13] Whether organic or inorganic, -*e* was sometimes pronounced in poetry after it had been given up in more general use. We have seen an example of the custom in a passage from Chaucer (pp. 118–19).

Except for -*s* and -*es* the most tenacious of the old suffixes was the -*en* of the past participle, which remains in use today. In the plural and possessive -*es*, the past -*ed*, and the present singular -*est* and -*eth*, the vowel was lost and the final consonant became nonsyllabic, although we still have syllabic endings in plurals like *churches* and in some participial forms used as adjectives, as in the expressions *not a blessèd thing, along a crookèd path, a learnèd man, our belovèd son.*

---

[12] [ə] may have varied with [i] or [ɪ], as is indicated by common ME spellings, especially in the North, -*is*, -*ith*, -*id*, -*ir*.

[13] Not to be confused with the purely "orthographic" -*e*, which was never pronounced. This was a scribal affectation in spelling, very common in the fifteenth and sixteenth centuries.

Adverbs

One other morphologic feature is of special interest—the derivation of adverbs. These were formed in Old English by various suffixes. The one most familiar to us is *-ly*, from the Old English *-līce*, which when added to nouns formed adjectives, as in modern *friendly* and *manly*, but when added to adjectives formed adverbs. This remains, of course, the commonest adverb-forming suffix, but, as pointed out earlier, there were other suffixes as well, vestiges of which remain in such words as *darkling* and *sidelong*.[14] Some others have disappeared but not without leaving behind some misunderstanding. Adverbial functions could be expressed by a noun or adjective with an oblique case ending.[15] If this happened to be the genitive in *-es*, the ending might survive as in *once*, *twice*, and *thrice*, in which the spelling preserves also the original voiceless pronunciation, or in *against*, *amidst*, *amongst*, *whilst*,[16] where the genitive ending is supported by the excrescent *-t*. The endings of adverbial datives and accusatives, however, were generally reduced to *-e* by the fourteenth century. They would then be indistinguishable from adverbs, of which there were a number formed in Old English by adding *-e* to the adjective. Thus *ȳfel* 'evil' used adverbially became *ȳfele*. Moreover many adjectives normally ended in *-e* like *clǣne* 'clean,' *nīwe* 'new,' and *sōfte* 'soft.' In these instances the adjective and adverb already had identical forms, but after the fourteenth century the *-e* disappeared from the pronunciation, and all adverbs with *-e* endings of whatever origin became indistinguishable in form from the corresponding adjective. Thus we have good historical precedent for such well-known idioms as "He got *clean* away," though the **flat,** or uninflected, adverb is often regarded as grammatically objectionable. Undoubtedly the injudicious use of the flat adverb is a characteristic of nonstandard speech, but, on the other hand, it occurs in respectable literary usage throughout the Modern English period.[17]

---

[14] See pp. 19–20.

[15] I.e., any case but the nominative.

[16] Note also the vulgar pronunciation *onst*, which, though analogous to these forms in *-t*, has not been accepted in cultivated speech.

[17] See pp. 189–92.

Chapter 12

EARLY ENGLISH

Vocabulary Enrichment

Borrowing from French

The extent to which English grammar was affected by contact with the French language in the post-Conquest period is open to debate, but there is very little question about the extent of French influence upon the vocabulary.

As we have already learned, one of the ways by which the vocabulary of a language is enriched is by borrowing. This may take place at the social level by contact between speakers of both languages, or at the literary level by the tendency of native writers to use words which they consider necessary importations from a foreign literature for which they have great respect.

FRENCH WORDS IN CHAUCER

During the Middle English period words continued to be borrowed from Latin at the second level but from French at both. The following is a short passage from a translation made by Chaucer of Boethius' famous philosophical work, *De Consolatione Philosophiae*.[1]

---

[1] Geoffrey Chaucer, *Boece*, in *The Works of Geoffrey Chaucer*, ed. F. N. Robinson, 2d ed. (Boston, 1957), p. 323.

Whoso it be that is *cleer* of *vertu*, sad* and wel *ordinat*† of lyvynge, that hath put under fote the proude weerdes,‡ and loketh, upright, upon either§ *fortune*, he may holden his *chere*‖ *undesconfited*.# The *rage* ne the *manaces* of the see, *commoevynge*** or *chasynge* upward hete fro the botme, ne schal nat *moeve* that man. Ne the *unstable mowntaigne* that highte†† Visevus, that writhith‡‡ out thurw his brokene *chemeneyes* smokynge fieres, ne the wey of thonderleit,§§ that is wont to smyten hye *toures*, ne schal nat *moeve* that man.

---

* serious, sober † ordered ‡ destinies § i.e., good or bad ‖ behavior
# undisconcerted ** commotion †† is named ‡‡ writhes, i.e., throws out in wreaths §§ thunderbolt, lightning

---

The italicized words here are of French origin. The style of the passage is serious and reflective, with an interesting blend of abstract meanings with concrete images; and the French words used are nicely suited to the style, though some of them (*cleer, chere, chasynge, moeve, toures*) have become so familiar to us that they are hardly distinguishable from words native in origin.

In a different passage, the well-known first lines of the Prologue to the *Canterbury Tales*, the style is lyrical, and the vocabulary, though revealing just as much French as the passage from *Boece* (here the words in roman type are of French origin), gives an impression of still greater ease and appropriateness:

Whan that Aprille with his shoures soote
The droghte of March hath perced *to the roote*
And bathed every veyne *in swich* licour
Of which vertu engendred *is the* flour;
Whan Zephirus eek with his sweete breeth
Inspired *hath in every holt and heeth*
The tendre *croppes, and the yonge sonne*
Hath in the Ram his halfe cours *yronne,*
And smale foweles maken melodye,
That slepen al the nyght with open yë,
So priketh hem nature *in hir* corages;
Thanne longen folk to goon on pilgrimages,
And palmeres *for to seken* straunge *strondes,*
To ferne halwes kowthe in sondry londes;

> *And* specially *from every shires ende*
> *Of Engelonde to Caunterbury they wende,*
> *The hooly blisful martir for to seke*
> *That hem hath holpen whan that they were seeke.*

One indication that the borrowed words we find in these passages were quickly anglicized is the extent to which they behaved like native words in taking English prefixes and suffixes, whether inflectional or derivational. Notice *undesconfited, unstable, engendred, inspired, specially.* Of particular interest in this regard is *commoevynge,* which may have been so recently borrowed as to have been introduced by Chaucer himself. At least it is not recorded earlier than his own time.[2] In other places of the *Boece* we find *assegeden, digneliche, falsnesse, likerousness* 'lechery,' *misaccounted, misaventure, mischance, unable, uncurteisly;* and among Chaucer's contemporaries *outpassage, outpassing, gentleman, gentlewoman,* and many similar combinations in this period and earlier.

It would be a mistake, however, to suppose that the language had given up its basically Germanic character. Reckoning "frequency" in terms of the occurrence of words in context, the spoken language preserves an impressive numerical superiority of native words. This fact also can be seen in many of Chaucer's passages where his smooth conversational tone often conceals the technical skill of his narrative style. The following passage from *Troilus and Criseyde* describes the hero who has recklessly disregarded the power of the god of love:

> *So ferde* it by this* fierse *and proude knyght:*
> *Though he a worthy kynges sone were*
> *And wende† nothing hadde had swich myghte*
> *Ayeyns his wille that shuld his herte stere,‡*
> *Yet with a look his herte wax a-fere§*
> *That he that now was moost in pryde above,*
> *Wax* sodeynly *moost* subgit *unto love.*

---

* fared † weened, supposed ‡ steer § on fire

Here the French element is limited to three words (in roman type here), and these are fully at home in their English context.

---

[2] See *OED,* s.v. "commoven"; *MED,* s.v. "commeven."

EXTENT OF FRENCH BORROWING

If, however, we consider separately all the French words that came into English in the Middle English period, their number is truly remarkable.[3] Some came in early from Norman French and reveal their Norman background in forms different from those of Central French, which became more influential as time went on. Compare, for example, English *war* with modern French *guerre*. The difference is due to the fact that our word is from Norman French, which preserved the sound of *w* while it was modified in Central French. Some words were borrowed twice, earlier from Norman French and later from Central French, and thus formed **doublets;** that is, two words in the same language from the same source, but with different phonological histories and frequently some difference in meaning. By this process we have in Modern English such pairs as *warden/guardian, reward/regard, warranty/guarantee.* A similar difference between Norman French *ca-* and Central French *cha-* gave us *cattle/chattel.*

The French infiltration touched not only the language of literature but the technical language of professional life, such as government, church, law, and warfare, and the many-sided activity of social life at all levels. Many of these borrowed words have remained technical or specialized. Few people, for example, speak much of courts of *oyer and terminer, mainpernor, malice prepense,* and *mortmain,* though the words are well known to lawyers. However, we have in this and other special vocabularies such words as *caitiff, chantry, crosier, cloister, homily, lectern, legate, plaintiff, schism, simony, surplice.* Some others, once well known, are, with the passing of old customs, growing unfamiliar to the general public, such as *arras, buckler, chandelier, dais, hauberk, joust,* and *palfrey.* A very large number of borrowed words, however, have become part of the common speech and have, as usually happens in such cases, modified and multiplied their meanings. The following words are so often used, and in different senses, both literal and figurative, that they raise no suspicion of foreign origin or specialized usage: *adore, blame, clerk, court, crown, damage, faith, force, hermit, lesson, miracle, noble, plead, revenue, sacrifice, summons, tally, tax,* and *vessel.*

The leisure occupations of the upper classes have given us *chase, falcon, track, quarry,* but other pastimes and their nomenclature were more

---

[3] See Baugh, pp. 200–22, for a detailed account of the chronology and extent of French word borrowings in Middle English. Another such account is given by Otto Jespersen, *Growth and Structure of the English Language,* 9th ed. (Oxford, 1960), pp. 78–105.

common to all classes: *ace*, *cards*, *champion*, *checkers*, *chess*, *dance*, *deuce*, *dice*, *minstrel*, and *music*. And at the commonest level, the language of kitchen and dining hall, we have *bacon*, *beef*, *biscuit*, *boil*, *cream*, *dinner*, *feast*, *fry*, *gravy*, *mutton*, *pork*, *roast*, *stew*, *supper*, *toast*, and *veal*.

Latin Influence

At the same time that English was borrowing heavily from French, it remained under the continuing direct influence of Latin, though in the Middle English period it is not always easy to determine from which of these two sources a given word was taken. It will be remembered from what we learned earlier about the Indo-European family of languages that the French language was an evolution of the popular speech of Romans and Latinized Gauls, as spoken in the first centuries of our era in the Roman province which was to become France. Latin words, therefore, that became French by the slow process of language evolution underwent the phonological changes that can be expected in any language in a long period of time. Thus Latin *incantare* became French *enchanter* by normal descent. In later times, however, when French and Latin had become virtually different languages and Latin was read as the language of learned men, Latin words were sometimes taken into French a second time, now in their ancient forms as learned borrowings. Thus Latin *incantationem* appears in medieval French in the thirteenth century as *incantation*. When the same word appears in English in the fourteenth century, are we to believe that it came from French or from Latin sources? In this instance, the source was probably French, but the decision is not always clear or certain. Consider this passage in Chaucer's "Tale of Melibee":

> Thanne, by the conseil of his wyf Prudence, this Melibeus leet callen* a greet *congregacioun* of folk; as surgiens, phisiciens, olde folk and yonge, and somme of his olde enemys *reconsiled* as by hir semblaunt† to his love and into his grace; and therwithal ther coomen somme of his neighebores that diden hym reverence moore for drede than for love, as it happeth ofte. Ther coomen also ful many *subtille* flatereres, and wise *advocatz* lerned in the lawe.[4]

---

* had, or caused to be, called   † according to their appearances

---

[4] Robinson, p. 168.

Of the four words here (in italics) which have the appearance of direct Latin borrowing, all had corresponding forms in French. Two had double forms, one of which was borrowed from or influenced by the Latin: *soutil/subtil* and *avocat/advocat*. All four of these are found in English, the first pair occurring in Modern English with different meanings.

Nevertheless, there were many words which we can be quite certain came directly into English from Latin. Such borrowings were naturally stimulated by the influence of Latin works of a learned or technical character translated into English or commonly used by specialists. From their technical jargon the most frequently used words would find their way into more popular speech, as we often see today in specialized interests such as psychology, economics, aeronautics, etc. One such field of interest abundantly cultivated in the Middle Ages was astronomy or its application to astrology. Here in all probability were first used in English such importations from Latin as *aspect, diurnal, direct, equator, equinox, erratic, exaltation (MED;* also *exalt), horizon, opposition, retrograde, revolution,* and *zenith.* From various types of Latin borrowing Baugh[5] lists some eighty-seven examples which have become commonplace, including *contempt, history, include, index, minor, nervous, picture, polite, private, quiet, suppress,* and *ulcer.*

By the end of the fourteenth century, then, the character of the English vocabulary had been extensively modified by borrowing from both Latin and French. The remarkable extent of the French borrowing is accounted for by the fact that a large part of it occurred in the living speech of a great number of people, for the evidence[6] is that the most abundant borrowing took place during the period when the families of French ancestry were gradually relinquishing the French language; that is, between 1250 and 1400. In these years there must have been an extended period of bilingualism, in which French words were frequently put into English context.

However, it must not be supposed that the influence of French ended at the close of the fourteenth century. France continued, because of its importance in the intellectual life of Western Europe, to exert a strong

---

[5] P. 223.

[6] Statistics are given by Baugh, p. 214 and by Jespersen, *Growth and Structure,* pp. 86–87. The figures from these two authorities are not identical, but their implications do not differ.

cultural influence. Its language was cultivated in England and its literature widely read in the fifteenth and succeeding centuries, but word borrowing was then less abundant and largely confined to the cultural level.

Scandinavian Influence

In our discussion of French and its influence we have ignored for the moment another linguistic event of great importance, which in its beginnings really antedated the French influence. As remarked earlier, the presence of the descendants of the Viking invaders who had settled in the North and East Midlands modified permanently the state of the language in several ways. Their gradual adoption of the language of the majority of their neighbors must have had two effects. In the first the uncertainties of such a large number of speakers about the traditional grammar of the language accelerated the rate of morphological change, which was already in progress at the time of their settlements and which was to be further hastened by the conditions following the Norman Conquest. Secondly, social intercourse among large numbers of speakers of two similar languages enjoying equal social status encouraged the continued use of Norse and the eventual transfer of some of its characteristics to English.

Some features even of syntax and morphology may have been the result of the extensive use of the Old Norse language in England. Jespersen[7] suggested that the large number of contact clauses (that is, subordinate clauses in which the introductory conjunction or relative pronoun does not occur) in Middle English parallels Norse syntax, as does the use of *shall* and *will* in the future, and some special uses of *should*. In Northern Middle English the use of inflectional -*s* in the present tense of the verb was Norse.[8] Also the present form of the third person plural pronoun, which has initial *th*- (*they, their, them*) in place of the native English *h*-, is a Norse borrowing.

The permanent lexical influence has been quite extensive. It is most striking in the language of Middle English literature produced in the North and Northeast Midlands. Here the depth of the Norse influence

---

[7] *Growth and Structure*, pp. 75–77.

[8] Only the third personal singular -*s* has become a permanent feature of English, but in Northern Middle English it was also, in many constructions, used in all the numbers of the plural.

may be judged by the borrowing of function words, usually not transferred in this way. *Till* (formerly used with the meaning *to*) was common in the North. *Fro*, though now heard only in the phrase *to and fro*, was once a frequent variant of *from*. Both of these are Norse in origin, but in neither instance was the borrowing as important as the introduction of *are* for the present plural of the verb *to be*. This also was a regional variant in the North until the late Middle English period, when it began to spread southward.

Accurate measurement of the real extent of Norse usage is made difficult by the similarity of many words in both languages. When a descendant of Norse settlers used the words *father, folk, house, man, mother, summer, wife, winter*, was he speaking the language of his ancestors or of his English relatives by marriage? It would be impossible to say, since the words were so alike in Scandinavian and English. However, other words of very commonplace application supply clues to their foreign origin and indicate the extent to which the two cultures intermingled: *anger, call, die, egg, fellow, gate, haven, hit, husband, root, take, want, wing*. In an interesting number of instances the Norse origin of a word can be detected by phonological criteria. One fairly widespread type is the Norse words with [sk], which in a native word would have been fronted to [ʃ]: *scant, scare, scowl, scream, scrape, scrub, skill, skirt, skulk, sky*.[9] Also Scandinavians retained [g], which in native words was fronted to [j] in Old English and Middle English. Some native cognates of this class, *yeven, yaf, foryeten, yate, yift*, eventually were ousted by the borrowed words *give, gave, forget, gate, gift*. Similarly, retention of palatal [k], which in Old English became [tʃ], appears in the doublets *kirk/church* and *dike/ditch*.

Some doublets have remained because, in one way or another, the native word serves a purpose different from that of the borrowed word: *from/fro, rear/raise, shirt/skirt, shot/scot, edge/egg* (i.e., 'to egg on'); and if we included the English of Scotland, we should find more numerous vestiges of the Scandinavian influence.[10]

At this point it is proper to add that the English language lost something during the medieval period. The addition of words from French and Scandinavian did indeed supply many new and useful things, but it

---

[9] This is not, however, an exclusively Norse feature. A number of words with *sk-* are from Old French.

[10] For additional details on the Norse element in English see Baugh, pp. 107–24; Jespersen, *Growth and Structure*, ch. 4.

rendered obsolete some native assets, and many words fell into disuse and have been forgotten. In the short Nativity story from St. Luke some two dozen of the Old English words, not counting function words and inflectional variants, have fallen out of use. True, some of them were replaced by other words of native origin; nevertheless, the loss has been considerable.

It has sometimes been said that the English language lost some of that power of compounding native elements which it enjoyed in the Old English period. The loss is more apparent than real; that is, it can be seen in the learned written language, which for several centuries has affected a style more or less freighted with Latinity. To those, however, who are given to observing popular speech phenomena today, it must be evident that if the power of shaping vivid compounds was ever moribund in the spoken language it has enjoyed a miraculous recovery.

It has also been maintained that words of native English origin are more concrete, more vivid, and more forceful than borrowed words. Here again it is quite true that when we discuss topics of a high level of abstraction, the rate of occurrence of words of Latin origin will be relatively high. It is equally true that exquisite poetic expression can be achieved by simple words of Anglo-Saxon stock. Consider, for example, Wordsworth's familiar lyric:

> *She dwelt among the untrodden ways*
> > *Beside the springs of Dove,*
> *A Maid whom there were none to* praise
> > *And very few to love:*
>
> *A* violet *by a mossy stone*
> > *Half hidden from the eye!*
> —*Fair as a* star, *when only one*
> > *Is shining in the sky.*
>
> *She lived unknown, and few could know*
> > *When Lucy* ceased *to be;*
> *But she is in her grave, and, oh,*
> > *The* difference *to me.*

This poem is remarkable for the simplicity of its expression. Though the borrowed words (in roman type) can hardly be distinguished from the native words for power of expression, it is true that they are relatively few. Perhaps Wordsworth's theory of poetic diction weights the scales to some degree. Compare then two other poems, much admired sonnets of Shakespeare, and with them Wordsworth's poem:

That time of year thou mayst in me behold
When yellow leaves, or none, or few, do hang
Upon those boughs which shake against the cold:
Bare ruin'd choirs, *where late the sweet birds sang.*
In me thou see'st the twilight of such day
As after sunset fadeth *in the west,*
Which by and by black night doth take away,
Death's second *self, that seals up all in rest.*
In me thou see'st the glowing of such fire
That on the ashes of his youth doth lie,
As the deathbed whereon it must expire,
Consum'd *with that which it was* nourish'd *by.*
   This thou perceiv'st, *which makes thy love more strong*
   To love that well which thou must leave ere long.

Here, in Sonnet 73, the rate of occurrence of borrowed words is about the same as in Wordsworth, but again it would be difficult to prove that they are less "poetic" in either poem than the native words. But consider Sonnet 29:

When in disgrace *with* fortune *and men's eyes,*
I all alone beweep *my* outcast *state,*
And trouble *deaf heaven with my* bootless *cries,*
And look upon myself and curse my fate;
Wishing me like to one more rich in hope,
Featur'd *like him, like him with friends* possess'd,
Desiring *this man's* art, *and that man's* scope,
With what I most enjoy contented *least;*
Yet in these thoughts myself almost despising,
Haply I think on thee, and then my state,
Like to the lark at break of day arising,
From sullen *earth, sings* hymns *at heaven's gate;*
   For thy sweet love remembered *such wealth brings*
   That then I scorn *to change my* state *with kings.*

In the second sonnet the number of words borrowed from Latin and French is noticeably greater, though it does not appear evident that they contribute less to the poetic effect of a great poem. A comparison of the three poems does suggest that in the passages which are rich in visual imagery the ratio of native to borrowed words increases, but this is not the same as saying that they carry a greater weight of concrete meaning. The truth of the matter is that the value of a word owes less to its origin than to the closeness of its association with the emotional experiences of the people who use it.

In summary, then, the grammatical changes that the English language underwent in the post-Conquest period were radical in their nature,[11] the lexical changes were abundant and far-reaching in their effect, but by comparison the phonological changes, though numerous, were less important to the future of the language.

Exercises

1. Why was dialect difference in Early English an important historical and literary fact? How did it originate? What has become of these differences in modern times?

2. How do you account for the linguistic difference between Chaucer's *Canterbury Tales* and *The Vision of Piers Plowman?*

3. Discuss the meaning of "standard language." What standards arose in Old English and in Late Middle English and under what circumstances?

4. Since Old English times our language has passed from the synthetic to the analytic state. What does this statement mean, and how did the change come about?

5. Make a list of the kings of England from the Norman Conquest to the end of the Middle Ages, with their regnal years. With which of these can you associate important influences on the English language?

---

[11] This radical change can be described by saying that English passed from the **synthetic** to the **analytic** state; that is, from a language that expressed its grammatical relations by the addition of inflectional suffixes, thus building up words into a more or less complex cluster of grammatical signals, to one in which such grammatical meanings are expressed by use of function words and by reliance on word order.

6. The following is one of the best-known passages in the Bible, the Twenty-third Psalm, or Psalm 22 in an older numbering. V represents a modern edition of the Latin Vulgate, the text which was read in the Middle Ages. From this were translated independently:

OE An Old English version known as the West Saxon Psalms.

R   A translation made with a commentary in the early fourteenth century by Richard Rolle in the language of the North of England.

M   A Midland version made about the same time as Rolle's or shortly after, once erroneously called the West Midland Psalter.

W1 The first Wyclif translation, which adhered very closely to the Latin text.

W2 The second Wyclif, or Purvey, version, in which the language is truer to the English idiom. It is Southeast Midland and therefore "King's English."

The last two versions printed here, KJ and J, are not simple translations of the Vulgate but were made with the assistance of earlier Greek and Hebrew texts:

KJ The Authorized Version, also called the King James Bible, which illustrates the finest Early Modern English tradition.

J   The Jerusalem Bible, a new English translation which embodies the results of modern biblical studies by Jewish, Catholic, and Protestant scholars. It is an excellent example of simple but dignified contemporary English.

VERSE 1

V   *Dominus regit me, et nihil mihi deerit.*

OE *Drihten mē ræt, ne byð mē nānes gōdes wan.*

R   *Lord gouerns me, and nathynge sall me want.*

M   *Our Lord gouerneþ me, and noþyng shal defailen to me.*

W1 *The Lord gouerneth me and no thing to me shal lacke.*

W2 *The Lord gouerneth me, and no thing schal faile to me.*

KJ *The Lord is my shepherd; I shall not want.*

J   *Yahweh is my shepherd, I lack nothing.*

VERSE 2

V   *In loco pascuae ibi me collocavit. Super aquam refectionis educavit me.*

OE *And hē mē geset on swȳðe good feohland. And fēdde mē be wætera staðum.*

R   *In sted of pasture thare he me sett. On the water of rehetynge forth he me brought.*

M   *In þe stede of pasture he sett me þer. He norissed me vp[on] water of fyllyng.*

W1 *In the place of leswe where he me sul sette. Ouer watir of fulfilling he nurshide me.*

W2 *In the place of pasture there he hath set me. He nurshide me on the water of refreischyng.*

KJ *He maketh me to lie down in green pastures; he leadeth me beside the still waters.*

J   *In meadows of green grass he lets me lie. To the waters of repose he leads me.*

VERSE 3

V   *Animam meam convertit. Deduxit me super semitas (semitam) iustitiae, propter nomen suum.*

OE *And mīn mōd gehwyrfde of unrōtnesse on gefēan. Hē mē gelædde ofer þā wegas rihtwīsnesse for his naman.*

R   *My soule he turnyd. He led me on the stretis of rightwisnes for his name.*

M   *He turned my soule fram þe fende. He lad me vp þe bistiȝes of riȝtfulnes for his name.*

W1 *My soule he conuertide. He broȝte doun me vpon the sties of riȝtwisnesse, for his name.*

W2 *He conuertide my soule. He ledde me forth on the pathis of riȝtfulnesse; for his name.*

KJ *He restoreth my soul; he leadeth me in the paths of righteousness for his name's sake.*

J   *There he revives my soul. He guides me by paths of virtue for the sake of his name.*

VERSE 4a

V   *Nam, et si ambulavero (ambulem) in medio umbrae mortis, non timebo mala quoniam tu mecum est.*

OE *Þeah ic nū gange on midde þā sceade dēaðes, ne ondrǣde ic mē nān yfel; for þām þū byst mid mē, Drihten.*

R   *ffor whi, if i had gane in myddis of the shadow of ded i sall noght dred illes, for thou ert with me.*

M   *For ȝif þat ich haue gon amiddes of the shadowe of deþ, y shal nouȝt douten iuels, for þou art wyþ me.*

W1 *For whi and if I shal go in the myddel of the shadewe of deth, I shal not dreden euelis, for thou art with me.*

W2 *For whi thouȝ y schal go in the myddis of the schadewe of deeth, Y schal not drede yuels, for thou art with me.*

KJ *Yea, though I walk through the valley of the shadow of death, I will fear no evil for thou art with me.*

J   *Though I pass through a gloomy valley, I fear no harm.*

VERSE 4b

V   *Virga tua, et baculus tuus; ipsa me consolata sunt.*

OE *Þīn gyrd and þīn stæf mē āfrēfredon, þæt is þīn þrēaung* [rebuke] *and eft þīn frēfrung* [comfort].

R   *Thi wand and thi staf thai haf confortyd me.*

M   *Þy discipline and þyn amendyng conforted me.*

W1 *Thi ȝerde and thy staf, tho han confortid me.*

W2 *Thi ȝerde and thi staf, tho han coumfortid me.*

KJ *Thy rod and thy staff they comfort me.*

J   *Beside me your rod and your staff are there, to hearten me.*

VERSE 5a

V   *Parasti in conspectu meo mensam, adversus eos, qui tribulant me.*

OE *Þu gegearwodest beforan mē swīðe brādne bēod wið þara willan þe mē hatedon.*

R   *Þou haś graþid in my syght the bord agayns thaim that angirs me.*

M   *Þou madest radi grace in my siȝt oȝayns hem þat trublen me.*

W1 *Thou hast maad redi in thi siȝte a bord aȝen hem that trublyn me.*

W2 *Thou hast maad redi a boord in my siȝt aȝens hem that troblen me.*

KJ *Thou hast prepared a table before me in the presence of mine enemies.*

J   *You prepare a table before me under the eyes of my enemies.*

VERSE 5b

V   *Impinguasti in oleo caput meum: et calix meus* (poculum tuum) *inebrians quam praeclarus est!*

OE *Þu gesmyredest mē mid ele mīn hēafod; Drihten hū mǣre þīn folc nu is, ǣlce dæge hit symblað.*

R   *Thou fattid my heued in oyle, and my chalice drunkynand what it is bright.*

M   *þou makest fatt myn heued wyþ mercy; and my drynk makand drunken ys ful clere.*

W1   *Thou hast myche fattid in oile myn hed; and my chalis makende ful drunken, hou riʒt cler it is.*

W2   *Thou hast maad fat myn heed with oyle; and my cuppe, filling greetli, is ful cleer.*

KJ   *Thou anointest my head with oil; my cup runneth over.*

J   *You anoint my head with oil, my cup brims over.*

VERSE 6a

V   *Et misericordia tua subsequetur (subsequitur) me omnibus diebus vitae meae.*

OE   *And folgie mē nū þīn mildheortnes ealle dagas mīnes līfes.*

R   *And thi mercy sall folow me all the dayes of my lif.*

M   *And þy merci shal folwen me alle daies of mi lif.*

W1   *And thi mercy shal vnderfolewe me alle the daʒis of my lif.*

W2   *And thi merci schal sue me in alle the daies of my lijf.*

KJ   *Surely goodness and mercy shall follow me all the days of my life.*

J   *Ah, goodness and kindness pursue me, every day of my life.*

VERSE 6b

V   *Et ut inhabitem in domo Domini, in longitudinem dierum.*

OE   *Þæt ic mæge wunian on þīnum hūse swīþe lange tiid oð lange ylde.*

R   *And that i won in the hows of lord in lenght of dayes.*

M   *And þat ich wonne in þe hous of our lord on lengþe of daies.*

W1   *And that I dwelle in the hous of the Lord in to the lengthe of daʒis.*

W2   *And that Y dwelle in the hows of the Lord in to the lengthe of daies.*

KJ   *And I will dwell in the house of the Lord for ever.*

J   *My home the house of Yahweh, as long as I live.*

(a)   Richard Rolle was a Yorkshireman and therefore used the Northern dialect. Can you detect obvious Northern characteristics in phonology (*a/o, s/sh*), morphology (*-s/-th*, pronoun forms), and lexicon? Check *OED* for words which seem peculiar to R.

(b)   Explain the grammatical features of

      v. 1: OE, *ne byð mē nānes gōdes wan;* R, *nathynge sall me want*
      v. 2: OE, *be wætera staðum*
      v. 3: OE, *ofer þā wegas rihtwīsnesse*

v. 5a: OE, *wið þara willan þe mē hatedon*

v. 5b: OE, *þu gesmyredest mē mid ele mīn hēafod;* M, *makand,* W1, *makende* (suffix)

v. 6a: OE, *folgie mē nū þīn mildheortnes (folgie,* though without the *-að* ending, may have indicated either subjunctive or present tense with future meaning.)

(c)   W1 was retranslated as W2 to achieve a more truly English idiom. By comparing each of these with the Latin, you should be able to discover contrasts between Latin and English syntactic structures of the fourteenth century.

(d)   What practices would now be considered substandard in v. 4a: OE; v. 4b: R, W1, W2, KJ?

(e)   What evidence of semantic change do you find from the study of v. 2: OE, *feohland;* v. 2: R, *in sted of;* v. 3: R, *stretis;* v. 3: OE, *mōd;* v. 5a: OE, *wið;* v. 5b; R, M, W1, W2, *fatt, fattid?*

(f)   Medieval manuscript books frequently contain changes and interpolations introduced by the individual scribe. By comparing the English translations with the Latin, find such an interpolation in v. 3: M and a more prominent one in v. 4b: OE. The latter reveals a misunderstanding which impairs the poetic imagery of the whole psalm. Can you explain this? What feature of word meaning has misled the translator? How does v. 4b: M betray the same misunderstanding? (One reason that vernacular translations of the Bible were not encouraged in the High Middle Ages was the danger of such distortions. A different type appears in v. 5b: R [notice that the Latin word *quam* is ambiguous]. Observe in the widely different translations the difficulty that this clause presented to the translators.)

7.   Considering the fact that KJ and J are based upon different textual originals, do you find significant differences in meaning between them and the medieval versions?

Part III

MODERN ENGLISH

Chapter 13

THE RENAISSANCE

The study of any phase of modern culture in Europe is almost certain to touch at least some of the effects of the Renaissance, a historic phenomenon complex and far-reaching in the changes it produced, though often poorly understood by students of general history. Fortunately, we need be concerned with only some elements of this revival: the humanist movement with its interest in ancient culture, which provided a new impetus to the study of both Latin and Greek language and literature, the invention of printing and the consequent spread of literacy, and later the dispersal of English throughout the world in the age of discovery and exploration.

The word *Renaissance* appears to have been used in English in the middle of the nineteenth century, when it referred to Italian art and architecture; but in 1873, Walter Pater wrote, "The word Renaissance is now generally used to denote . . . a whole complex movement of which that revival of classical antiquity was but one element or symptom."[1] It was the influence of classical learning, however, that stimulated the entire movement. In the Middle Ages there was an abundance of literature in the Latin language, but many of the works of the great authors of pre-Christian Rome had been lost or lay neglected. The Greek language was little known in Western Europe, and Greek literature was known only in very imperfect adaptations in Latin. On the other hand, in the Eastern Empire, whose capital was Byzantium or Constantinople, the prevailing

---

[1] Quoted in *OED*, s.v. "Renaissance."

language had remained Greek, and here the ancient Greek literature had not been lost. A wall of religious difference, however, separated the East from the West, so that interchange of culture remained at a minimum. In the fourteenth century increasing commerce and travel between Constantinople and the great commercial centers of Italy resulted in a stirring of interest in Greek, which was shared by Boccaccio and Petrarch. When the Eastern Empire was overrun by the Turks and Constantinople taken in 1453, Greek scholars in large numbers fled westward, bringing with them their knowledge of Greek and of ancient literature. An enthusiasm for the recovery of ancient literature spread rapidly, first in Italy and then further westward. The full power of the movement reached its peak in England in the sixteenth century, and influenced the English language in important ways.

Another event of the greatest consequence to the English language and its literature as well was the invention of printing, which dates from the middle of the fifteenth century. In 1476 William Caxton set up a printing press in Westminster, at that time outside the city of London. It would be difficult to overestimate the importance of his innovation. For our purposes, however, the principal effects may be reduced to these: (1) Books were made in greater numbers and therefore more cheaply. Many people, especially of the less wealthy classes, could now afford to own them. The result was an extension of literacy. (2) Because of Caxton's sympathy for the native language, many works were translated from Latin, French, and Italian, and later from Greek also, thus bringing some of the substance of humanistic and other literary interests to the knowledge of those who lacked a classical education. (3) The growth of the printing industry fostered a general desire for the standardization of language, particularly in vocabulary and spelling. (4) The role of the native language in the dissemination of books tended to improve its status in competition with Latin, now more firmly than ever entrenched as the language of learned men.

The multiplication of books in the vernacular and the enthusiasm of scholars for Latin learning came together in an interesting way. Authors whose education and interests were predominantly classical were finding it more and more possible in the sixteenth century to write in English. Some of them, however, were not quite satisfied with the resources of their native language. They felt that things could be much improved by using learned Latin words in English contexts, and they did not hesitate to do so. Some felt also that the character of English writing could be greatly improved by submission to the precepts and examples of ancient rhetoricians. Not all literate people shared this attitude, but there was a sufficient interest in it to bring about a pronounced effect upon the English style and vocabulary. These matters we will return to later.

Despite the importance of the great events of this time, it is not to be taken for granted that the transitions in political, social, and even literary history coincide with the transitions in linguistic history. In fact, not all of the several phases of linguistic history itself keep a uniform pace in their changes. The history of English sounds had certainly entered into the "modern" period earlier than the sixteenth century, and modernization of English morphology was even earlier. Nevertheless, the events of the later fifteenth and of the sixteenth century were so monumental, and their impact upon men's thoughts and words was so strong, that we may accept the conventional practice of dating the Modern English language from some convenient point in the latter fifteenth century—say, the establishment of Caxton's printing press at Westminster in 1476, or the accession of Henry Tudor (Henry VII) in 1485.

Chapter 14

MODERN ENGLISH

The Sounds

Vowels

THE GREAT VOWEL SHIFT

The great events recorded in the general history of the fifteenth and six-teenth centuries had little to do with the changes that took place in the sounds of English in that period, and yet these changes, at least insofar as the long vowels are concerned, are striking enough to mark the passage from Middle to Modern English. Called collectively the Great Vowel Shift, they have already been partly explained in the description of the vowel sounds of Middle English.

Sometime near the end of the fourteenth or the beginning of the fifteenth century, all of the long vowels began to undergo the process of raising. More explicitly this means that in all words which contained a long vowel, this vowel was pronounced with a more elevated tongue posi-tion. The change at first would have been so slight as to remain unnoticed by any one generation of speakers, but, continued over a period of one or two centuries, the cumulative effect was considerable.

The changes must all have begun about the same time, or at least each vowel must have begun to shift before the next lower vowel had com-pleted its evolution; otherwise the two sounds would have fallen together. Under such circumstance the Middle English word for *boat*, spelled *boot* but pronounced [bɔːt], would have become a homonym with the word *boot* [boːt], but since the words remained different in sound *boot* [boːt] must also have begun to shift upward towards its present sound [buːt], which was reached by about 1500, before [bɔːt], became [boːt].

Some vowel shifts, however, took a much longer time for completion. Thus, though the words *feed* and *food* reached approximately their present pronunciation at the beginning of the sixteenth century,[1] the present sounds of *find* and *foul* were not reached until the end of the seventeenth century or later; in fact, intermediate stages of the sound change are still to be heard in some regional varieties of English.

We have said that all of the long vowels were raised. There is one exception to this. Both the high front vowel *ī* and the high back vowel *ū* would have become consonants if the tongue had been further raised. Instead, the vowels underwent diphthongization. Perhaps because of extreme length, both developed a double sound, the front element consisting of a lax on-glide producing a result which can be represented as [ɪi] and [ʊu], with stress on the second element. As the first element became more prominent in both new diphthongs it was centered to [ə] and the stress shifted forward. This stage was reached in the sixteenth century and therefore represents Shakespeare's pronunciation, [əɪ] and [əʊ]. The present sounds [aɪ] and [aʊ] were not heard in Standard English before the end of the seventeenth century.

The general character of the Great Vowel Shift can be seen in the following table:

EXAMPLES OF THE GREAT VOWEL SHIFT

Middle English	14th–16th Century	17th–19th Century	Present English
ī [iː]	> [əɪ]	> [aɪ]	find
ē [eː]	> [iː]	> [iː]	feet
ę̄ [ɛː]	> [ɛː]/[eː]	> [eː]/[iː]	great/seat
ā [aː]	> [æː] > [ɛː]	> [eː]	late
ū [uː]	> [əu]	> [au]	out
ǭ [oː]	> [uː]/[ʊ]	> [uː]/[ʌ]/[ʊ]	food/flood/foot
ǭ [ɔː]	> [oː]	> [oː]	old

---

[1] The assumptions followed here are substantially those of Dobson; see esp. vol. 2.

SHORT VOWELS

The history of the short vowels in this period is, as usual, much simpler than that of the long vowels. Short *i* and *e* remained unchanged, so that *sit* and *set* were pronounced by both Chaucer and Shakespeare as they are today. Chaucer's *a* [a] had probably become [æ] by Shakespeare's time, as it is today in words like *sat, happy*, etc. The short *o* and short *u* were both kept rounded in the sixteenth century (as in the present sound in *for, pull*), though since the seventeenth century *u* has been unrounded to [ʌ] as in present *dull, mud, rut*, except after labial stops and fricatives: *put, full, bush*. The short *o* remains rounded in modern British usage, but is generally unrounded [a] in the United States as in *pot, top, mob*, etc.

Diphthongs

The behavior of diphthongs between Middle and Early Modern English is sometimes difficult to explain, because not all words which at first glance appear to belong to the same class have the same sound history, as we see in the records of *-ough-* in *though, thought*, and *through*. To make the confusion more perplexing, the sound we are accustomed to may have had a very irregular history, as in *cough*, where *-gh* represents not the normal evolution but a substitution from a nonstandard dialect.

We see in the period from the fifteenth to the eighteenth century two opposite tendencies: the simplification of old diphthongs and emergence of new ones. It has been pointed out that a number of digraph spellings which now represent a monophthong were diphthongs in Middle English. One of these was *au/aw* [aʊ], found in Chaucer's language, not only in words like *cause, daunt*, and *dawn*, but in other words now spelled *-a-*, like *chamber, dance, damper*. Words with *au* in Middle English occur in Present English in three main classes. In some, by reciprocal assimilation,[2] the diphthong was simplified to [ɔ:].[3] In others the simplification took

---

[2] That is, modification of each of the two elements by the other to an intermediate position: *a* was raised and *u* lowered.

[3] Also ME *ou* [ɔʊ], like *au*, was simplified before [x] and fell together with it as [ɔ:]. This accounts for the PE spellings *au* and *ou* for the same sound.

place early,[4] the diphthong was simplified to coincide with Middle English *a*, and if the vowel remained long, it shared the usual evolution of Middle English *ā* to [e:] as in *ancient, chamber, change, danger,* and *strange.* However, in a considerable number of instances the vowel was shortened. This short vowel has largely remained in American English as [æ] but appears in the Received Standard of Great Britain as [ɑ:] in such words as *dance, demand, example, grant.*

Several Middle English diphthongs have fallen together in Modern English as [ju], though they retain different spellings as in *new, feud,* and *cute.* First, in the earlier Middle English period *iu* and *ęu* fell together as [iu] (*blew, knew, new, true*). To these were eventually added words from French in which the French *ū* [y:] was modified to [iu] (*cute, cure, pure, use*). In the meantime Middle English *ęu* [ɛu] was kept distinct from the *iu/ęu* diphthong and remained so perhaps until the middle of the seventeenth century, when at the latest all of these sounds became [ju] and have shared the same later history. A number of these remain unchanged in Present English (*new, few, cute*). In others the first element has been lost, especially after *r* as in *rude, cruel, true,* or after a consonant and *l* as in *blew, blue, glue.*[5] Loss of [j] in words like *news, due, duty, deuce* is also common today, but likely to be viewed suspiciously by educated people. In still other words [j] has been lost by reciprocal assimilation with the preceding consonant (*sure, sugar*), especially in suffixes (*nature, creature, pleasure*). It is worth noting that the suffix *-ure* had a simple unstressed vowel [ə] until the eighteenth century, when it was changed to [ju] under the influence of the spelling.[6] One should not therefore be surprised to encounter such rhymes in this early period as *nature/creature/traitor.* Shakespeare rhymes (*Venus and Adonis,* l. 628) *venture/enter,* and reflects the same pronunciation in puns.[7]

Other changes in the diphthongs have been less spectacular, though

---

[4] But see Otto Jespersen, *A Modern English Grammar on Historical Principles,* 7 vols. (Heidelberg, 1909–49), I, 110–11.

[5] After initial *l* practice in this country is divided, but the English custom seems to be more conservative. Compare Kenyon and Knott with Jones, *English Pronouncing Dictionary,* s.v. "lubricate," "lucid," "lunar," "lute," etc.

[6] The early pronunciation explains the dialectal form *critter,* and perhaps also the still current but nonstandard ['fɪɡɚ] for figure.

[7] See Helge Kökeritz, *Shakespeare's Pronunciation* (New Haven, 1953), esp. p. 271.

it is perhaps useful to take note of the Middle English *ei/ai* diphthong, if for no other reason than to illustrate once and for all how persistent old spellings can be and therefore how unsafe a guide spelling is to pronunciation. Although *ei* fell together with *ai* as early as the thirteenth century, the old spelling was sometimes retained. In the Early Modern period, ME *ā* passed through the stages [æ:] and [ɛ:] before becoming [e:]. At some point the diphthong *ai/ei* [æɪ] fell together with the long vowel. Possibly the diphthong was retained by conservative speakers in the sixteenth century, but in time it fell in with the reflex of ME *ā*, and thereafter both the original long vowel and the original diphthong shared the same phonological history.[8] Nevertheless, the old spellings are still with us as in *eight* beside *ate*, *main* beside *mane*, and *weight* beside *wade*.

Consonants

A number of consonants which remained voiceless in terminal positions, like *th* [θ] in *bath*, were voiced when followed by an inflectional syllable, like *th* [ð] in ME *bathen*. Thus we have the voiced consonant in Chaucer's line "And bathéd every veyne in swich licour." Now, since verbs retained inflectional endings later and more frequently than nouns, a general pattern was established that now distinguishes a number of noun-verb pairs by the feature of voice: *bath/bathe, breath/breathe,[9] half/halve, house/house, mouth/mouthe, peace/(ap)pease, price/prize, strife/strive, wreath/wreathe*.

Voicing of the final consonant of the stem is also a feature of the plural of some nouns of which the ending, *-es*, was originally syllabic: *calf/calves, half/halves, leaf/leaves*. Some nouns which once followed this pattern of voicing have assumed a new plural and now fluctuate between two forms. In *bath* and *hoof* we vary between [bæθs] and [bæðz] and between [hʊfs] and [hu:vz]; or, in some instances, the older plural may have been lost, as *troves*, plural of *trough*. Obviously lengthening may also occur in the inflected form of nouns: *staff/staves*. A new plural has developed for *cloth* since the original plural, *clothes*, has undergone semantic separation. In general, final position favors voicelessness in words of this type, but a few words do not conform: *blithe, lathe,[10] scythe, smooth*.

---

[8] The PE vowel is, of course, a new diphthong, [eɪ].

[9] In *bathe* the long vowel resulted from open position (see pp. 128–30). *Breath* is one of a number of words in which ME [ɛ:] was shortened before [d], [t], and [θ].

[10] I.e., 'turning-lathe,' not related to *lath*.

Final -*s* has become voiced after vowels (*eyes*), after voiced consonants (*buds*), and in -*es* plurals, when the ending is syllabic (*witches*). Medial *s* likewise became voiced under the influence of neighboring voiced sounds: *cosmic, dismal, gooseberry, muslin, pansy, quinsy, raspberry, schism*. This Early Modern voicing was quite general and, as occasional phonetic spelling shows, included words which now have voiceless *s*: *discourse, mistletoe, wristband*. In words of more than one syllable there is a tendency to voice the sound at the beginning of the stressed syllable before a vowel as in *resent* and *observe*, but it is by no means consistent; it does not occur in *precise* and *presage* (v.), and practice is divided in *absorb* and *absurd*.

The most protean of all English sounds in recent history is *r*. It varies through historical periods, across dialect areas, and at different positions in the same word from a strongly trilled consonant to a midcentral vowel. Originally it was a trilled phoneme consisting of a small and closely related group of allophones, but even in prehistoric times it tended to assume some vowel quality by becoming syllabic. In Old English the syllabic *r* generated the syllable -*er* [ər] as in Old English *æcer* 'acre.' Through the Middle English period it retained a firm consonantal quality. Chaucer's *r* was probably trilled, at least to a moderate extent. Shakespeare's *r* between vowels was probably lightly trilled, and in other positions was close to that now heard in the Midlands and in Western America. The ancient sound, however, has been well preserved in the English of Scotland.

The important varieties of sound represented by the letter *r* in Modern English are:

1. Trilled *r* preserved in Scotland
2. Glide *r* used initially or before vowels
3. Fricative *r* which replaces the glide in some varieties of both British and American
4. Flap which in RP replaces the glide common in American speech in intervocalic positions[11]
5. Syllabic *r* as in ladder
6. Vocalized *r* which varies according to region from the "*r*-colored" vowel to the vowel off-glide (It occurs in final or preconsonantal positions.)

---

[11] RP is the Received Standard Pronunciation of England. To unaccustomed ears, the flap sometimes sounds like intervocalic *d* as in "veddy, veddy Ameddican."

Those parts of the English-speaking world in which the vocalized *r* has completely lost its *r* coloring are called the "*r*-less" regions. Loss of *r* had already occurred in some Middle English areas in Late Middle English by assimilation to [s] or [ʃ] in words like *burst, cursed, first, horse, harsh,* but though these pronunciations survived into modern times they are different in origin from the more general loss of preconsonantal *r* in the late seventeenth and of final *-r* at the end of the eighteenth century.

The original trilled quality of the consonant is partially preserved in the intervocalic flap as heard in RP, but the most extensive uniformity among English speakers is to be found in the glide *r* used initially.

One variety of *r* which occurs only in the *r*-less regions but which merits special attention is the "linking *r*" and its attendant, the "intrusive *r*." Though final *-r* in these areas has completely disappeared as a consonant, the spelling remains, and the *r* is restored to the pronunciation before a vowel. Thus the usual pronunciation of *father* would be [fɑːðə], but in the pairing *father and mother* we would have [fɑːðər ən mʌðə]. The restored *r* because of its connective function is called the "linking *r*."

However, there are many words with a final vowel pronounced [ə] which do not result from loss of *-r* and have therefore no *-r* in the spelling. When these words occur before other vowels the force of analogy leads to the insertion of an *r* which has no historical basis and is not represented in the spelling. For example, where *sofa* [sofə] has an ending like *father* [fɑːðə], the pairing *sofa and chair* follows the analogy of *father and mother* to give us [sofər ən tʃeə]. This analogical *r* is called intrusive.

There is a mistaken assumption prevalent among some people outside the *r*-less regions that the intrusive *r* is characteristic only of the uneducated speakers. It is indeed widespread among such speakers, especially in the metropolitan area of New York and in parts of New England, but it is also heard among educated people of those areas and in England as well.[12]

Another consonant whose loss, like that of *-r*, has produced compensatory lengthening of a preceding short vowel has left its traces in the spelling *-gh-* (*light, naught*). Actually there were two different allophones of the phoneme represented by this spelling, a palatal fricative [ç] after

---

[12] Concerning the status of intrusive *r* Bronstein (pp. 121–22) is suspicious. Other authorities are more lenient. See John S. Kenyon, *American Pronunciation*, 10th ed. (Ann Arbor, 1950), pp. 164–65; Jespersen, *Modern English Grammar*, (1: 370–72); Kenyon and Knott, pp. xxxv–xxxvi; Jones, *English Pronouncing Dictionary*, pp. xxiv–xxv.

front vowels (*light*) and a velar fricative [x] after back vowels (*naught*). Among conservative speakers [ç] may still have been heard in the sixteenth century, but in Shakespeare's language both sounds had been lost. In words like *light* the short vowel was lengthened to [əɪ].[13]

Early loss of [x] after *u* gave rise to the lengthened vowel [u:], and this followed in due course the history of Middle English *ū* to [əʊ] and later [aʊ] as in *bough, drought,* and *plough.* In still other words a diphthong spelled *au* resulted from the vocalization of [x] and this became in regular development [ɔ:] as in *caught, naught, brought, daughter.* However, among words of this group a displacement occurred from a nonstandard dialectal source in which [x] > [f], frequently with shortening of the vowel to [ʊ], later [ʌ]: *rough, tough, slough, chough, cough, laugh, trough.* In *dwarf* (OE *dweorȝ, dweorh*) the spelling has been modified, but in another instance, *draft* and *draught,* both spellings have survived. In Early Modern speech, a pronunciation with *f* was also used in words not now so pronounced. In *The Winter's Tale* (IV.i.27–28) Shakespeare rhymes *daughter* with *after,* though this possibly was [dɑ:ter] and [ɑ:ter].[14]

Consonant loss occurred also in Early Modern English in the combination *ng.* Originally *n* in this sequence was a front nasal [n]. By assimilation to [g] the nasal became velar [ŋ] in Old English, but merely as a positional allophone of the *n* phoneme. Chaucer also preserved [g] in words like *sing* [sɪŋg] and *thing* [θɪŋg]. Eventually, however, the velar quality of the nasal was felt to be sufficient to show phonemic[15] contrast, and the final [g] was lost, though it has been preserved in the spelling· As a result *ng* is now an ambiguous spelling. In final position it is always [ŋ]: *strong, long, sing, ring.* With the comparative and superlative suffixes, [ŋg] has survived, as in *stronger, strongest, longer, longest,* but with other suffixes [g] is lost: *ringer, ringing, singer, singing.* Quite often before syllabic *l* and *r* the sound is [ŋg]: *anger, angle, finger, mingle, single.*

A further stage of development is seen in the history of the present participle suffix *-ing,* in which the velar nasal [ŋ] was fronted to [n] under the influence of the front vowel [ɪ]. Swift, who was certainly not one to tolerate carelessness, wrote:[16]

---

[13] Kökeritz, p. 148, s.v. "light."

[14] See Dobson, 2: 519, n. 2; Jespersen, *Modern English Grammar,* 1: 286–88.

[15] As between *sing* and *sin* or *thing* and *thin.*

[16] *Journal of a Modern Lady,* pp. 178–79.

All mad to speak, and none to hearken,
They set the very lap-dog barking.

This pronunciation, which was current as early as Shakespeare's time, certainly remained fashionable through the nineteenth century, as suggested by rhymes similar to Swift's in the poetry of Wordsworth, Byron, Shelley, and Tennyson.[17] Its status since then has been justly defined by the eminent historian of language, the late Henry C. Wyld: "At the present time [1914] thousands of the best speakers still use *-in* forms, but it seems that since the thirties of the last century this was one of the 'mistakes' against which governesses and schoolmasters successfully waged war, and the result has been a widespread adoption of *-ing* to agree with the spelling."[18] In the United States the *-in* form is very common in popular speech, though many educated people regard it as evidence of slovenly speech habits, a judgment hardly warranted by its history.[19]

Loss of a somewhat different character has occurred in words spelled *wh-*. This originally consisted of a labial element represented by *w*, strongly aspirated, as shown by the *h*-spelling.[20] In a few words of this class the labial element disappeared, as in *who* and *whole*, but more generally it is the aspiration that has disappeared, leaving [w]. At least this has been the case in the standard language since the early eighteenth century, if not as early as the sixteenth. Consequently, the following pairs have became homonyms: *what/watt, wheel/we'll, where/wear, whet/wet, whether/weather, whey/way, which/witch, while/wile, whine/wine.* In many parts of the United States, however, voiceless *wh-* remains.

A voiceless but very weakly aspirated labial [w̥] is heard after voiceless stops as in *twin* and *queen*, but the more prominently aspirated sounds occur normally only in Scotland and Ireland. Partly from the influence of the Scotch and Irish segments of the American population and partly because of the spelling, it has commonly been taught in schools that [w̥]

---

[17] Wordsworth, *Helwellyn/dwelling;* Byron, *children/bewildering;* Shelley, *pursuing/ruin;* Tennyson, *treading/wed in;* quoted in Jespersen, *Modern English Grammar,* 1: 356–57.

[18] *Short History*, p. 209.

[19] The *-in* suffix for *-ing* is frequently heard among educated speakers in the Southeastern states.

[20] In Old English the spelling was the reverse, *hw-*. The phonetic symbol for the voiceless sound, if preserved, is [w̥].

is "correct" in these words, but it is very doubtful that all of those who preach the doctrine practice it habitually.

Other consonant loss in or shortly before Early Modern English may be listed as follows:

kn- > n: *knave, knew, knife, know,* etc. (17th century)
wr- > r: *write, wrap* (15th century)
wl- > l: *lisp* (Middle English *wlispen*) (15th century)
gn- > n: *gnash, gnat, gnaw* (16th century)
-mn > n: *damn, hymn, solemn* (15th century or earlier)
-ln > l: *kiln* (15th century)
-lm > m: *alms, calm, palm, psalm*[21] (15th century)
-lk > k: *folk, walk, talk* (16th century)
-mb > m: *dumb, lamb, thumb* (15th century or earlier)

Medial *t* has been lost between consonants: *apostle, castle, chasten, Christmas, epistle, fasten, listen, wrestle;* and often in *acts, defects, reflects.* In similar contexts both *nd* and *nt* have suffered erosion: *handsome, handkerchief, landscape;* and in unstressed position: *patients, assistants.*

The introduction of new consonants is less common than the loss of old. We have already become familiar with the excrescent *t* which arose in final position in words like *amidst, against.* Other examples include *ancient, pageant,* and *parchment.* In the same way intrusive sounds arose in medial positions: [d] in *spindle, thunder, kindred* (also finally in *sound*); [p] in *empty;* [b] in *bramble, nimble, shambles,* and *thimble;*[22] and [n] in *messenger, nightingale.*

Of special interest is the modern pronunciation of the numeral *one* and its inflected form *once.* A few words beginning with *ǭ* in Middle English developed an on-glide consisting of labialization from overrounding. By the sixteenth century the standard pronunciation was [wɔ:n]. In some Middle English dialects, however, a second change took place; *ǭ* became *ọ̄* and was carried in the Great Vowel Shift to [u:], then shortened

---

[21] Usually loss of *l* results in lengthening of the preceding vowel, but in these words a short vowel was retained by some speakers and remained in use in America in the nineteenth century as in *alms* [æmz], etc. It is now uncommon.

[22] Note also the illiterate *chimbley,* in which *b* arose by this same process after [n] > [l] by dissimilation.

to [ʊ] and by regular development became [ʌ]. In Shakespeare's time this was considered vulgar, but it eventually displaced the standard form. The earlier regular development of the vowel is preserved in *only, alone,* and *atone.*

A few additional consonants arose by the restoration of original Latin spelling features to words which earlier had come into English from French; thus *c: perfet > perfect, verdit > verdict; b: dette > debt, doute > doubt; l: faute > fault, vaute > vault.* In the second group *b* remains a spelling anomaly, but with the exception of *victuals* (OF *vitaille*), the pronunciation of the other groups was modified in the eighteenth century to conform to the spelling.

Regional Influence

Descriptions of sound change have sometimes been called "laws" of sound change, the term being used here as in the physical sciences when we speak of Boyle's law or the law of gravity. Unfortunately, since laws of sound change are descriptions of the behavior of human beings rather than of inanimate matter, they are not altogether consistent in their operation. Moreover, they are historical events which occurred in a given time, and therefore their causes are sometimes lost to our view.

The failure of a sound law to operate may result from mixed practice among speakers, consisting of variation in either regional or social characteristics, which is a common condition in a living language. In any metropolitan American city, for example, educated speakers may be found, some of whom have [ɑ] in words like *call, fall,* while others have the rounded vowel [ɔ:]. Paradoxically the first group may have a rounded vowel in *forest* and *moral,* while the second group have [ɑ]. No one can say whether one of these pronunciations will prevail and become the single general pronunciation or under what circumstances.

Substitution

Similar variations must have existed in earlier times. In Middle English there were two classes of words spelled with the same vowel symbol, but in one group it represented Middle English *ẹ̄* [e:] and in the other, Middle English *ẹ̄* [ɛ:].

In the standard language the sounds were kept distinct until the eighteenth century, so that words with a vowel from Middle English *ẹ̄*, such as *sea* and *teach* had [ɛ:] or [e:] rather than the present sound [i:]. Shakespeare has rhymes like *peace/face* and *defeated/created*. Swift rhymed *tears*(n.)/*forswears*, and Pope, *obey/tea*. Since the eighteenth century, however, words of this class, that is, like *peace, defeat,* and *tea* (usually spelled *ea*), have been pronounced with [i:]. This shift illustrates a change explained earlier (p. 55) due to **substitution** or displacement, by which a feature from the standard language was driven out by one from a different dialect tradition—in this instance, one in which Middle English ẹ̄ and ę̄ had fallen together, both becoming [i:] in the modern era. The displacement has affected all words with the reflex of ME ę̄ except *break, great, steak,* and words in which the change to [i:] was inhibited by combinative factors, as in *bear* and *swear*.

Combinative Change

Either the operation of a sound law or its apparent failure to operate may be due to the influence of neighboring sounds. In this event, we have a second law, if it describes a set of conditions which operate consistently. Thus we can formulate a rule which says that OE short *i* remained in Middle English, but we find that OE *cild* 'child,' though it had a short vowel in Old English, has a long vowel in its subsequent history. Extended observation of many words reveals that a short vowel was lengthened when it fell before *ld*. This illustrates how neighboring sounds influence change, but it is also to be observed that lengthening did not take place if a third consonant followed *ld*. This is also a rule, and it explains why we have one vowel phoneme in the singular form of this word but a quite different phoneme in the plural, *children*.

One development in which both combinative change and displacement played a part was the appearance of a new pronunciation [ar] for spellings of *er*, to which we referred earlier (p. 55). The change, which consisted simply of the lowering of *e* before *r*, appeared in Northern English in the fourteenth century but was not adopted in the standard language until somewhat later. In Chaucer words of this kind had both *er*-spelling and *er*- pronunciation: *bern, derk, fer, ferme, ferther, sterre, sterve, werre*. During the following century, however, the new pronunciation began to spread. Some words affected by this change took modified spellings to agree, and in such instances both the spelling and the sound have remained: *barn, dark, far, farm, farther, star, starve, war*. Other words pronounced with [ar] preserved the older *er*-spelling through the sixteenth and seventeenth centuries and have now reverted to a spelling pronunciation: *clerk, certain, convert, desert, sermon, serve, swerve.* Notice, for example, Shakespeare's rhyme in Sonnet 17 of *deserts* and *parts.* In the light of these facts we are enabled to explain several linguistic oddities, such as the discrepancy between the spelling and pronunciation of *sergeant,* between the common noun *clerk* and the proper noun *Clark,*[23] the background of some early American dialectal spellings and pronunciations—*larnin'* 'learning,' *'tarnal* 'eternal,' *sartin* 'certain,' and *varmint* 'vermin'—and finally several pairs of doublets: *errant/arrant, Henry/Harry,*[24] and *person/parson.*

Some consonants seem to be especially fruitful in producing combinative change. One of these is *r*, which, as we have seen, has strong vowel characteristics. These tend to attract neighboring vowels to lower or more open articulation, as one can demonstrate by contrasting such pairs as *fate* and *fair, deed* and *deer, moon* and *moor.* The Early Modern lowering of *er* to *ar* is an historic illustration of this tendency. Another is the influence of *r* in preventing in some words the Late Modern shift of the vowel from Middle English $\bar{ę}$ to [i:], as in *bear, swear, tear* (v.), and *wear.* Even words with Middle English $\bar{ẹ}$, which was raised quite early to [i:], retained the lower vowel before *r*, fell in with the *ea* words, commonly adopted their spelling, and were pronounced like them until the eighteenth century, as numerous rhymes attest.[25]

In a somewhat similar way, *r* has inhibited raising to [u:] in *floor, fourth,* and *sword,* and has prevented diphthongization to [aʊ] in *bourn, course, court, pour, source.*

A special instance of combinative change with important regional variation is the history of Middle English *a* [a] before the voiceless fricatives [s], [f], and [θ]. The normal development of Middle English *a* [a] to [æ] was extensively carried out even before these consonants. Among some speakers, however, the consonants inhibited the shift to [æ], and the vowel remained [a]. These two pronunciations now constitute the two American reflexes of Middle English *a* in this position, [a] being heard

---

[23] In England the common noun has [ɑ], as have some proper nouns: *Derby, Hertford, Berks,* etc.

[24] From earlier *Herry* by assimilation of the French *n* to *r.*

[25] For illustrations in Shakespeare, see esp. *Rape of Lucrece,* ll. 610–12, 1290–92; Sonnets 61, 84, 102, 110.

in parts of New England. In England, however, the retracted [a] has undergone further retraction and lengthening to [ɑ:]. This sound, heard in such words as *staff*, *pass*, and *path*,[26] constitutes one of the prominent differences between American English and RP.

Vowels have been influenced by preceding as well as by following vowels. Two instances of this process are important enough to call attention to.

1. The labial *w* favors rounding of *a* when it is followed by *r*. In *war*, *warm*, *warn*, *quart*, the vowel was rounded in the seventeenth century, though Dryden, who died in 1700, rhymed *scars/wars*. The rounding, however, is not universal. It generally fails before [g], [k], and [ŋ], as in *wag*, *wax*, *wangle*, and *swank*. In American English practice varies in *warrior*, *warble*, *warrant*, *wash*, *wasp*, and *water*.[27]

2. Finally the rounded [ʊ] from Middle English *u* generally remains after the labials *b, f, p, w* if the vowel is followed by the alveolar consonants *d, l, t, sh: bull, full, pull, wood, push*, etc.

Changes in Phonemic Structure

In light of the changes described here the phonemes in use among the educated classes of London at the end of the sixteenth century may be enumerated as follows.

CONSONANTS

The consonants:

/p/ /t/ /k/ /f/ /θ/ /s/ /ʃ/ /tʃ/ /h/
/b/ /d/ /g/ /v/ /ð/ /z/ /dʒ/ /j/
/m/ /n/ /ŋ/ /w/ /r/ /l/

The new phoneme /ŋ/, which in Middle English had been only a positional allophone of /n/, resulted from loss of [g] in final *-ng*. By the middle of the seventeenth century another new phoneme, /ʒ/, the voiced counter-

---

[26] This pronunciation extends also to *a* before [ns] and [nt] as in *dance, grant, chant*, etc.

[27] "Unrounded forms," says Dobson (2: 717), "apparently still survived in *wan, quality*, etc., in the late eighteenth century." Surely they are current in American English today, as recorded by Kenyon and Knott, though not by Jones, *English Pronouncing Dictionary*.

part of /ʃ/, made its appearance when [z]+[j] became [ʒ] by reciprocal assimilation in words like *vision*.

LONG VOWELS

The long vowels resulting from the Great Vowel Shift:

$$\text{/i:/} \quad \text{/e:/} \quad \text{/ɛ:/} \quad \text{/u:/} \quad \text{/o:/} \quad \text{/ɔ:/}$$

Combinative factors contributed also a lengthened vowel [a:] or [æ:], which we may designate /a:/. The distribution, dating, and precise phonetic character of this phoneme are the subject of considerable difference of opinion, especially with respect to words of three different classes: those with ME *a* before *n* plus a consonant, as in *dance* and *grant;* those with ME *a* before *l* plus a labial before which *l* was later lost, as in *calm* and *alms;* and those with ME *a* before the voiceless fricatives /s/, /f/, and /θ/. In the first two classes diphthonging to [aʊ] was normal, leading to merger with /ɔ:/, but diphthonging may not have been universal, and the vowel would then have remained a front vowel, [a], with long and short variants, as the history of all three classes of words in American English seems to indicate. However Dobson (2: 790) believes that in the first two classes diphthonging was general but generated two reflexes, [ɔ:] and [a:]. The latter, he thinks, was restricted in the sixteenth century to vulgar usage. If so, it had certainly attained reputable status by the end of the seventeenth century, when [a:], later [ɑ:], became standard in these words as well as before the voiceless fricatives.

The separate phonemic status of [e:] and [ɛ:] is also uncertain. The enumeration given here is based on the assumption of the development of ME *ę̄* to [e:] and of ME *ā* and *ai/ei* to [ɛ:]. All three sounds eventually merged as one phoneme, but whether as /ɛ:/ in the sixteenth century or as /e:/ in the seventeenth is an open question.

SHORT VOWELS

The short vowels:

$$\text{/ɪ/} \quad \text{/ɛ/} \quad \text{/æ/} \quad \text{/ʊ/} \quad \text{/ɔ/} \quad \text{/ə/}$$

The phoneme /ɔ/ was probably realized as [ɒ] in the best London speech; but unrounding to [a] was also current, and later become standard in many parts of America. As noted above, [a] was retained from ME *a* in variation with [æ]. An important difference of opinion exists as to the unrounding of /ʊ/ to /ʌ/. Hans Kurath[28] places this development in the sixteenth century, with a significant role in his reconstruction of the Early Modern phonemic system. Kökeritz (pp. 240–44) also supposed that ME *u* was already unrounded and had become approximately [ʌ] by the end of the sixteenth century, but Dobson (2:585–88) seems firm in his opinion that this pronunciation was vulgar at that time, though certainly reputable by the latter seventeenth century.

DIPHTHONGS

The diphthongs:

/ɪu/ and /eu/   /əɪ/ and /əu/   /ɔɪ/ and /ʊɪ/

Of the first pair, /eu/ had survived as a separate phoneme from ME /ɛu/, but not later than the seventeenth century the two diphthongs fell together and remain today as /ju/. In the second pair the first element of each has been lowered so that they are now heard in the standard speech as /aɪ/ and /au/, though the earlier intermediate stages of these diphthongs is preserved in some regions. The last pair were both spelled *oi/oy* and have since fallen together as /ɔɪ/, but for a time in Early Modern English [ʊɪ] survived. When [ʊ] was unrounded in the seventeenth century [ʊɪ] became [əɪ], and many *oi* spellings of both diphthongs were pronounced that way. Under these conditions they had the same sound as the reflex of ME *ī*, which was then also pronounced [əɪ]. For that reason it is not unusual to find rhymes like *line/join* as late as the age of Pope. However, the *oi* spelling eventually determined the pronunciation and has given the present [ɔɪ], whether from earlier [ɔɪ] or [əɪ].

Recent Changes

In the system of vowel and diphthong phonemes the most important modifications since the seventeenth century[29] are those produced (1) by

---

[28] *A Phonology and Prosody of Modern English* (Heidelberg, 1964), p. 23.

[29] The chronology given here is the traditional one, but in the opinion of some scholars diphthongization of the long vowels began earlier than has been generally supposed. For example, Kurath (*A Phonology*, pp. 25–26) places it in the pre-Shakespearean period on the theory that, when the reflexes of ME *ā* and *ǭ* merged respectively with those of *ai* and *ou*, they merged as diphthongs. This theory avoids the awkward assumption of a sound change's reversing itself.

the diphthongization of the long vowels and (2) by the vocalization of preconsonantal and final *r*.

The first cannot yet be said to have altered the structure of the language. Some linguists are satisfied to classify the glide diphthongs of this development as allophones of the long vowels, whereas others do not recognize the existence of the long vowels at all. At any rate we must recognize the following current trends:

$$[i:] > [ɪi], \quad [e:] > [eɪ], \quad [u:] > [ʊu], \quad [o:] > [oʊ],$$
$$[ɔ:] > [ɔə]$$

Among some speakers in England and the United States /ʊu/ has an allophone [ɪu] or [y:], and generally in England the RP pronunciation for /oʊ/ is [əʊ], a trend which also seems to be becoming more prevalent in Middle States American speech. These developments seem to make mandatory the recognition of the diphthongal character of the long-vowel phonemes.

The second important change has generated a set of new diphthongs, which varies somewhat in different parts of the so-called *r*-less regions. A concise statement of these has been enumerated for American English by James H. Sledd:[30]

/ɪə/ (*beard, dear*)	/oə/ (*core, door*)
/ʊə/ (*boor, poor*)	/ɑə/ (*are, car*)
/ɛə/ (*air, care*)	/ɔə/ (*for, war*)

To these we should add /ɜɪ/ (*bird, earl*, metropolitan New York).

Conclusion

From this survey, which is by no means exhaustive, we can gain some understanding of the routes by which the sounds of our language have approached their present state. Their paths of development are not always rigidly straight and uninterrupted. Main lines of change may be clearly marked, as in the operation of the Great Vowel Shift, but their application to particular words or groups of words may be deflected by combinative

---

[30] *A Short Introduction to English Grammar* (Chicago, 1959), p. 53. See also at greater length Bronstein, ch. 10; Thomas, pp. 219ff.; Gimson, pp. 121ff.

factors or thwarted by dialectal substitution. Sometimes also a bypath
may return to the main course, leaving in the present form of a word no
reliable testimony to its circuitous history. On the other hand, since during
the earlier Modern period our spelling has become gradually more
standardized and resistant to change, it has preserved clues to the varied
and complex history of English sounds.[31]

More important to the general reader, however, is the light which
a knowledge of the earlier sounds of English casts upon the character of
the language which the great masters of our literature turned to their
purpose. The fact that we can derive eminent satisfaction from Shakespeare's plays by reading his words as if they were our own, disguises the
extent of the difference between his sounds and ours. The following transcription of Sonnet 73 will illustrate the point (cf. p. 155).

ðæt təɪm əv jiːr ðəu meːst ɪn miː bɪˈhoːld
wen ˈjɛloː leːvz ɒr nʊn ɒr fɪu* du hæŋ
əˈpɑn ðoːz bəuz wɪtʃ ʃeːk əˈgeːnst ðə koːld
beːr ruːɪnd kwəɪrz wer leːt ðə swiːt bɪrdz sæŋ
ɪn miː ðəu siːst ðə ˈtwəɪˌləɪt əv sʊtʃ deɪ†
æz ˈæftər ˈsʊnˌset ˈfeːdəθ ɪn ðə west
wɪtʃ bəɪ ən bəɪ blæk nəɪt dʊθ teːk əˈweɪ†
deθs ˈsekənd self ðət seːlz ʊp ɔːl ɪn rest
ɪn miː ðəu siːst ðə ˈgloːɪŋ‡ əv sʊtʃ fəɪr
ðæt ɒn ði ˈæʃəz əv ɪz juːθ dʊθ ləɪ
æz ðə ˈdeθˌbed ˌwerˈɒn ɪt mʊst ɛksˈpəɪr
kənˈsɪuːmd wɪθ ðæt wɪtʃ ɪt wɒs ˈnʊrɪʃd bəɪ
ðɪs ðəu pərˈseːvst wɪtʃ meːks ðəɪ lʊv mɔːr strɔːŋ
tə lʊv ðæt wel wɪtʃ ðəu mʊst leːv er lɔːŋ

* If Shakespeare was conservative in his speech habits, he may have
   retained [feu] for *few*.
† The diphthong may have been by this time raised to [eɪ].
‡ Final [ŋ] in *-ing* may have been fronted to [n] as early as Shakespeare's
   time.

[31] Such clues can also be misleading. In *delight*, for example, the *-gh-* is merely a spelling
introduced by analogy with *light*. Having been adapted from Old French *delit*, this
word did not have the fricative [x].

Exercises

1. Copy the above transcription, pronouncing each word as you copy it.

2. Write a transcription as you would read the sonnet in the sounds of your own speech.

3. Write a pair of similar transcriptions for Sonnet 29 (p. 155).

Chapter 15

MODERN ENGLISH

Grammatical Forms, Old and New

In the Early Modern period a few important but by no means radical changes took place in the English inflectional system. These consist for the most part of the completion or extension of tendencies already fully established at the end of the Middle English period.

Nouns

The simple inflection of the noun [s], [z], or [ɪz], now spelled 's in the possessive singular and -s or -es in the plural, became the standard form, though exceptions survive from earlier times: some persistent umlauted plurals (*men* and *geese*), some nouns with unchanged plurals (*fish* and *deer*), and some with plurals in *n* (*oxen, children, brethren,* and *kine*). Of these only *oxen* goes back to an Old English plural and only *oxen* and *children* are still in general use.[1]

Two features of nominal inflection call for special mention in Early Modern English. The title page of the first printed edition (first quarto) of Shakespeare's *Midsummer Night's Dream* refers to the play as having been acted by the "Right honorable, the Lord chamberlaine his seruants."

---

[1] The widespread use of singular *kind* after *these* and *those* is commonly condemned by handbooks of usage, but as Pyles has pointed out (*Origins and Development*, p. 182), it may very well be due to persistence of the older inflection according to which, either as a feminine or neuter noun, the plural had no -s. (See also Porter G. Perrin, *Writer's Guide and Index to English* [Chicago, 1959], p. 572.)

The use of *his* after a proper noun to denote the possessive case was common in the sixteenth century. One explanation for this practice is that it arose as an error. In Late Middle English the genitive ending in *-es* became nonsyllabic in most words, but when retained was sometimes written as a separate word rather than as a final syllable; thus, *a knyght es sone*. In this circumstance the ending was phonetically similar to the unstressed pronunciation of the possessive *his*. Many examples of this miswriting are to be found in fifteenth- and even fourteenth-century manuscripts. However, it is also true that the use of *his* after a proper name, especially the name of God, is found as early as the Old English period, and many later medieval uses are of this kind.

Whatever its origin, the *his* genitive was common in Shakespeare's age with such nouns as *King of England* or *Duke of York*. Chaucer's genitives would have been *the Kinges sone of Engeland* and *the Dukes sone of York*, but in the sixteenth century *the King of England his sone* and *the Duke of York his sone* were preferred. This custom survived into the seventeenth century and, when given up, was replaced by *'s*, for the association of the older genitive ending with *his* had been firmly, though erroneously, established. As a consequence, the useless apostrophe has become a permanent graphic feature of our nominal inflection.

Some older genitive forms occurred in Early Modern English which have since become obsolete or archaic. Henry C. Wyld[2] gives examples of the omission of possessive inflection before a word beginning with *s-*: *for his country sake;* in feminine nouns: *our lady belle;*[3] in words ending in *r*: *my father and mother souls;* and in words ending in [s]: *for conscience sake.* The last of these has held on the longest, though it is now perhaps old-fashioned.

Adjectives and Adverbs

The form of the adjective has changed but little except for inflection of the comparative and superlative degrees. The older system of comparison required the use of suffixes. In Middle English, however, *more* and *most* (or their variants) were used as intensives and therefore might occur before the comparative and superlative as well as before the positive.

---

[2] *History of Modern Colloquial English*, 3d ed. (Oxford, 1936), pp. 316–17.

[3] As already noted, fossilized remnants of this feature turn up in the modern *Lady Day* and *Lady chapel*.

Under such conditions the usage was not felt to be redundant, and this attitude remained in Early Modern English, as readers of Shakespeare remember from *Julius Caesar* (III.ii.187), "This was the most unkindest cut of all." In our present use, when *more* and *most* precede the adjective they are considered to be the equivalent of -*er* and -*est*. In fact, they are the only inflections now acceptable in words of more than two syllables. This attitude must have crystallized soon after Shakespeare's time, for we find Dryden writing about 1668,[4] "I think few of our present writers would have left behind them such a line as this—'Contain your spirits in more stricter bounds.' But that gross way of two comparatives was then ordinary, and, therefore, more pardonable in Jonson."

The adjective *far* has developed two comparisons. One of these was borrowed from OE *fore* 'before': *fore, furðra, fyrrest*. The superlative *fyrrest* became specialized in form as *first* and in meaning as the ordinal corresponding to the numeral *one*, its place being supplied by the new analogical formation *furthest*. The Middle English adjective *fer* 'far' also assumed a new comparative and superlative by analogy: *fer (ferre), ferther, ferthest*. These were modified to their present sound and spelling in the fifteenth-century shift of *er* to *ar*.

Another irregular comparison which may be mentioned here is that of the adverb *near*, in Old English *nēah* 'near,' *nēarra, nēhsta*, which became in Middle English *nygh* 'nigh,' *nẹre* or *nerre, next*. Although *nigh* has continued to be used until comparatively recent times, the Middle English *nẹre* developed a positive meaning which led to new analogical formations in the comparative and superlative. The old superlative *next*, like *first*, was separated by semantic change.

There existed also in Old and Middle English a number of umlauted (mutated) comparatives and superlatives.[5] Thus *long, lenger, lengest; strong, strenger, strengest; old, elder, eldest*. Of these only the last has survived.

FLAT ADVERB AND -*LY*

From Early English adverbial use Modern English derived the standard adverbial suffix -*ly* (from OE -*lic*) as well as an adverb without a suffix (the "flat adverb"). The latter originally had a suffix consisting simply

---

[4] In the *Essay on Dramatic Poesy*, quoted in Wyld, *Colloquial English*, p. 326.

[5] The Proto-Germanic suffixes were *-iʒon* and *-isto*. See pp. 91–92.

of -*e*, but when -*e* was lost in Late Middle English many adverbs assumed the same form as the adjective. The flat adverb was perhaps more freely used by Shakespeare and his contemporaries than it is today, but on the whole, the -*ly* suffix was approaching the standard frequency with which it occurs in present educated usage. The succession of adverbs through the first act of *Hamlet* illustrates the point:

You come most carefully *upon your houre.*

[i.6]

Your better wisdomes which haue freely *gone.* . . .

[ii.15]

Who . . . scarcely *heares*
Of this his nephew's purpose. . . .

[ii.29–30]

From whence though willingly *I came to Denmark.* . . .

[ii.52]

That he might not beteem the windes of heauen
Visit her face too roughly.

[ii.141–42]

Beside these we have:

Wee'l teach you to drink deepe⁶ *ere you depart.*

[ii.175]

Indeed my lord, it followed hard *upon.*

[ii.179]

A figure . . .
Goes slow *and* stately *by them.*

[ii.202]

The will of my most seeming *virtuous queene.*

[v.46]

Oh day and night, but this is wondrous *strange!*

[v.165]

How strange *or* odde *so'er I bear myself.* . . .

[v.170]

---

⁶ The phrase *drink deep* has become a fixed idiom, perhaps with the help of Pope's well-known line "Drink deep, or taste not the Pierian spring." See *OED*, s.v. "deep," adv.

In other places Shakespeare makes frequent use of *new* as an adverb:

I Richard's body have interred new. . . .

[Henry V: IV.i.311]

Methinkes I am a prophet new inspir'd. . . .

[Richard II:II.i.31]

A station like the herald Mercury
New lighted[7] on a heaven-kissing hill. . . .

[Hamlet: III.iv.58–59]

Similar examples can be found from the sixteenth century to the present time, even in quite formal poetic expression, for example, in Tennyson's "Lotos-Eaters":

There is sweet music here that softer *falls*
Than petals from blown roses on the grass.

In current usage the speech of educated people is studded with terse, vigorous phrases like *go slow, buy cheap and sell dear, sunk deep, laugh loud and long, walk straight and true, live high.*

The adverbial genitive in *-s* continued from Middle English to Modern in expressions in which it had already been established. Some adverbs with this ending (*agenes, amiddes*) were modified by excrescent *-t* and have survived as *against, amidst, amongst,* with which we may group the similarly modified *betwixt.* In one instance two forms have been preserved, *whiles* and *whilst.* The former, however, seems to be losing ground in the United States, although it still quite common in England. The suffix *-way* and its genitive form *-ways* have also continued a vigorous life side by side despite the fact that Samuel Johnson's judgment of *ways* to be a corruption of *wise* has given the latter a preferred status of dubious credit.

Other adverbial suffixes used in Old and Middle English became dormant in Early Modern practice. *Darkling* was to be found in Shake-

---

[7] " New lighted" is sometimes hyphenated by modern editors. If, however, we can rely on the First Folio and Second Quarto texts as Shakespeare's pointing rather than the printer's, "new lighted," being in graphic contrast to "heaven-kissing," should be taken as two words, since the adverb *new* is well attested in sixteenth-century usage.

speare and Milton, and after them in other literary use, but for common use *-ling* has since dropped out of fashion,[8] so that words like *endling*, *headling*, and *sideling* have been replaced by their corresponding forms in *-long*. The suffix *-meal*, which was quite active in Middle English, produced in Early Modern such forms as *fitmeal*, *jointmeal*, and *lumpmeal*, but of this class only *inchmeal* and *piecemeal* survive, and only the latter with relative frequency in colloquial speech. The old dative plural ending, *-um*, used adverbially, survived in *whilom*. This was once a commonplace in narrative style but by the nineteenth century had become archaic or at least restricted to literary use, whereas its parallel form *seldom* is part of the vocabulary of all levels of contemporary speech.

Little needs to be said about the article. Before the end of the fourteenth century both definite and indefinite articles had approximated their modern forms. As explained earlier, *an* developed its present status as an article from the OE numeral *ān* 'one,' used in positions of weak sentence stress. Here the vowel was shortened and almost immediately *n* was dropped before consonants.[9] In Early Modern English, and indeed until very recent times, *an* was used before *h* in such words as *hotel* and *hermitage*. This practice is a vestige of an earlier pronunciation when initial *h* was silent in all words derived from French, as it remains in *hour* and *honor*. Today *an hotel* would be considered old-fashioned.

In Late Middle English handwriting, when word spacing was not yet standardized, *a* was sometimes written as part of the following word, giving such combinations as *anoke* 'an oak,' *anapron*, *anadder*, *anewt*. In the resulting uncertainty, metathesis of juncture occurred when *n* was either wrongly attached to the article to produce such different forms as *adder* and *apron*, or wrongly detached from the article to give *newt* and *nickname*.[10]

---

[8] The likelihood of confusing *-ling* with the verbal suffix *-ing* may have contributed to its disuse. See pp. 19–20.

[9] A form of the numeral with loss of the consonant (that is, *o*) occurred in Chaucer and is recorded as late as Caxton's time, but does not seem to have been used in the sixteenth century. In any case, it would not have been likely to remain in use after the formation of the initial labial consonant in *one*.

[10] See p. 54. A similar metathesis took place when the neuter form of the definite article *that*, which survived for a time in standard English, stood before a vowel. The shift gave such forms as *the tone* and *the tother* which, however, survive only in dialectal usage.

Pronouns

By the end of the Middle English period, the first person singular pronoun was established as *I*. Chaucer occasionally uses the older *ich*, but by Shakespeare's time only vestiges of it remained in the speech of rustics, such as in *chill* 'I will,' or *chud* 'I would.' The second person singular *thou* continued to be used but was restricted to communication with intimates or social inferiors. As the general use of *thou* declined, the polite use of the plural pronoun with singular reference became more widespread. Eventually *ye/you* rather than *thou/thee* became mandatory in polite address. The significance of this change is reflected in the occasional use in the sixteenth century of *thou* as a verb, meaning 'to insult': "I thou thee, thou traitor." (*OED*)

For a time a distinction was maintained between the nominative *ye* and the objective *you*,[11] as readers of the King James Bible remember. The two cases probably began to fall together in the fourteenth century because their unstressed forms in weak sentence position were much alike, as illustrated by Chaucer's rhyme *Troie/joie/fro ye*, where the pronoun object of *fro* was pronounced [jə]. At any rate *you* in nominative positions became more frequent in the fifteenth century and was formally established in the sixteenth, although *ye* continued to be used into the seventeenth century.

At the same time the spelling *ye* for the objective case occurs in Shakespeare and other sixteenth-century writers. This may have represented a weakened vowel [ə] or a restressed pronunciation with a long vowel. Both *ye* and *you* accusatives may be found in the same passage, as Shakespeare illustrates:

> *Stand, sir, and throw us that you have about ye!*
> *If not, we'll make you sit, and rifle you.*

> [*Two Gentlemen of Verona:* IV.i.3–4]

---

11 By normal historical change the vowel of ME *you* should have become diphthongized to [əu], and evidence exists that such a pronunciation was to some degree prevalent in the sixteenth century. The most probable explanation of our current pronunciation is that ME [juː] had a weakly stressed variant [jʊ], which by restressing became [juː] again before Early Modern short *u* was unrounded. The history of *your* parallels that of *you*.

The unstressed accusative is, of course, still in common use, though never represented in the spelling, except in dialogue when attention is called to its colloquial character. It may also be noted in passing that it is this form of the pronoun that is preserved in *good-bye*, a contraction of *God be wi' ye.*

Today, then, the second person pronoun has inflection only for the possessive. The uninflected pronoun, however, has both a stressed form [juː] and an unstressed variant [jə] in all positions. The possessive adjectives *your* and *their* have two similar variants. Shakespeare's language had also an unstressed variant of *my*, that is, [mɪ], but this is often avoided today in educated speech because it is mistaken for an illiterate substitution of *me* for *my*.

In the third person singular *his* continued in Early Modern English for the possessive of *it*, as illustrated in the familiar King James passage "if the salt have lost *his* savour." The ambiguity, however, must have been felt as an inconvenience, for the nominative form *it* is found in possessive use to some extent during the fifteenth and sixteenth centuries. In *King Lear*, the fool says

> *The hedge-sparrow fed the cuckoo so long*
> *That it had* it *head bit off by* it *young.*

[I.iv.235–36]

The new possessive *its* is an invention of the late sixteenth century, though it does not seem to have had either Shakespeare's favor[12] or Milton's and was not used at all in the King James Bible. Its popularity grew rapidly, however; it was fully established in literary usage by the end of the seventeenth century.

The relative pronoun *that* came into use in Early English as an extension of the function and meaning of the demonstrative pronoun. It was common in Old and Middle English as a simple relative. In the sixteenth century it was still used as the equivalent to *that which*, a function which we now reserve to *what;* for example, Shakespeare has in *Titus Andronicus*

> *Meanwhile am I possess'd of that is mine.*

[I.i.408]

---

[12] A few instances are to be found in the First Folio (1623).

Which, sometimes preceded by the article, appeared as a relative in the Middle English period. In conservative practice it could refer to persons well into the seventeenth century, though it is now restricted to animals and things. The most familiar example of its earlier use is the prologue to the Lord's Prayer, as contained in the Authorized Version: "Our Father, which art in heaven," but it is also to be found in Shakespeare, as, for example, in *Henry V:*

> *King Pepin, which deposed Childeric . . .*
> *Of Blithild, which was daughter to King Clothair.*
>
> > [I.ii.65–68]

Who was originally only interrogative in use. Its transition to relative use is illustrated in constructions without an antecedent, that is, equivalent to *he who.*

> Who that holdeth it ageynst it we wille slee hym.
>
> > [Malory, *Le Morte d'Arthur*]
>
> *Who steals my purse steals trash. . . .*
>
> > [*Othello:* III.iii.157]

As a simple relative referring to an antecedent, *who* is recorded as early as the end of the thirteenth century, but it was only rarely so used before the sixteenth, when it became much more common. Thus, beside other forms of the relative, Shakespeare has:

> · · · I would not hang a dog . . . much more a man who hath anie
> honestie in him.
>
> > [*Much Ado about Nothing:* III.iii.68]
>
> *I should do Brutus wrong, and Cassius wrong,*
> *Who, you all know, are honorable men.*
>
> > [*Julius Caesar:* III.ii.128–29]

Even a few lines below those quoted above from *Henry V* to illustrate the use of *which,* Shakespeare writes:

> *Hugh Capet also—who usurp'd the crown. . . .*

The possessive *whose* in its Old English form was used as the genitive of both interrogatives, *hwā* and *hwæt.* Since in these connections it always denoted both animate and inanimate things it became the possessive of the relative *which*, whatever its meaning. Thus the Wyclif translation of the Latin Vulgate (late fourteenth century) has:

> the loond of oyle and hony . . . whose stones ben yren . . . ,

and readers of Shakespeare remember his famous passage in *Hamlet:*

> For any thing so overdone is from the purpose of playing, *whose* end, both at the first and now, was and is, to hold, as 'twere, the mirror up to nature. . . .
>
> [III.ii.22–25]

This usage remains in Present English despite some tendency to look upon it with disfavor and to prefer *of which* to *whose* when the reference is to inanimate things or to abstract ideas, but many examples can be cited which demonstrate the value of both:

> Something had happened during his absence *of whose nature* he was ignorant.
>
> [William Locke, *A Study in Shadows*]

> She saw events coming, *whose* very shadow I scarce guessed; yet *of which* the faint suspicion sufficed to impart unsettled sadness.
>
> [Charlotte Brontë, *Villette*]

Obviously there are some constructions in which the neuter *whose* is justified by convenience.

In addition to *ye*, unstressed varieties of other pronouns occur from time to time in plays and narratives of Early Modern English in the speech of rustics or even in the familiar speech of cultivated folk.[13] One of these is *a* or *ha* for *he*, and *em*, later *'em*, for the third person plural. The latter is probably a survival of the old Southern *hem* rather than a reduced form of *them*. Also unstressed forms of possessive adjectives must have been as common in Early Modern English as today, if we are to judge by Milton's spelling *thir* as shown in the first printed editions of *Paradise Lost* (*OED*, s. v. "their"). See the *OED* for examples also of unstressed *my* [mɪ].

---

[13] As exemplified by Beatrice (*Much Ado about Nothing:* I.i.90): "It will cost him a thousand pounds ere *a* be cur'd."

PRONOUNS AND CASE

Concerning the use of the pronoun the modern reader may be surprised to discover that the grammatical regularity so well known to, if not popular with, the American schoolboy was not in the sixteenth century a matter of great anxiety. Forms such as the following from Shakespeare were commonplace among all sorts of people:

> *Her I love now*
> *Doth grace for grace . . . allow.*
>
> > [*Romeo and Juliet:* II.iii.86]

> *'Tis thee (myself) that for myself I praise.*
>
> > [Sonnet 62]

> She *. . . that you wrong'd look you restore.*
>
> > [*Measure for Measure:* V.i.531]

> *Lay on, Macduff,*
> *And damn'd be* him *that first cries, "Hold, enough!"*
>
> > [*Macbeth:* V.viii.33–34]

> Who *does he accuse?*
>
> > [*Antony and Cleopatra:* III.vi.23]

> *And that no man might draw short breath today*
> *But* I *and Harry Monmouth.*
>
> > [*1 Henry IV:* V.ii.49–50]

> *You know my father hath no child but* I.
>
> > [*As You Like It:* I.ii.18]

> *Earth hath swallow'd all my hopes but* she.
>
> > [*Romeo and Juliet:* I.ii.14]

> *And yet no man like* he *doth grieve my heart.*
>
> > [*Romeo and Juliet:* III.v.83]

> *All debts are cleared between you and* I.
>
> > [*Merchant of Venice:* III.ii.322]

> *Is she as tall as* me?
>
> > [*Antony and Cleopatra:* III.iii.13]

These practices are, of course, not peculiar to Shakespeare. His friends and fellow-actors wrote in the Prefatory Matter to the First Folio, "And so we

leave you to other of his friends, *whom*, if you need, can bee your guides."
Ben Jonson has in *The Alchemist*, "He has been with my cousin Edward and
I, all the day"; and the learned translators of the King James Bible have,
in Matthew 19:11, "All men cannot receive this saying, save *they* to whom
it is given."

It would be a serious misjudgment to label such locutions "errors"
on the assumption that they indicate ignorance. Some, like the "her I
love" quotation from *Romeo and Juliet*, represent the principle of **attraction,** which is common in educated speech.[14] Furthermore, case forms
were often chosen for considerations other than simple grammatical
agreement. Rhetorical factors such as euphony or emphasis might play
a part, as in a statement of Biron in *Love's Labour's Lost*, where the two
case forms side by side must have been used for calculated effect:

> It kills sheep; it kills me—I a sheep.
>
> [IV.iii.7–8]

Moreover, the era of strict grammatical legislation was still in the
future. Gentlemen and the educated middle class accepted their linguistic
tradition and used it with confidence and skill. They had as yet no need
for guidebooks in matters of cultivated speech. This traditional attitude
survived even the rigors of eighteenth-century standardization, as may be
judged from many passages in the works of well-known authors down
to our own time. The following instances,[15] none of which can be interpreted as representing vulgar speech, illustrate this freedom:

> A stone is heavy, and the sand weighty, but a fool's wrath is heavier
> than *them* both.
>
> [Proverbs 27:3, Authorized Version]

> *Belial came last, than whom a spirit more lewd*
> *Fell not from heaven.*
>
> [Milton, *Paradise Lost*, I, 490]

---

[14] It has, likewise, a place in the grammar of classical Latin.

[15] Quoted by Jespersen in *Modern English Grammar*, 7: passim; and in *Essentials of English Grammar* (New York, 1933), pp. 132 ff. Quotations are given here in sufficient number to demonstrate that the usages illustrated are not merely rare or inadvertent lapses.

Did you never hear of Dryden Leach, *he* that prints The Postman?
[Swift, *Journal to Stella*]

Who should I see there but the most artful procuress?
[Addison, *The Spectator*]

Who, I exclaimed, can we consult but Miss P?
[Thackeray, *Vanity Fair*]

Our cousin, who was himself in little better circumstances than *me*. . . .
[Goldsmith, *Vicar of Wakefield*]

Be thou me, *impetuous one.*
[Shelley, "Ode to the West Wind"]

. . . the servants, *who* she would never allow to sit up for her.
[Thackeray, *The Newcomes*]

Our noble Arthur, him
Ye scarce can overpraise, will hear and know.
[Tennyson, *Idylls of the King*]

. . . the . . . people were quite as badly off as *us*, only they were poorer than *us*.
[Trollope, *The Duke's Children*]

If I was *her*, I would not have put up with it.
[Austen, *Pride and Prejudice*]

She, whose happiness you most desire, you choose to be your victim.
[Stevenson, *Virginibus Puerisque*]

It wasn't *me*, it wasn't the real *me*.
[Maugham, *The Painted Veil*]

In general, in present-day written English such instances as these do not appear in print except in the representation of realistic dialogue. They are avoided by careful prose stylists or edited out by their publishers, but there is no doubt that they remain characteristic of the informal speech of educated people.

Compound Personal Pronouns

In addition to the simple personal pronouns, the compound forms with -*self* are to be accounted for. In Present English these are limited to the possessive pronoun and *-self* in the first and second person: *myself, ourselves, (thyself), yourself (-ves);* and to the objective with *-self* in the third person: *himself, herself, itself, themselves.* The substandard *meself* is probably in origin not an illiterate confusion of case forms, but the preservation in popular use (with or without restressing) in nonstandard dialects of the shortened vowel from ME *my* [mi:] when the word occurred in weak sentence position. In these circumstances the shortened vowel would not have been diphthongized.

Prescriptive tradition today limits the compound pronouns to reflexive and intensive uses:

> He will do himself an injury.
> He himself will be to blame.

There is a persistent survival, however, even among educated speakers, of compound in place of simple pronouns, especially as the second element of compound subjects and objects:

> Leave the remainder of the food for Hal and myself.
> Jenny said no one was home but her mother and herself.

Although the history of the compound forms supports the priority of the intensive and reflexive uses as in the first pair of sentences, those exemplified in the second pair are rooted deeply in the literate tradition despite their frequent condemnation.[16] From the Old English to the Early Modern period all reflexive uses could be expressed by the simple pronoun:

> Ða beþohte he *hine.* ('Then bethought he himself.')

> And therefore if ye governe *you* by sapience, put away sorwe.
> > [Chaucer, "Melibee"]

> *Uprist this july lovere Absolon*
> *And* hym *arraieth gay.*
> > [Chaucer, "Miller's Tale"]

> Richarde, the duke of Normandy . . . recommendeth *him* [i.e., himself] humbly to you.
> > [Caxton, *Sonnes of Aymon*]

---

[16] E.g., "Wrong: 'one of the party and myself'" (Margaret Nicholson, *A Dictionary of American English Usage* [New York, 1952], p. 356).

And now I do bethink me, *it was she.* . .

[*Twelfth Night:* V.i.356]

Let every soldier hew him *down a bough.* . . . .

[*Macbeth:* V.iv.4]

In the nineteenth century similar constructions seem to be limited to verse:

And I awoke and found me *here.*

[Keats, "La Belle Dame sans Merci"]

Where can I get me *harbourage for the night?*

[Tennyson, *Idylls of the King*]

In Present English the simple reflexive occurs only after prepositions:

He had the horses led before him.
They took everything with them.

However, the custom was common in Old English of using *self* adjectivally (and therefore with adjectival inflection) after a noun for emphasis and thus generated the form we call intensive; and in turn specialized uses of the intensive produced both the reflexive use and the use of the compound pronoun independently. The following passage on the death of Cædmon illustrates both the simple adjectival and the reflexive use of *self:*

Ond	sēo	tunge	þe	swā	monig	hālwende	word	in	þæs
And	*that*	*tongue*	*that*	*so*	*many*	*holy*	*words*	*in*	*the*

Scyppendes	lof	gesette	hē	ðā	swelce	ēac	þā	ȳtmæstan
Creator's	*praise*	*composed*	*he*	*then*	*likewise*	*(did)*	*the*	*last*

word	in his	herenisse,	*hine seolfne*	segniende	ond his	gāst	in	his
words	*in His*	*praise*	*him-self*	*blessing*	*and his*	*soul*	*into*	*his*

honda	bebēodende	betȳnde.	Eac	swelce	þæt	is	gesegen	þæt	hē	wǣre
hands	*committing*	*died.*	*Thus*		*it*	*is*	*seen*	*that*	*he*	*was*

gewis	his *seolfes*	forðfōre	of þǣm	þe	wē	nū	secgan	hȳrdon.
certain	*of his own*	*death*	*by*	*what*	*we now*		*have heard.*	

[King Alfred, *Bede's Ecclesiastical History*]

As a qualifying adjective with intensive force it is illustrated in:

> Þonne is to   geðencanne   hwæt Crist   self   cuæð on his
> *Then is to (be) remembered what Christ (him) self said in His*
>
> godspelle.
> *gospel.*

[King Alfred, Pastoral Care]

and with inflection in a reflexive construction as in the Cædmon Passage above: "hine seolfne segniende." Both intensive and reflexive compounds are to be encountered in all periods since:

> Þah [though] ӡe ӡour-self be talenttyf [desirous] to take it to ӡour-selven.

[Sir Gawain and the Green Knight]

> *Jalous he was . . .*
> *And demed himself been lik a cokewold.*

[Chaucer, "Miller's Tale"]

> I doubt not but to do myself much right. . . .

[Twelfth Night: V.i.315]

In early usage similar constructions illustrate the compounding of *his* and *self*. These occur today as well, but are generally rejected as illiterate except when a qualifying word intervenes, as in *his very self, his true self*, etc.

Compound in place of simple pronouns began to be used at least as early as the end of the thirteenth century, probably by simple elision of the noun or pronoun before the intensive:

> Mony was þe gode body þat hym self slou þat day.

[Robert of Gloucester, Chronicle]

> *This is to seyn, myself have been the whippe.*

[Chaucer, Prologue, "Wife of Bath's Tale"]

> *Myselven cannot telle why*
> *The sooth. . . .*

[Chaucer, Book of the Duchess]

> *Ther was also . . .*
> *A maunciple and myself. There were namo.*

[Chaucer, Prologue, Canterbury Tales]

Her father and myself . . .
Will so bestow ourselves. . . .

[*Hamlet:* III.i.32–33]

. . . myself and Toby
Set this device against Malvolio here. . . .

[*Twelfth Night:* V.i.367–68]

Myself have letters of the self-same tenure.

[*Julius Caesar:* IV.iii.171]

Myself when young did eagerly frequent
Doctor and Saint. . . .

[Fitzgerald, *Rubaiyat*]

The compound pronoun as the equivalent of the simple pronoun is used with much less freedom than in the Early Modern period. Nevertheless in one construction it is both common and reputable, that is, as the second element in coordinate combination with a preceding noun or pronoun:

> My sister and myself were the only ones not down with
> the flu.
> There has always been complete understanding between
> his father and himself.[17]

Verbs

PRESENT-TENSE INFLECTION

The inflection of the verb in Early Modern English has been slowly modified to assume its present character. In the present tense of the second person singular the ending *-est* disappeared from general use with the loss of the pronoun *thou*, but both continued to be used to some extent until the eighteenth century, when they became, for the most part, restricted to the liturgical and biblical idiom. In the third person *-eth* was the standard ending of Chaucer's language and remained so for about three hundred years after his time. In the fifteenth century *-s/-es* occurred occasionally in the emerging standard language, in the sixteenth century more frequently, and in the seventeenth century it spread quite rapidly.

---

[17] R. W. Zandvoort, *A Handbook of English Grammar* (1966), pp. 145–46.

Wyatt and Surrey used the -s ending for rhymes. In Spenser, Marlowe, and Shakespeare -s and -th may be found in the same passage:

> MACBETH.   *Hath he ask'd for me?*
> LADY MACBETH.   *Know you not he has?*
>
> [*Macbeth:* I.vii.30]

As to formal prose, the King James Bible retained -th, but other contemporary prose was not so consistent, as can be judged from the following sentence from Sir Thomas Browne's *Religio Medici:*

> . . . for I am of a constitution so general that it consorts and sympathiseth with all things.

Although by the end of the seventeenth century -s forms were predominant, -th forms were used even in the informal prose of conservative speakers, surviving perhaps most tenaciously in the auxiliaries *hath* and *doth*.[18] The origin of the -s ending in the third person singular verb is not clear. In Middle English it was the common ending in the North and is thought to have entered the Southeast Midland speech from that source, though not all authorities adopt this explanation.[19]

It is clear, however, that London speech accepted other regional verb inflections, such as -th and -s plurals. The present-tense plural endings in Chaucer's time were -e/-en. These fell into disuse in the fifteenth century, though Ben Jonson[20] reported that they were used until the time of Henry VIII. The -eth plural, which was derived from the Old English -aþ, survived in the Southwest, and, since some Southwestern features penetrated London English, it is not surprising to find this inflection in the conservative speech of London in the sixteenth century. Examples are to be found in writings of Cranmer, Latimer, Wolsey, Queen Elizabeth, and Spenser. On the other hand, the same speakers also have -s plurals, which we would expect to find only in the language of the North. Thus

---

[18] See Sir Henry Ellis, *Original Letters of Eminent Literary Men* (London, 1843), *passim*. The mid-eighteenth-century grammars continue to list -s and -th as alternate forms of the third person singular of the present tense.

[19] See Wyld, *Short History*, pp. 255–57.

[20] Quoted in Wyld, *Short History*, p. 257.

Queen Elizabeth in her translations:

> . . . roaring winds the seas perturbs. . . .
>
> . . . as hunters rates their hounds. . . .

And even later Sir Richard Verney wrote:

> Covenanters has forbidden any man to read it.

The social status of those who used -*s* and -*th* plurals forbids us to regard these examples as solecisms.

PAST TENSE

In the past tense distinctions of person and number did not survive Middle English. However, the -*ed* of the weak verbs retained its syllabic character in the sixteenth and seventeenth centuries more generally than in Present English. This was particularly true in verse, where the syllable served the purpose of meter. The existence of syllabic and contracted forms side by side led eventually to the spelling of the contracted forms with an apostrophe, as, for example, from the First Folio edition of *Hamlet:*

> *My honor'd Lord, you know right well you did,*
> *And with them words of so sweet breath compos'd. . . .*
>
> [III.i.97–98]

The contracted forms were not, however, universally accepted in conservative use even in the early eighteenth century, for they were among the popular tendencies of his day to which Jonathan Swift objected. In Present English the syllabic form occurs in verbs which end in -*t* and -*d* (*counted, ended*) or in certain attributive forms sanctioned by time and custom: *cursed, blessed, beloved, learned.* After voiceless consonants the suffix was devoiced to [t], though the spelling -*ed* is generally retained. Thus there is only a spelling difference between the verb *passed* and the adjective *past.*[21]

Concerning tense forms it has already been pointed out that English

---

[21] From the sixteenth to the eighteenth century modified spellings occurred in words like *jumpt, whipt, stept* (*OED,* s.v. "-*ed,* suffix").

inherited from its Germanic origin only the present and past tenses. The inflection of the past tense was of two kinds: internal inflection, or gradation, which gave the strong verbs; and terminal inflection, which gave the weak verbs. Each of these in turn contained a number of different types.

The verb system of Present English contains a mixture of these earlier types. Many verbs originally strong now have weak inflection, while the reverse is true for a few verbs; some have preserved irregularities due to phonological change (*catch/caught*), while others of the same type have made new regular forms (*work/worked*); in some strong verbs the past tense has retained a vowel from the old past singular form (*drove*), while others have kept the vowel of the past plural or participial form (*bit*);[22] some have kept the -*en* suffix in the past participle, while others have dropped it or even formed a new past participle from the past (*stood*).

Early Modern English was of course marked by similar inconsistencies, but it also preserved forms now obsolete or reduced to nonstandard usage:

(a) old past-tense forms: *flang, gat, span, swang, wan; bare, drave, sate* 'sat,' *spake, stale; chese* 'chose,' *leese* 'lost,' *stroke* 'struck,' *rid* 'rode,' *writ* 'wrote,' *holp* 'helped.'[23]

(b) variation between normal and contracted inflection: *bended, builded, catched; lift* 'lifted,' *start* 'started.'

(c) old participial forms: *geven, holpen, sitten, snowen, speken, waxen; broke, spoke, wrote, frore* 'frozen,' *lorn* 'lost,' *yclept* 'named.'[24]

---

[22] Cf. the Early Middle English principal parts:

INFINITIVE	PAST	PAST PARTICIPLE
drīven	drōf, drĭven	drĭven
bīten	bōt, bĭten	bĭten

[23] This list does not include verbs in which educated speakers still vary between two forms, such as *sang/sung, rang/rung*, or more striking still, *ate*, which in America is [e:t] but in England very commonly [ɛt], though the same spelling is retained.

[24] *Y*- was a survival of the participial prefix *ge*- which is represented in Present English only in fossilized form in *handiwork* (OE *handgeweorc*).

EXPANDED TENSES

Tenses other than the simple present and past are called expanded tenses or periphrastic tenses. These have evolved during the course of history from combinations of finite verbs such as *have*, *be*, and *do* with a complementary infinitive or a participle.

VERBALS AND THE EXPANDED TENSES

The participle was originally a modifier. As such, it could be added to the object of a finite verb and if inflected was in agreement with the object. Thus it resembled to some extent the modern structure, "We had the door painted." In modern German it remains the custom to place participles and infinitives in terminal position, but in English the rule has been that they have become more closely connected with the finite verb, which, though reduced in semantic value, retains the inflection and becomes a function word.

The periphrastic passive forms have been in use since Old English times, though the Old English passive auxiliary *weorðan* has been given up.

PROGRESSIVE FORM

A construction resembling the progressive is illustrated in the Old English translation of St. Luke:

> Et pastores erant in regione eadem *vigilantes*, et *custodientes* vigilias noctis super gregum suum.

> And hyrdas wǣron on þām ylcan rīce *waciende* and nihtwæccan *healdende* ofer heora heorda.[25]

Obviously if the participle is moved to a position after the verb, the resulting form closely resembles the progressive. In another passage, a translation of *Orosius*, King Alfred wrote:

> Þæt sēo ea biÞ flowende ofer eal Ægypta land.
> *That this river is flowing over all the land of Egypt.*

---

[25] The participial suffix in Old English was *-ende; -ung* was restricted to the verbal noun.

And in another part of the same work not directly influenced by Latin structure he wrote:

> Wulfstan sǣde . . . þæt þæt scip wæs ealne　weg yrnende under
> *Wulfstan said*　　*that the ship was the whole way running under*
>
>　　segle.
>　　*sail.*

However, since progressive constructions are uncommon in Middle English writings which survive, we may surmise that these instances in Old English were features of a literary style and were not preserved in the popular tradition. In Late Middle English, however, they were certainly used, for we have in Chaucer:

> *We han ben waitynge al this fourtenyght.*
>
> ["Knight's Tale"]

Whatever the actual beginning of the progressive form, its popularity was probably stimulated from a different direction. In Old English the verbal noun in *-ung* was frequently used in prepositional phrases beginning with *on: þā he wæs on sawlunga* 'when he was dying,' *he wæs on huntunge* 'he was hunting.' Eventually the preposition, weakened to *a*, became a prefix: "He rode a-huntynge." In Late Middle English the *-nd* participial suffix was discontinued, and the participial and gerund suffixes fell together as *-ing*. Thereafter the popularity of the progressive form as we know it today resulted from, or coincided with, the loss of the prefix *a-*. Thus *he is a-running* became *he is running*.[26] Forms with the prefix remained in general use through the sixteenth century.

> . . . where Mistress Page is, at a farm-house a-feasting.
>
> [*Merry Wives of Windsor:* II.iii.91]
>
> *I kill'd the slave that was a-hanging thee.*
>
> [*King Lear:* V.iii.274]

These forms have become less common and are now seldom heard except in dialectal speech. The progressive form, on the other hand, has

---

[26] The origin of the progressive form is still the subject of some difference of opinion. See Tauno F. Mustanoja, *A Middle English Syntax* (Helsinki, 1960), 1: 584–90.

become one of the most important features of Present English. It was fully developed in the sixteenth century:

Upon a certeyne daye, as I was heryng the devyne service. . . .
[More, *Utopia*, trans. Ralph Robinson]

. . . hither are they coming to offer you service.
[*Hamlet:* II.ii.331]

The periphrastic tenses with the auxiliary *do* have had a continuous history from Old English times,[27] but they did not drive out the simple forms in the interrogative and negative structures until the later Modern period. In both the informal usage and the literary style of the sixteenth and seventeenth centuries the emphatic form was extensively used in the affirmative, where today the simple or progressive form would be used:

Which . . . do fashion the whole island. . . .
[More, *Utopia*, trans. Robinson]

As the fashion . . . doth partly show.
[*Ibid.*]

Our great physicians do wink at the matter.
[Ascham, *The Schoolmaster*]

Those be counted the noblest knights that do kill most men.
[*Ibid.*]

With all my love I do commend me to you.
[*Hamlet:* I.v.184]

However, in contrast to Present English, the simple forms of the present and past tenses were widely used as negatives and interrogatives. In this respect Chaucer's usage was preserved by Shakespeare and his contemporaries:

How fares thy doghter and thy wyf?
[Chaucer, "Reeve's Tale"]

Aleyn, welcome . . . what do ye heer?
[*Ibid.*]

---

[27] See *OED*, s.v. "do," 25–30.

Where rydestow under this grene-wode shawe?

[Chaucer, "Friar's Tale"]

"Why," quod the somonour, "ryde ye thanne or goon?"

[*Ibid.*]

 And saw'st thou not
Mine Argosie at Alexandria?

[Marlowe, *Jew of Malta*]

Bring you scripture to confirm your wrongs?

[*Ibid.*]

How chances it they travel?

[*Hamlet:* II.ii.343]

All three forms, simple, emphatic, and progressive, are found in sixteenth-century verse, sometimes in the same passage where the choice of one over the other may occasionally have rested upon metrical requirements:

GLOUCESTER. Why so earnestly seek you to put up that letter?
EDMUND. I know no news, my lord.
GLOUCESTER. What paper were you reading?
EDMUND. Nothing, my lord.
GLOUCESTER. No? What needed, then, that terrible dispatch of it into your pocket?

[*King Lear:* I.ii.28–32]

What dost thou profess? What wouldst thou with us?

[*King Lear:* I.iv.13]

OLIVIA. Did he write this?
CLOWN. Ay, madam.
OLIVIA. This savors not much of distraction.

[*Twelfth Night:* V.i.320–22]

Among the perfect tenses the intransitive verb of motion was formerly conjugated with the auxiliary verb *to be*, as it still is in some other modern languages. Thus:

 And all the merchants
With other merchandise are safe arrived.

[Marlowe, *Jew of Malta*]

And here, I take it, is the doctor come.

[*Merchant of Venice:* IV.i.68]

This idiom was continued through the eighteenth century and even, though with diminishing frequency, in the nineteenth:

Mr. Addison and I are entered into a new confederacy.

[Lord Halifax, letter to Swift]

Lady Ann and her nursery were now returned to London.

[Thackeray, *The Newcomes*]

Today, however, this idiom is out of date. In such expressions as *he is gone* and *the years are passed*, the participles would probably be felt as predicate adjectives.

Chapter 16

MODERN ENGLISH

Syntax, Word Order from Old English to Modern

The history of the changes that have taken place in the English verb has carried us into the field of syntax insofar as it has touched upon phrasal verbs and their word order. Our account of Early English omitted its syntactic features to allow for their inclusion here as part of the story of the changing pattern of the English sentence. Let us see how Early and Modern English differ in this respect and to what extent one is the product of the other.

SVO Order and Its Variations

The basic order of the English sentence is subject-verb (SV) or subject-verb-complement (SVC) or subject-verb-object (SVO):

> The flowers faded.
> We watered the flowers.

If the verb is followed by an indirect object, this precedes the direct:

> We gave them every care.

If, however, the indirect object is expressed as the object of the preposition, it follows the direct:

> Give this your close attention.
> Give your close attention to this.

The order SVO was fully established in Old English and undoubtedly constituted the basic pattern of speech. At any rate, it gradually came
to prevail over all others. The following passage from the *Ancrene Wisse*,
written about 1200 or 1225 and illustrating an accomplished prose style,
follows a word order strikingly like that of modern English:

> Ure Louerd, hwon he iðoleð þet we beoð itented, he plaieð
> *Our   Lord,   when he suffers that we   be   tempted, he plays*
>
> mid us, ase þe moder mid hire ȝunge deorlinge, vlihð from him,
> *with us, as the mother with her young   darling,   flees from him,*
>
> and hut hire, and let hit sitten one, and loken ȝeorne abuten and
> *and hides,   and lets it   sit alone, and look longingly about and*
>
> cleopian, Dame! Dame! and weopen one hwule.
> *call   Mother! Mother! and   weep   a   while.*

Classic Old English, however, more often varied the word order. One
reason for this was that Old English retained much of the Indo-European
system of inflections, which made it possible to express many grammatical
relations by inflectional endings. Old English thus inherited a syntax
which allowed greater freedom of order than was convenient in later
stages of the language, but it is likely that even in that period the earlier
conservative word order was rather a refinement of literary style than a
reflection of colloquial usage.

INVERSION AND TRANSPOSITION

One of the most frequent variations in Old English style was the inversion
of subject and predicate, which today would sound like a question, as in
the following, from the *Anglo-Saxon Chronicle:*

> Næfde sē   here,   Godes þonces, Angelcyn ealles for swīðe
> *Had not the (enemy) host, by God's mercy, the English   wholly*
>
> gebrocod.
> *destroyed.*

Also, as this same passage illustrates, complementary infinitives and
participles were put off to the end of the clause. This does does not occur in
Modern English except when adverbial modifiers intervene between the
parts of the verb. When the participle follows the object, it is construed as

an objective complement rather than as part of the verb, as, for example, in "He had the grass cut."

Notice the order of the verb elements in the following sentences from the Old English version of the Gospel of St. Mark:

And eft hē *ongan* hī æt þǣre sǣ *lǣran.* And him *wæs*
And again he began them at the sea to teach. And to him was

mycel menegu tō *gegaderod,* swā þæt hē on scip ēode, and on þǣre
a great multitude gathered so that he on a ship went and on the

sǣ wæs; and eall sēo menegu ymbe þa sǣ wæs on lande. And hē
sea was; and all the multitude about the sea was on land. And he

hī fela on bigspellum lǣrde, and him tō cwæð on his
them many things in parables taught, and them to said in his

lāre, Gehȳrað: Ūt ēode sē sǣdere his sǣd to sāwenne.
doctrine, Listen: Out went the sower his seed to sow.

This passage illustrates also another type of sentence in which the object precedes the verb to give the order SOV or OVS:

And him wæs mycel menegu tō gegaderod. . . . And hē hī fela
to him *them*

. . . lǣrde. . . .

Still another possibility is OSV, as in

Hæstenes wīf ond his sona twēgen mon brōhte.
Hæsten's wife and his sons two one brought [= were brought].
[*Anglo-Saxon Chronicle*]

Though this construction was not as common in Old English as the preceding, it is not unusual in Present English in such emphatic expressions as "This one thing I am sure of" or "That I will not tolerate."

EXPLETIVE *THERE*

The usual position of the verb *to be* has been quite generally preserved as it occurred in Old English structure:

Ond hīe wǣron on twǣm gefylcum: on ōþrum wæs Bāchsæg
And they were in two divisions: in one was Bachseeg

and Halfdene, þā hæþnan cyninges, ond on ōþrum wæron þā
and   Haldane,   the   heathen   kings,   and   in the other   were   the

eorlas.
earls.

[Anglo-Saxon Chronicle]

In one important respect, however, a new idiom has developed in
the use of the copulative verb. A sentence like the following would not
occur in Present English with the obviously intended meaning:

Hit gelamp gīo ðætte ān hearpere wæs on ðǣre ðīode ðe Ðrācia
It happened once that a harper was in the   land that Thrace

    hātte.
    is called.

[King Alfred, Boethius]

Today *a harper was* would become *there was a harper*.

It is possible that the modern idiom was already in the process of
formation, for we have such sentences as this of King Alfred:

And þǣr is   mid Estum   ðēaw, þonne þǣr bið man dēad,
And there is among the Estonians a custom, when   there is (a) man dead,

    þæt hē lið inne unforbærned mid his māgum and frēondum
    that he lies indoors   unburned   with his relatives and   friends

    mōnað.
    a month.

[King Alfred, Orosius]

In this passage the second *þǣr* may be construed 'when a man is
dead there,' but the first *þǣr* as a pure adverb is redundant. Consequently
in such constructions the weakened force of the adverb would naturally
lead to its later use as a simple expletive. At any rate, when Wyclif wrote
in the fourteenth century:

As þou3 þer were no lif but only in þis wrecchid world . . . ,

he was certainly using a structure similar to that of Modern English. By the sixteenth century the idiom was a commonplace, and in Shakespeare it occurs with contraction:

> . . . *for many miles about*
> *There's scarce a bush.*
>
> [*King Lear:* II.iv.304–5].

In the same way *there* was used as an introductory word before other verbs, as in this sentence from Chaucer's "Melibee":

> Ther coomen also ful many subtille flaterers.

At this time it was also possible to use the introductory *there* before a transitive verb, as in the following from Hoccleve:

> There may no martirdom me make smerte . . . ,

but this usage is obsolete.

Simple Inversions

Patterns of order from Old and Middle English now extinct are preserved to some extent in Early Modern, as the plays of Shakespeare illustrate. Inversion of the simple verb in questions, giving the order VS or VSO, is common:

> Came he not home to-night?
>
> [*Romeo and Juliet:* II.iv.2]
>
> *Think'st thou I jest?*
>
> [*Comedy of Errors:* II.ii.23]
>
> *Went he hence now?*
>
> [*Othello:* III.iii.50]
>
> Where lies your text?
>
> [*Twelfth Night:* I.v.240]
>
> Sconce call you it?
>
> [*Comedy of Errors:* II.ii.35]
>
> *When spake I such a word?*
>
> [*Ibid.:* II.ii.13]
>
> . . . what blessing brings it?
>
> [*Much Ado about Nothing:* I.iii.8]

With two pronoun objects the order DO/IO occurs frequently, a structure which survives in British usage but sounds archaic to most Americans today, who would be more likely to use the prepositional phrase than the indirect object:

> *Upon what bargain do you give it me?*
>
> > [*Comedy of Errors:* II.ii.25]
>
> *Dromio my man did bring them me.*
>
> > [*Ibid.:* V.i.385]
>
> *I'll yield him thee asleep.*
>
> > [*The Tempest:* III.ii.68]

In a passage from *The Merchant of Venice* (V.i.143–65) contrasting structures, with and without the preposition, occur side by side:

> *. . . I gave it to the judge's clerk.*
>
> *You swore to me when I did give it you. . . .*
>
> *Gave it a judge's clerk?*
>
> *I gave it to a youth. . . .*
>
> *I could not for my heart deny it him.*

Shakespeare also preserves old dative forms now unused:

> *I can buy me twenty at any market.*
>
> > [*Macbeth:* IV.ii.40]
>
> *. . . he pluck'd me ope his doublet. . . .*
>
> > [*Julius Caesar:* I.ii.265]

Adverbs and Negatives

The English adverb has always been more free in its position than other parts of speech. From the earliest periods it was used at the beginning of a sentence:

> Hēr cuōm sē here tō Rēadingum.
> *This year came the host to Reading.*
>
> > [*Anglo-Saxon Chronicle*]

Þā sōna æfter þǣm com Hæsten ūp on Temese mūðan.
Then soon after this came Hæsten up into the Thames mouth.

[*Ibid.*]

As these sentences illustrate, the introductory adverb was followed by subject-verb inversion. Except in verse this is not usual in Modern English, although it does occur to a limited extent. After *so* in quasi-pronominal use inversion is common:

> He refused the offer; so did I and so will all of us.

After introductory negatives inversion is mandatory:

> Never had I seen the like.
> Hardly has he ever succeeded.
> At no time is this permitted.

It is also mandatory after *there* and *here:*

> There goes your opportunity.
> Here comes the band.

Other instances of inversion are likely for purposes of style or emphasis:

> Down goes the hammer.
> Out went the light.

In the early period of Modern English, however, such inversions after introductory adverbs were more common:

Then is doomsday near.

[*Hamlet:* II.ii.242]

Now could I drink hot blood.

[*Ibid.:* III.ii.408]

Now might I do it pat.

[*Ibid.:* III.iv.73]

Then art thou damned.

[1 *Henry IV.:* I.ii.134]

These inversions are not confined to verse:

> Though I bee not to receive any favor . . . yet is your excellente
> herte . . . worthie to showe favour.
> > [Nicholas Udall, correspondence, c. 1542]

The position of *not* in Present English is illustrated in these sentences:

> We do not speak of such things.
> We must not speak of such things.
> Don't you ever speak of them?

In other words it occurs only with an auxiliary verb unless the main verb
is *be* or *have*, or with *do* when used as a substitute for a preceding verb:

> He isn't ready yet.
> He hasn't much time.
> He talks too much, doesn't he?

In Early Modern usage the situation was different. Then *not* might follow
the subject and simple verb:

> *Ha! I like not that.*
> > [*Othello:* III.iii.35]

> What secret hath held you here, that you followed not to Leonato's?
> > [*Much Ado about Nothing:* I.i.206–7]

Or it might come after SVO:

> *This bird you aim'd at, though you hit her not.*
> > [*Taming of the Shrew:* V.ii.50]

> I saw him not.
> > [*Much Ado about Nothing:* II.i.2]

As we have seen above, the expanded tenses with the auxiliary *do* had
become so common in the sixteenth century that they were often used in
places where today only the simple form would occur. It is not unusual

therefore to find that the negative may occur with either simple or expanded forms. At one place in *Hamlet* (I.ii.177) we have:

I prithee, do not mock me, fellow student.

And at another (II.ii.571) we have:

—and look you mock him not.

After the sixteenth century the use of the emphatic forms in simple affirmative statement gradually died out, but with the negative it has remained. Thus *I do fear him* and *I fear him not* as simple statements of fact are now archaic, but *I do not fear him* is common and standard.

Occasionally in Shakespeare *not* is found in the unusual position before the verb, as in:

. . . *it not appears to me.* . . .

[2 *Henry IV:* IV.i.107]

. . . *I not doubt*
He came alive to land.

[*Tempest:* II.i.121–22]

However this construction is a departure from the original and traditional use. In Old English the negative adverb was *ne*, placed before the verb:[1]

Hī hine ne mehton ferian.
They him not might   carry.

[*Anglo-Saxon Chronicle*]

Ne ondrǣd þū þē, Maria.
Not   fear   thou thee, Maria. [*Fear not, Mary.*]

[Luke 1:30]

The negative, however, was frequently doubled for emphasis:

Ne ondrǣde ic mē nān yfel.
Not   fear   I   me no evil.

[Psalm 22/23]

---

[1] The particle *ne* was sometimes compounded to give such forms as *nam* 'am not,' *nere* 'were not,' *nolde* 'would not.' Of such contracted negative verbs only *willy-nilly* is heard today.

One such emphatic double negative was *nawiht,* which became *no3t* in Middle English and was subsequently weakened to *not.* After *no3t* became an established part of the common negative idiom, *ne* was less important to the sense. Consequently it was gradually given up in the later Middle Ages, though the *OED* records it in poetic use as late as Byron. Thus, *not* inherited both the full negative function and the postverbal position.

Other varieties of double negatives, or even an accumulation of negatives, remained a completely acceptable form of rhetorical emphasis until well into the Modern period:

Nan heort ne   onscunede   nænne leon, ne nan hara nænne hund.
    hart   shunned [feared]   lion   hare   dog.
[King Alfred, *Boethius*]

He nevere yet no vileynye ne sayde
In al his lyf unto no maner wight.
[Chaucer, Prologue, *Canterbury Tales*]

Ne never shal none be born fairer than she.
[Caxton, *Blanchardyn*]

I will not budge for no man's pleasure, I.
[*Romeo and Juliet:* III.i.58]

Man delights not me; no, nor woman neither. . . .
[*Hamlet:* II.ii.321]

Since the seventeenth century, however, the emphatic double negative has been frowned upon by educated speakers, though it remains common in nonstandard usage.

Adjectives

The position of the adjective has never been so free in English as has the adverb. In Old English the normal position was before the noun,[2] though occasionally inverted order was used as in King Alfred's language:

Hē hæfde . . . tamra dēora unbebohtra syx hund.
He had   of tame deer   unsold six hundred.
[King Alfred, *Orosius*]

---

[2] Except, of course, the predicate adjective and the objective complement.

And þǣr sint swīðe micle meras fersce geond þā mōras.
And there are very large lakes fresh beyond the moors.

[Ibid.]

In Early Modern English similar structures occur from to time to time in the writing of the educated:

> If these persones, and others innumerable of like sort had been taken.
> [Nicholas Udall, correspondence, c. 1542]

Still other examples of inverted order, many of which remain in Present English, have a different origin. In French, descriptive adjectives commonly follow nouns. Through the influence of Anglo-Norman, especially in matters pertaining to law and government, we have inherited such patterns of speech as *heir-apparent* and *blood-royal*, and a number of expressions have been formed on the same pattern: *court-martial, adjutant-general body-politic, time immemorial, president-elect, proof positive, poet laureate, for the time being, on Thursday next,* etc.

Adjectives follow nouns when they are accompanied by qualifying phrases, as in:

> He has money sufficient for all his whims but not time
> enough to spend it.

In this connection notice also:

> He doesn't have time enough,

in which *enough* implies an ellipsis. Other inversions, though not common in the general colloquial speech, may occur in literary contexts:

> *My lady sweet, arise.*

[Cymbeline: II.iii.28]

> *Friends both, go join you with some further aid.*

[Hamlet: IV.i.33]

> *No light, but rather darkness visible.*

[Milton, Paradise Lost, I,63]

It is perhaps a whim of history that *thing* is frequently followed by its adjective, as in *all things foul* (Shakespeare), *things evil* (Shakespeare), *something new*, etc. And, of course, inversion is to be found wherever it may acceptably serve the needs of meter, rhyme, or rhetorical heightening:

> *The Right Divine of kings to govern wrong.*
>
> [Pope, *Dunciad*]

> *And from the flower-inwoven soil divine.*
>
> [Shelley, *Prometheus Unbound*]

> *There she weaves by night and day*
> *A magic web with colors gay . . .*
> *And moving through a mirror clear*
> *That hangs before her all the year.*
>
> [Tennyson, *Lady of Shalott*]

Verbals

An important feature of the English sentence is the use and function of verbals. Old English had a noun-forming suffix, *-ung*, which was later modified to *-ing*, and a present participle suffix *-ende*, which appeared in various Middle English dialects as *-end*, *-ind*, or *-and*. In the standard language the *-nd* suffix was displaced, and the gerund and participle have since shared the common suffix *-ing*.[3]

In Old English the *-ung* suffix formed a true verbal noun rather than a gerund. Such expressions as *Ic wæs on huntunge* were preserved in the idiom *I was a-hunting*, which we have pointed out is assumed to have contributed to the spread of our modern progressive verb forms.[4] In Late Middle English, however, the verbal noun came to be accompanied by adverbial modification and objective complements, thus evolving into a true gerund, as exemplified in

> *Confessioun and knowlechyng and crauyng þy mercy*
> *Shulde amende us.*
>
> [*Piers Plowman*]

---

[3] It has been suggested but not definitely proved that the colloquial [ɪn] for [ɪŋ] in the present participle is a survival of the *-end* form with loss of the final consonant.

[4] See above, pp. 207–9.

She koude muchel of wandrynge by the weye.

[Chaucer, Prologue, *Canterbury Tales*]

However, the gerund inherited a feature of its earlier life as an abstract verbal noun which led to a problem in modern usage. In Old English the subject (if we may call it that) of a verbal noun was in the genitive case:

Up cymð deofles costnung.
Up comes the devil's tempting.

There are already instances in Middle English[5] which suggest that the objective case precedes the gerund:

þoru [through] corn wanting. . . .

[*Cursor Mundi*]

Speke we of þe children fiȝting.

[*Arthur and Merlin*]

But genitives without -*s* are so common in Early English that we cannot be certain of the significance of these examples. At all events, the possessive before the gerund seems to have been preferred in Shakespeare if it could be used without awkwardness:

. . . unless it be to report your lord's taking of this.

[*Twelfth Night:* II.ii.11]

. . . he will chafe at the doctor's marrying my daughter.

[*Merry Wives of Windsor:* V.iii.9]

In some constructions, however, a possessive case form is not available:

You seem to understand me,
By each at once her choppy finger laying
Upon her skinny lips.

[*Macbeth:* I.iii.43–45]

He would not hear of that being possible.
In spite of those three telling the same story, I could
not believe it.

---

[5] See Mustanoja, 1: 574.

A change in general practice has therefore developed so that from the seventeenth to the nineteenth century we find uninflected forms before the gerund with increasing frequency, even among authors of repute.[6] Thus Swift, who was usually demanding in matters of propriety:

> But by the noise increasing, I knew their numbers were greater.

Or Thackeray:

> I have not the least objection . . . to a rogue being hung.

Or De Quincey:

> No man ever heard of opium leading into delirium tremens.

Or Shelley:

> I have no objection to the author being known.

Apparently, then, this construction is justified by eminent precedent, but recently handbooks of usage have been endeavoring to establish a prejudice against it.[7]

The participle in constructions other than the expanded tenses referred to earlier has also undergone some change in modern usage. It was used freely in Old English as an adjective, and when referring to the subject frequently followed the verb:

> And hyrdas wæron on þām ylcan   rīce waciende, and nihtwæccan
> *And shepherds were   in   the   same country watching, and nightwatches*
>
> healdende ofer heora heorda.
> *holding   over   their   flocks.*

As we have seen, structures such as this bear some resemblance to the modern progressive form. In other instances the construction remained a

---

[6] A strong defense of this construction is offered by G. H. Vallins, *The Pattern of English* (London, 1956) pp. 128–33, where he cites a number of illustrations.

[7] A reasonable statement of present reputable practices is given by Perrin, pp. 541–42.

purely adjectival relationship, as in the following, in which *heriendra* and *cweþendra* agree in gender, number, and case with *werydes:*

> And þā wæs fǣringa geworden mid þām engle   mycelnes
> *And then was suddenly* . . .   *with the angel (a) multitude*
>
> heofonlīces werydes, God heriendra and þus cweþendra. . . .
> *of the heavenly   host,   God   praising   and thus   saying.* . . .

Many participial phrases of this kind are found in the early periods of the language but usually in the middle of the sentence modifying the object:

> They fond the feyrest corps lyenge in a ryche bedde,
> [Malory, *Le Morte d'Arthur*]

Or the subject:

> He, lyk a mad man, rentynge his clothes, gan to wepe and crye.
> [Chaucer, "Melibee"]

The participial phrase preceding the subject, however, became common in cultivated prose in the sixteenth century:

> Musing with myself . . . how I might be well employed I could find nothing either mor fit. . . .
> [Lyly, *Euphues*]

> Having thus the champion tied to his villainous determination by oath, he prosecuted the intent of his purpose thus.
> [Lodge, *Rosalynde*]

Apparently the use of the participial phrase in the introductory position led almost immediately to that *bête noire* of the later grammarians, the dangling participle, called also "loose" or "unattached," for we find in Lyly:

> Seeing therefore the very blossom of love is sour, the bud cannot be sweet.
> [*Euphues*]

Perhaps the most familiar example is from Shakespeare's Hamlet:

> *'Tis given out that, sleeping in my orchard,*
> *A serpent stung me.*

> [I.v.35–36]

Similar constructions have been frequent in literary contexts from the sixteenth century to the present time, of which the following are fair examples:

> *Wondering at my flight and change*
> *To this high exaltation, suddenly*
> *My guide was gone, and I, methought, sunk down.*
> [Milton, *Paradise Lost*, V, 89]

Then he walked about the room, and taking me by the hand, I walked with him.
> [Defoe, *Moll Flanders*]

I wrote . . . and having got it copied fair, with an elegant frame, it was placed over the chimney-piece.
> [Goldsmith, *Vicar of Wakefield*]

Having left daughters only, the property was sold.
> [Boswell, *Life of Johnson*]

Looking up the river, the character of the scene was varied.
> [Scott, *Old Mortality*]

He felt himself gently touched on the shoulder, and turning round, his father stood before him.
> [Dickens, *Pickwick Papers*]

Looking out of the window, there were the flower beds in the front garden.
> [Butler, *Way of All Flesh*]

But lying in bed, everything seemed so difficult.
> [Galsworthy, *On Forsyte 'Change*]

In the light of present opinion some of these passages are indeed surprising. However, the extent to which earlier writers were unaware of any impropriety in these constructions can be judged from a particularly appropriate passage written by William Cobbet, of whom *The Dictionary of*

National Biography says that he "wrote with exceptional perspicuity and force, on grammar":

> Having been taught the rule of *Etymology*, what are the relationships of words, how words grow out of each other . . . , Syntax will teach you how to give to all your words their *proper* situation or place.[8]

The custom today forces us to be somewhat more discriminating, at least to the extent of avoiding possible ambiguity. It is quite relevant, however, to the point out that most of the passages cited to illustrate the loose participle among earlier writers occur in larger contexts which make the meaning so clear that only the more captious readers would take exception. Even among rigid purists today certain loose participial phrases are commonly accepted as sentence modifiers:

> Strictly speaking, he ought to have been punished.
> Speaking of Jones, what do you expect him to do next?
> Judging by his labored breathing, he must have run a
>   great distance.
> Considering the difficulties, you have done well.

Terminal Prepositions

From the end of the seventeenth century to very recent times, objection has sometimes been voiced against the preposition in terminal position. Vallins (pp. 113–14) refers to evidence which rather accurately dates the beginning of this attitude. In 1684 Dryden revised his *Essay of Dramatic Poesie*, and, among the changes, "tucked in" his terminal prepositions. However, such prepositions had been used in all earlier periods of the language from King Alfred to Shakespeare:

> . . . for ðæm hy   foð   þā   wildan   hrānas   mid.
> *because they capture the   wild   reindeer with (them).*
> [King Alfred, Orosius]

---

[8] *Grammar of the English Language in a Series of Letters* (New York, 1818), p. 16. Cobbet's *Grammar* carries the interesting subtitle "Intended for the Use of Schools and of Young Persons in general; but, more especially for the use of Soldiers, Sailors, Apprentices, and Ploughboys." The work is dedicated to "Mr. Benbow, Shoe-maker, of Manchester." See further on the loose participle Jespersen, *Essentials*, pp. 94–95, and *Modern English Grammar*, 5: 407–11.

. . . preciouse stanes þat he myght by a kingdom with.

[Rolle, *English Writings*]

And of that word took heed Troilus,
And thoughte anon what folie he was inne.

[Chaucer, *Troilus and Criseyde*]

It is an honor that I dream not of.

[*Romeo and Juliet:* I.iii.66]

My father was that Sebastian of Messaline whom I know you have
heard of.

[*Twelfth Night:* II.i.18–19]

What fashion will you wear the garland of?

[*Much Ado about Nothing:* II.i.195–96]

Terminal prepositions like the last seem to be unavoidable when a clause
is introduced by an interrogative word, as in "What are you looking at?"
Examples also abound among reputable writers of similar constructions
in which the appropriate case of the pronoun is ignored:

Who would you speak with?

[Johnson, *The Alchemist*]

Who do you think t'other was from?

[Swift, *Journal to Stella*]

Well, Jane, who is it from?

[Austen, *Pride and Prejudice*]

Although terminal prepositions are comparatively rare in formal writing,
they are so much a part of the tradition of the spoken language that in
Present English the prejudice against them is disappearing, if it has ever
been much respected in practice.

Subordination and Subordinating Words

As we have seen earlier, most of the important features of Modern English
syntax were already well established at the end of the Middle English
period. A few points, however, may be made about longer sentences containing more than one clause. These are of two general types: one in which
clauses are loosely connected by simple coordinating words or not explicitly

connected at all (**parataxis**), and one in which the clauses are subordi-
nated, usually but not invariably by means of introductory words (**hypotaxis**). The latter clauses have a function in the syntactic structure of the
clause to which they are attached and are therefore considered dependent
or subordinate.

Hypotaxis is usually thought of as a later stage of syntax, developing
out of parataxis. Some evidence of this appears in the fact that subordinating words often originated as other parts of speech. The relative and conjunctive *that* seems first to have been used as a demonstrative and to have
derived its present character from its frequent use in quasi-connective
positions. For example:

> An hearpere wæs on ðære ðiode ðe Ðrācia hatte,   *sīo*   wæs
> *A   harper   was in   that   nation that   Thrace is called, this (which) was*
>
> on   Crēca rīce.
> *in (the) kingdom of Greece.*

[King Alfred, Boethius]

The pronoun *sio* as it is used here was a demonstrative (feminine nominative), which, from its frequent use in passages of this kind, was extended
to relative meaning, equivalent to modern *which;* but among all the inflectional varieties of the demonstrative, only *that* has been retained as a
relative.

Similarly, as was pointed out earlier, *what*, *which*, and *who* were
interrogatives which ultimately acquired the subordinating relative function, probably by way of the indirect question. The shift from one function
to the other is accompanied by a change in word order:

> What is your name?
> I asked him what his name was.

This word order has been characteristic of relative use from an early
period. We find an example of it in the Anglo-Saxon Gospel of St. Luke:

> Ne rǣdde ʒē þæt hwæt Dauid dyde?
> *Not read   ye that what   David did?*

An interesting point about this passage is that it is a translation of a Latin
phrase, *quod fecit David*, containing the word order which in English was
appropriate to questions.

In its early uses *which*, when introducing a relative clause, was often accompanied by the article and not uncommonly used adjectivally:

> *Now was ther of that chirche a parrish clerk*
> *The which that was ycleped Absolon.*
>
> > [Chaucer, "Miller's Tale"]

> *Thou seydest eek that ther ben thynges thre,*
> *The whiche thinges troublen al this erthe.*
>
> > [Chaucer, Prologue, "Wife of Bath's Tale"]

By the end of the sixteenth century we have relative clauses introduced by *who*, *which*, *that*, and *where*, referring to antecedents. As in present use, *what* referred to antecedents only after an intervening connective:

> *And draw no swords but what are sanctified.*
>
> > [2 *Henry IV:* IV.iv.4]

Who, sometimes accompanied by *that*, was used without an antecedent, as in the instances quoted above (p. 195):

> Who that holdeth ageynst it we will slee him.
>
> > [Malory, *Le Morte d'Arthur*]

> *Who steals my purse steals trash.* . . .
>
> > [*Othello:* III.iii.157]

In Present English the introductory relative *who* is not common except in the form *whoever*.

An early feature of complex sentence structure was the "contact" clause. This is, of course, a form of parataxis in which subordination, though implicit, is clear. Undoubtedly its continuing popularity is due to the influence of the colloquial idiom, in which the syntactic relation is signaled by elements of intonation which are not part of the written language:

> Is this the book you want?
> I know a case you would be interested in.

Sentences of this type are sometimes explained as due to omission of the pronoun, which is then said to be "understood." There are serious objections to this explanation, especially if it carries the suggestion that contact clauses are inferior. Their widespread and long use in the English tradition contradicts such an implication. They are found to some extent in Old English, but are abundant in Middle and Early Modern English, (a) with "omission of pronoun object":

> *Besyde a town men clepen Baldeswelle. . . .*
> > [Chaucer, Prologue, *Canterbury Tales*]
>
> *Where is the thousand marks I gave thee, villain?*
> > [*Comedy of Errors:* II.i.65]
>
> Here she set up the same trade she had followed in Ireland.
> > [Defoe, *Moll Flanders*]

and (b) with end prepositions:

> *There is another thing I take of hede* (i.e., take heed of). . . .
> > [Chaucer, *Troilus and Criseyde*]
>
> *This wind you talk of blows us from ourselves.*
> > [*Romeo and Juliet:* I.iv.104]
>
> I remember a pretty jest your daughter told us of.
> > [*Much Ado about Nothing:* II.iii.141]

Contact clauses are found also with omission of the pronoun subject. Today such clauses are usually confined to colloquial usage:

> I know a man does that work cheap.

But in earlier periods, when authors drew a less sharp distinction between the cultivated colloquial and the formal style, they were more common:

> *With him ther was a Plowman, was his brother.*
> > [Chaucer, Prologue, *Canterbury Tales*]
>
> *For he hadde found a corn, lay in the yerd.*
> > [Chaucer, "Nun's Priest's Tale"]
>
> *My father had a daughter, lov'd a man. . . .*
> > [*Twelfth Night:* II.iv.110]
>
> He hath an uncle here in Messina will be very much glad of it.
> > [*Much Ado about Nothing:* I.i.18]

You are the first ever asked who he was.

[Addison and Steele, *Spectator*]

I am not the first man has carry'd a rod to whip himself.

[Swift, *Polite Conversation*]

Later instances demonstrate that such usage is current in colloquial contexts even at the cultivated level:

It was haste killed the yellow snake.

[Kipling, *The Jungle Book*]

I wonder who it was defined man as a rational animal.

[Wilde, *Sebastian Kelmoth*]

The great variety of complex sentences in modern style is also the result of the multiplication of subordinate conjunctions. These comprise original conjunctions (*if*, *though*) reinforced by adverbs which from use developed connective and subordinating functions (*as*, *since*) and the conjunction of widely varied use, derived from the demonstrative *that*.

To these have been added a number which originated as compounds. Phrases with connective function were frequent in Old and Middle English, though many of them have not survived: *þat time þat*, *whenne þat*, *whenne as* 'when', *þe while þat* 'while,' *wher-so*, *wher-as*[9] (as well as *ther-as* with relative meaning), *where that*, *for as muche as*, *for-þy* 'because', *but-yf* 'unless', *al be it* 'although.' A few conjunctions both simple and phrasal, now unused, were preserved in Early Modern English. One of these is illustrated in a couplet of Shakespeare's:

> *Indeed, a sheep doth very often stray*
> *An if the shepherd be a while away.*

[*Two Gentlemen of Verona:* I.i.75]

In this phrase *an* is a variant of *and*, which, in fact, is the First Folio reading. The origin of *and* with the meaning of *if* is uncertain, but it was so

---

[9] *Whereas* remains in use today as an adversative, but not as a relative. Notice also the continued usefulness of *that* in forming phrasal conjunctions: *now that*, *provided that*, etc.

used as early as the beginning of the thirteenth century, and was in general use in Chaucer's time:

> *Wo him that is allone*
> *For, and he falle, he hath non helpe to rise.*
>
> [Chaucer, *Troilus and Criseyde*]

and about that time the weakly stressed *an* occurs in *Piers Plowman:*

> *Mede . . . my3te kisse the kynge for cosyn, an she wolde.*

The phrase *and if* was therefore redundant, but perhaps *if* was felt to be a necessary support for the ambiguous *and*. At any rate we find in Shakespeare not only *and if* but other variants as well, including *an't*, a contraction of *an it*.

> *Nay, an you will not, sir, I'll take my heels.*
>
> [*Comedy of Errors:* I.ii.94]

> There, an't shall please you! a foolish mild man. . . .
>
> [*Love's Labour's Lost:* V.ii.584]

Similar redundant connective phrases are *or ere*, in which *or* is a variant of *ere* and *for because*, now quite out of use. Occasionally also we find *sith* and *sithence*, earlier forms of *since*, but most of the archaic conjunctions which occur in the sixteenth century are found in contexts suggestive of colloquial practice. In the use of connectives Early Modern literary prose is, on the whole, strikingly close to Present English.

Whatever conjunctive forms were used, adverbial clauses enjoyed the same freedom as the adverb itself; and their varied uses, together with those of the relative clauses, have directed the development of the English sentence in serious literary prose toward greater complexity, accompanied by variety and logical control. It should not be assumed, however, that the simpler types of parataxis and coordination are without significance in later English structure. In their proper use they are capable of remarkable power of expression. Consider, for example, one of the Early Modern translations of the Bible, the Rheims-Douay Version:

> I am the good shepherd. The good shepherd giveth his life for his sheep. But the hireling, and he that is not the shepherd, whose own

the sheep are not, seeth the wolf coming, and leaveth the sheep, and the wolf catcheth and scattereth the sheep; and the hireling flieth, because he is a hireling and he hath no care for the sheep. I am the good shepherd: and I know mine and mine know me, as the father knoweth me and I know the father: and I lay down my life for my sheep. And other sheep I have that are not of this fold: them also I must bring, and they shall hear my voice, and there shall be one fold and one shepherd.

Even in contemporary English, with its many sophistications, coordinate sentence structure varying with simple levels of phrase and clause subordination have served well the needs of poetry:

I passed along the water's edge below the humid trees,
My spirit rocked in evening light, the rushes round my knees,
My spirit rocked in sleep and sighs; and saw the moorfowl pace
All dripping on the grassy slope, and saw them cease to chase
Each other round in circles, and heard the eldest speak:
Who holds the world between His bill and made us strong or weak
Is an undying moorfowl, and He lives beyond the sky.
The rains are from his dripping wing, the moonbeams from his eye.

[Yeats, "The Indian upon God"]

Exercises

1. Go back to the versions of Psalm 23 designated KJ and J (pp. 157–60). Are these sufficiently alike in language for both to be classified as "modern"?

2. Compare a chapter from the King James Bible with a chapter from Lyly's *Euphues*. How would you describe the difference in language?

3. The following prose passages from *Much Ado about Nothing* illustrate cultivated standard English of the late sixteenth century. In the first passage we find Don Pedro planning to entrap Benedick in the snares of love. Benedick's state of mind is revealed in the second. Collect and classify the differences between this language and that of educated people today according to vocabulary, word meanings, word forms, and word order;

that is, according to lexical, semantic, morphologic, and syntactic differences.

(a) And Benedick is not the unhopefullest husband that I know. Thus far can I praise him: he is of a noble strain, of approved valour, and confirm'd honesty. I will teach you how to humour your cousin, that she shall fall in love with Benedick; and I, with your two helps, will so practise on Benedick that in despite of his quick wit and his queasy stomach, he shall fall in love with Beatrice. If we can do this, Cupid is no longer an archer. . . .

[II.i]

(b) I do much wonder that one man, seeing how much another man is a fool when he dedicates his behaviours to love, will, after he hath laugh'd at such shallow follies in others, become the argument of his own scorn by falling in love; and such a man is Claudio. I have known when there was no music with him but the drum and the fife; and now had he rather hear the tabor and the pipe. I have known when he would have walk'd ten mile afoot to see a good armour; and now will he lie ten nights awake carving the fashion of a new doublet. He was wont to speak plain and to the purpose, like an honest man and a soldier; and now is he turn'd orthography; his words are a very fantastical banquet—just so many strange dishes. May I be so converted and see with these eyes? I cannot tell; I think not. I will not be sworn but love may transform me to an oyster; but I'll take my oath on it, till he have made an oyster of me he shall never make me such a fool.

[II.iii]

4. Examine in the same way the following passage, written by Addison for the *Spectator* (No. 122) in 1711, and compare it with those above. How long a time elapsed between the writing of these specimens? Is Addison's language closer to ours or to Shakespeare's, and in what respects?

In our return home we met with a very odd accident which I cannot forbear relating, because it shows how desirous all who know Sir Roger are of giving him marks of their esteem. When we were arrived on the verge of his estate, we stopped at a little inn to rest ourselves and our horses. The man of the house had, it seems, been formerly a servant in the knight's family; and to do honor to his old master, had sometime since, unknown to Sir Roger, put him up in a sign-post before the door; so that the knight's head had hung out upon the road about a week before he himself knew anything about the matter. As soon as Sir Roger was acquainted with it, finding that his servant's indiscretion proceeded wholly from affection and good-will, he only told him that he had made him too high a compliment; and when the fellow seemed to think that could hardly be, added with a more decisive look that it was too great an honor for any man under a duke; but told him at the same time that it might be altered with a very few touches and that he himself would be at the charge of it. Accordingly they got a painter by the knight's directions to add a pair of whiskers to the face, and by a little aggravation of the features to change it into the *Saracen's Head*.

5.   The following passages are varieties of English from Early Modern to the present century. Rearrange them in chronological order and explain why you place each one in relation to the earlier and/or later passages. Classify your criteria as lexical, semantic, morphological, syntactic, or stylistic (though not all selections yield features in every one of these categories). The placement of the later pieces will be most difficult and more likely to rest upon stylistic than upon grammatical differences. (Identification of the passages will be found on p. 307.)

(a)   "I wish the good old times would come again," she said, "when we were not quite so rich. I do not mean that I want to be poor; but there was a middle state"—so she was pleased to ramble on—"in which I am sure we were a great deal happier. A purchase is but a purchase, now that you have money enough and to spare. Formerly it used to be a triumph. When we coveted a cheap luxury (and oh! how much ado I had to get you to consent in those times!)—we were used to have a debate two or three days before, and to weigh the *for* and *against*, and think what we might spare it out of, and what saving we could hit upon that should be an equivalent."

(b)   The poor countryman, hearing himself named by a man he knows not, marvels, and answers that he knows him not, and craves pardon.

"Not me, goodman Barton, have you forgot me? Why, I am such a man's kinsman, your neighbor not far off; how doth this or that good gentleman my friend? Good Lord, that I should be out of your remembrance! I have been at your house divers times."

"Indeed, sir," saith the farmer, "are you such a man's kinsman? Surely, sir, if you had not challenged acquaintance of me, I should never have known you. I have clean forgot you, but I know the good gentleman your cousin well; he is my very good neighbor."

"And for his sake," saith the verser, "we'll drink afore we part."

(c)   My regular school training was of the briefest, perhaps fortunately, for though my way of life had made me acquainted with all sorts and conditions of men, from the highest to the lowest, I deliberately affirm that the society I fell into at school was the worst I have ever known. We boys were average lads, with the same inherent capacity for good and evil as any others; but the people who were set over us cared about as much for our intellectual and moral welfare as if they were baby-farmers. We were left to the operation of the struggle for existence among ourselves, and bullying was the least of the ill practices current among us. Almost the only cheerful reminiscence in connection with the place which arises in my mind is that of a battle I had with one of my classmates who had bullied me until I could stand it no longer. I was a very slight lad, but there was a wild-cat element in me which, when roused, made up for lack of weight, and I licked my adversary effectually.

(d)   I walked towards White Hall, but, being wearied, turned into St. Dunstan's Church, where I heard an able sermon of the minister of the place; and stood by a pretty, modest maid, whom I did labor to take by the hand; but she would not, but got further and further from me; and, at last, I could perceive her to take pins out of her pocket to prick me if I should touch her again—which, seeing, I did forbear, and was glad I did spy her design. And then I fell to gaze upon another pretty maid, in a pew close to me; and I did go about to take her by the hand, which she suffered a little and then withdrew. So the sermon ended.

(e)   I had scarcely passed my twelfth birthday when I entered the inhospitable regions of examinations, through which for the next seven years I was destined to journey. These examinations were a great trial to me. The subjects which were dearest to the examiners were almost invariably those I fancied least. I would have liked to have been examined in history, poetry, and writing essays. The examiners, on the other hand, were partial to Latin and mathematics. And their will prevailed. Moreover, the questions which they asked on both these subjects were almost invariably those to which I was unable to suggest a satisfactory answer. I should have liked to be asked to say what I knew. They always tried to ask what I did not know. When I would have willingly displayed my knowledge, they sought to expose my ignorance. This sort of treatment had only one result: I did not do well in examinations.

(f)   There is no one thing so trifling, but which (if it is to be done at all) ought to be done well; and I have often told you, that I wished you even played at pitch, and cricket, better than any boy at Westminster. For instance, dress is a very foolish thing, and yet it is a very foolish thing for a man not to be well dressed, according to his rank and way of life; and it is so far from being a disparagement to any man's understanding, that it is rather a proof of it, to be as well dressed as those with whom he lives; the difference in this case between a man of sense and a fop, is, that a fop values himself upon his dress, and the man of sense laughs at it, at the same time that he knows he must not neglect it. There are a thousand foolish customs of this kind, which, not being criminal must be complied with, and even cheerfully, by men of sense. Diogenes the Cynic was a wise man for despising them, but a fool for showing it. Be wiser than other people, if you can; but do not tell them so.

(g)   A companion and I spent twelve hours perched on a tiny ledge rather too small for both of us, 1,500 feet up an overhanging rock wall in the Italian Dolomites. A storm had caught us; we had no food and no extra clothes; and we had to sit it out while the stars glinted with cold and our outer clothing froze on us. The huge, folded landscape below us was blue and deep. Both of us were convinced we would freeze to death, though neither of us mentioned the fact for fear of demoralizing the other. Since sleep lowers the body's temperature, it was important to stay awake; so we talked in a desultory way, swapped stories, recited limericks; we even tried singing. Occasionally we would slap each other about the back and chest—but tentatively, because of our precarious stance. Our minds, like our bodies, were in suspension, neither frightened nor grieving, just blank.

Part IV

ENGLISH "IMPROVED"

Chapter 17

EARLY QUALITATIVE
JUDGMENTS OF ENGLISH

In the material we have so far discussed, our main concern has been the language habits of the English-speaking people as they spoke from day to day, so far as these can be determined from the written records. There is also, however, a history of the conscious or deliberate effort to deploy the resources of language for special effect and even to modify it in such a way as to enlarge its possibilities. Early heroic and religious written poetry, perhaps growing out of a more primitive oral poetry, is the first evidence of such use.

The purposeful use of prose appears later in the development of a literary tradition and is consciously fostered by those who use the language for "professional" purposes. Such a tradition was established in Old English, as the quality of prose composition in the writings of Alfred and Ælfric amply demonstrates. The tradition has often been described as disintegrating after the Norman Conquest, but it has been shown that a literary style was maintained in the devotional prose of Middle English.[1] In the earlier period of Middle English this writing was found in dialects other than Southwestern, though the West Midlands writers seem to have been especially active and influential in this respect, if we consider the *Ancrene Wisse* evidence of such activity.

---

[1] See especially R. W. Chambers, *On the Continuity of English Prose*, Early English Text Society, no. 191A (1932). Chambers' evaluation is enthusiastic and has been thought by some to be exaggerated. But in the points made here he is reliable.

The difference between literary and colloquial prose in early periods is indeterminable because of the paucity of colloquial materials. It is also a matter of speculation to what extent Latin writing influenced English style. Latin influence might have been direct and have consisted of the actual imitation of features of Latin structure and style, but this seems not to have been extensive, for the most accomplished prose in Early English is quite native in its idiom. On the other hand an important indirect influence must be reckoned with. With very few exceptions Early English prose was written by authors for whom Latin was a second language. Now, medieval Latin is sometimes disparaged, but there is no doubt that the classical idiom and style were well known to educated men in Western Europe as early as the twelfth century.[2] As one twelfth-century author put it, in the prologue of a Latin collection of the *Miracles of the Virgin*,[3] the Ciceronian style was available to him, but a more simple style was suitable to the subject.

In fact, there had been in England from the time of Bede and Alcuin a knowledge of the grammatical and rhetorical works of antiquity, and a knowledge of these works flourished on the continent in the ninth and tenth centuries. In post-Conquest England one need only mention the great humanist John of Salisbury and the rhetoricians Geoffrey de Vinsauf and John Garland to show that the love of literary excellence and the refinements of style were cultivated in those times. True, this interest was more completely directed toward Latin poetry, but it would be strange if the study and critical use of Latin language materials did not promote a conscious desire to order the resources of English grammar and syntax with logic, clarity, and force, without at the same time imposing upon the English language an alien character.

At any rate, when the standard language was generally adopted in the fifteenth century it had already at hand a prose style in which these characteristics are evident. The following epilogue, written early in the fifteenth century by an anonymous cleric, is affixed to the translation of a devotional work of St. Catherine of Siena.[4]

---

[2] See C. H. Haskins, *The Renaissance of the Twelfth Century* (Cambridge, Mass., 1927); Helen Waddell, *The Wandering Scholars* (London, 1927), esp. chs. 4 and 5.

[3] British Museum, MS. Cotton Cleo., C. 10, f. 101.

[4] *The Orcherd of Syon*, ed. Phyllis Hodgson and Gabriel H. Liegey, Early English Text Society, o.s. 258 (1966). *Orcherd* here means 'garden' and refers to allegorical representations of the virtues of the religious life as flowers and herbs, arranged in a garden. Graphic features are slightly modernized in the quotation.

Now, reuerent modir and deuoute sustren, youre orcherd is plauntid and sett, and at my symple deuyes,* apparaylid, with the help and grace of oure merciful lord, by the gracious praier of his blessid modir, youre principall and glorious abbes. In this orcherd yee mowe† disporte you in oportune tyme. Heelful fruyt and heerbis ye mowen† fynde there, ful delitable to the soule. Sekith there than bisily the swetnes of the fruyt, that ye mowe fynde hem. Tasteth hem wel inwardly, that ye mowe sauoure hem. Whanne ye sauoure hem, chewith hem wel with a desier feruently that ye mowe be wel fed with hem goostly. And to declare you more opinly myn intent, I sey to you ayein, seekith this goostly mete with bisye and ofte redyng. Tasteth thenne with meditacioun and inward thinkyng. Aftir meditacioun sauoureth hem wel and cheweth hem wel in youre soulis with deuoute preiinge, that ye mowe ascende bi liȝt of contemplacioun to holy desires and parfiȝt loue of God euermoore lastynge. . . .

And whanne ye ben thus fulfilled with grace and siche goostly delicis, streecith forth youre charite and parteth forth youre holy desires to help and cumfort of that synful creature which began this werk; and in youre deuoute praieris haueth myn helper recomendid, youre brothir, Dan Iamys, which for the mooste partye hath laborid it to the eende of this goostly orcherd. If ony fruyt or heerbe be here myssett or plauntid, I commyte alle defautis or errouris to the correccioun of betir lettrid clerkis and of trewe feelynge fadris. And for my neclygence and ignoraunce, as I am wont to seye so I now write: A, Ihesu, mercy. Amen.

---

* device † may

This clear, well-ordered, but obviously rhetorical style is in sharp contrast to the pedestrian level of those persons of more elementary literary attainments who have left us some record of a different manner of writing —that, for example, found in the letters of the Paston family or the Stonor family. Until the first quarter of the fifteenth century such correspondence, as the Stonor remains show, was sometimes written in French. Thereafter, the familiar style in English became the rule, but it was clearly not reminiscent of a cultivated tradition.

On the other hand, the literary style inherited from the earlier devotional literature was steadily maintained in the fifteenth century, at the end of which it became the possession of St. Thomas More and was

adapted by him to more general purposes. Of his attainments, so convinced a Protestant and so strict a critic as Roger Ascham said, referring
to More's *History of Richard III*, that it "doth in most part . . . so content
all men, as, if the rest of our story of England were so done, we might well
compare with France, or Italy, or Germany in that behalf."[5]

Nevertheless, such "plain and open" writing did not please all, for
many considered the English tongue to be quite inadequate. As a consequence we find in the sixteenth century the first of a long series of efforts
to make the language "better" according to one or another concept of
excellence.

Renaissance Learning and Enrichment

In the sixteenth century great changes were taking place in education. The
universities, which in the Middle Ages had been the professional schools
of the clergy, were naturally much changed at the separation of the Church
of England. The older emphasis upon philosophy and theology gave way
to what have since been called "the humanities." The great literary works
of Greece and Rome became the staple of the curriculum. With these new
studies arose a new consciousness of style and "elegance" in language—
qualities in which many critics judged the English language impoverished.
Its deficiencies, it was thought, could be made up by importing stylistic
features of Augustan Latin.

RHETORIC AND STYLE

One early example of an effort to enrich the language is found in *The
Governor*, written in 1531 by Sir Thomas Elyot, who was disposed to
introduce or popularize English forms from the Latin vocabulary. For
rhetoric and style Quintilian and Cicero were admired and imitated, and
their ideas were exploited as early as 1528 by Leonard Coxe in *The Art or
Craft of Rhetoric* and again more influentially by Thomas Wilson in *The
Art of Rhetoric* (1551?) and *Rule of Reason* (1551). Though Wilson objected
strenuously to the excessive borrowing of Latin and Greek words, his
influence on the study of rhetoric was such that it has been said that the

---

[5] See Chambers, p. cxx.

Art of Rhetoric "deserves to be read in its entirety by anyone seeking to understand the underlying principles of Elizabethan literary art."[6]

Perhaps the most notable achievement in the development of a consciously ornate style is seen in the two novels of Sir Thomas Lyly, *Euphues* (1578) and *Euphues and His England* (1580). Here we find the assembly of all the blandishments of rhetoric from classical reference and allusion to the obvious play of alliteration, but, most notable of all, a balanced style so sedulously cultivated as to become monotonous to modern taste:

> If my lewd life, gentlemen, have given you offense, let my good counsel make amends; if by my folly any be allured to lust, let them by my repentence be drawn to continency. Achilles' spear could as well heal as hurt; the Scorpion, though he sting, yet he stints the pain; though the herb Nerius poison the sheep, yet it is a remedy to man against poison; though I have infected some by example, yet I hope I shall comfort many by repentence. Whatsoever I speak to men, the same also I speak to women; I mean not to run with the hare and hold with the hound, to carry fire in the one hand and water in the other, neither to flatter men as altogether faultless, neither to fall out with women as altogether guilty; for, as I am not minded to pick a thank with the one, so am I not determined to pick a quarrel with the other; if women be not perverse, they shall reap profit by remedy of pleasure. If Phyllis were now to take counsel, she would not be so foolish to hang herself, neither Dido so fond to love a bull, nor Phedra so unnatural to be enamoured of her son.

Not all Elizabethans admired the influence of Latin rhetoric or the affectations of Lyly, but whatever the opinion, Elizabethan or modern, of the beauty of this style, its importance in the history of English syntax should not be underestimated. Lyly's two narratives were widely read, especially in courtly circles, and its linguistic example, if not its moral precepts, was extensively followed.

This new fashion did not, to be sure, go unchallenged by precept or example. A new art of preaching fostered by John Colet, Dean of St. Paul's, John Fisher (now St. John Fisher), bishop of Rochester, and later by Hugh Latimer encouraged the use of the native tradition. Meanwhile, a similar trend is to be discovered in the language of Tindale and Coverdale, in their

---

[6] McKnight, p. 130.

translations of the Bible, which came to noble fruition in the Authorized Version, or King James Bible.

LATIN BORROWING

One phase of the movement to enrich the language consisted of the effort to enlarge the vocabulary by deliberately importing words from Latin. A notable person in this endeavor was Sir Thomas Elyot, whose work, *The Governor*, has already been mentioned.

The introduction of Latin words was, of course, no new thing. It had been going on more or less unobtrusively for hundreds of years. Concerted attention was paid to it in the fifteenth century in the well-known efforts of certain poets, particularly John Lydgate and the Scottish poets Henryson and Dunbar, to ornament their style by the use of words—called "aureate terms"—newly adapted from Latin. Later, during the sixteenth-century enthusiasm for Latin learning, this activity was renewed and enlarged. A number of learned classicists, especially Sir John Cheke, Roger Ascham, and Thomas Wilson, opposed these liberties and called the new words pretentious "inkhorn" terms, but the process went on. Even More, who is certainly marked by great clarity of style, shows the influence, for a number of now indispensable words occur first in his writings, such as *absurdly, dissipate, exact, explain, fact, monosyllable,* and *pretext.* But it is Thomas Elyot's *The Governor* which is usually thought of as illustrating most forcefully the effect of the contemporary affection for Latinity of style.

SPELLING

The spread of printing led also to the search for a third kind of improvement. In Middle English, spelling was presumably phonetic, but in a quite individual way. Each scribe consulted his own judgment and, to some extent, the tradition, but there was no fixed relation between sound and symbol accepted by the entire literate public. Professional scribes often adopted for themselves a fairly consistent practice, but this soon became insufficient. The spread of literacy during the fifteenth and sixteenth centuries and the multiplication of printed books stimulated a desire for standardization of spelling. Unfortunately, however, this development coincided with rapid changes in the sounds of English, and, as a result, when a fixed spelling finally took shape, it was characterized by two serious inconveniences: first, many spellings represented obsolete features of the language; and, second, the values of the vowel symbols were out of phase with the continental tradition.

Among men of letters in the sixteenth century, increasing efforts were made to bring about a consensus. John Cheke, an eminent Cambridge scholar, renowned for his valiant effort to reestablish the pronunciation of ancient Greek, showed an interest in spelling reform in his translation of the Gospel of St. Matthew. Thomas Smith, Cheke's fellow classicist at Cambridge, went further and devised an alphabetical system using diacritical marks.

William Bulloker, a man of less education and lower social status than his predecessors, devoted admirable energy and self-sacrifice to the cause, but without permanent effect, no doubt because the proposed orthography was too complicated and to some extent flawed by the author's personal dialectal habits of speech. Richard Mulcaster, whose *Elementarie* was published in 1582, was more successful than Bulloker, though his judgments also at times revealed his Northern provincial origin. His influence may have been due in part to his academic position in the Merchant Taylor's School and later in St. Paul's School but more to the fact that he took a very practical middle position on reform. He suggested an agreement based upon compromise rather than strict logic, which he rightly thought too difficult to achieve. He had the vision to see that a strictly phonetic spelling is not only difficult to obtain agreement upon but also impractical in view of the constantly changing character of language.[7] He offered some modifications, many of which are in use now, either because of his suggestions or because they were already part of the generally accepted system. Other recommendations, however, were not adopted. The *gu-* spelling as in *guilt* remains in spite of his proposal to omit the unnecessary *u*. The *u/v* and *i/j* ambiguity remained for some time, our present system becoming accepted in the seventeenth century. His suggested use of *-ie* for short, unstressed endings (*trewlie*) and *-y* for long, stressed endings (*deny*) did not finally take hold. On the other hand, we do follow his recommendations in dropping useless double consonants and

---

[7] It would be more difficult, he said in effect, to change a familiar inconsistency than profitable to try to introduce an unfamiliar reform. "It is a strange point of physik, when the remedie itself is more dangerous than the disease."

using the final -*e* as the signal of length. Other conventions made general during this period were the spellings -*ee*- or -*ie*- for the reflex of ME *ẹ̄* (*feel, believe*) and -*ea*- for the reflex of ME *ę̄* (*sea, head*).

EARLY ORTHOEPISTS AND GRAMMARIANS

Concern for the native English language led also to efforts by a number of sixteenth- and seventeenth-century orthoepists to examine the sounds of the English language and to describe them. This interest received support partly from the movement for spelling reform and partly from the need to supply schoolbooks for elementary instruction in English for foreigners and for schoolchildren. Contributions were made by John Cheke and Thomas Smith, whose scholarly attainments have already been mentioned. One of the most important of these linguistic pioneers was John Hart, to whose writings we owe a reasonable knowledge of the sounds of language at the time of Shakespeare's birth. In this early period he is surpassed in importance only by John Wallis, who, in the following century, brought to the subject one of the most scientific and versatile minds of that period.

Much less attention was paid to what we today call "grammar and usage." In Old English times Ælfric had composed a Latin grammar which he supposed would be useful as an English grammar, but it led to no permanent use in the formal study of English. In the High Middle Ages the ancient tradition of the Greeks as handed down through Dionysius Thrax was preserved in the early Latin grammars of Donatus and Priscian. Speculative grammar was also included among the interests of the Scholastic philosophers, but serious grammatical study of the English vernacular seems to have been wholly disregarded.

It was inevitable, however, that Renaissance scholars should take a more expanded interest in the whole subject of grammar, ranging from the reordering of the earlier Latin grammars to the search for a universal grammar; and among these interests English found a place. Some attempts were made, then, in the sixteenth and seventeenth centuries to compose grammars of English, based largely, it is true, upon Latin grammatical theory, but sometimes exhibiting an interesting degree of originality. One of particular interest to students of English literature was composed by Ben Jonson, friend and fellow playwright of Shakespeare, and printed in 1640. His account of the sounds of English is a repetition of the work of his predecessors, but he supplied also an analysis of forms and syntax which was quite individual. By modern standards Jonson's *Grammar* has, of course, many defects. Like so many observers before the nineteenth century, he did not distinguish between letters and sounds, and his account of the grammatical system was not based upon a knowledge of its historical background. On the other hand, he did attempt to be descriptive. Like all educated Londoners of his time, he recognized the difference between cultivated and provincial speech, but he accepted with tolerance the language of his educated peers, whatever its supposed deficiencies might be.

Concerning, for example, the occurrence of a double negative and a double superlative in a passage from the writing of St. Thomas More he observes:

> And this is a certain kind of English Atticism, or eloquent phrase of speech, imitating the manner of the *most ancientest and finest* Grecians, who for more emphasis and vehemencies sake, used so to speak.

A generation later Dryden was to look askance at such permissiveness as Jonson exhibited, but by that time an attitude was asserting itself that was to have a far-reaching influence upon the use of the English language by educated men and women.

Chapter 18

THE RISE OF THE
PRESCRIPTIVE TRADITION

John Dryden stood near the beginning of a movement toward an external regulation of language usage that we call "authoritarian" or "prescriptive" or simply "normative," for it looked toward the establishment and public acceptance of explicit rules of "correctness." Not that notions of propriety in the use of the language were unknown in earlier times. On one occasion, for example, More found fault with Tindale because he disregarded the customary distinction in the use of *yea* and *yes*. But such knowledge was assumed to be the inheritance of gentlemen and was fixed only by custom among them.

Prescriptivism and Its Causes

During the late seventeenth century, however, and through the eighteenth, serious attempts were made to replace the simple acceptance of the cultivated tradition in grammatical usage by regulation supposedly emanating from the rule of logic or reason. The reasons for the change were probably twofold. For one thing, the role of Latin and Greek studies had now dominated the schools for so long that it had become extensively formalized.

The use of Latin, once the tool of learning and scholarship, became also, to some extent, the showpiece of the educated gentleman. The conventions of Latin grammar acquired a superficial glamour thought to be lacking in the native tongue, and it was supposed that the English language could be made more appealing by adapting it to such a "grammar."

The force of tradition was undoubtedly weakened for another reason; that is, the increasing mobility within the English social structure, which had been noticeable since the mid-sixteenth century, when the confiscation of monastic wealth was redistributed in such a way as to make extensive changes in the English peerage and gentry. Also, with the growing prosperity of the middle classes rich citizens tended more and more to aspire to social elevation.

In the first half of the seventeenth century the growing political power of the middle classes was reflected in the success of the Puritan revolution and the establishment of the Commonwealth. Meanwhile England's expansion as a new colonial empire was laying the groundwork for an influx of vast new wealth from abroad. Naturally the beneficiaries of these changes who aspired to social betterment were forced to look outside their own traditions for guidance in modes of behavior which characterized the gentleman.

As a result, then, of these two conditions, the excessive regard for the surface values of classical education and the lack of confidence in one's own linguistic background, the appetite for an authoritative or "prescriptive" grammar was developed. It may also be said that the popular drift was quite in harmony with the eighteenth-century adulation of Reason and even with the more learned interests of philosophy, but for the most part the success of the authoritarian movement was the answer to popular demand, especially among the middle classes, as in our own time the success of the Emily Post type of handbook is due less to the love of gentility than to the simple need of someone to tell insecure people how to behave. At any rate, as the eighteenth century progressed the concept of grammar as a set of rules to eliminate "errors" became almost universal. The extent to which this growth became what might be called a "grass-roots" movement is reflected in the example of one Robert Baker, who, with only the barest elementary education and reading experience, contributed a successful publication on the "detection of many improper expressions used in conversation, and of many others to be found in authors."[1]

---

[1] Cited in Baugh, pp. 332–33. Ch. 9 of Baugh's *History* is the best survey available of this very important phase of the history of English.

Eighteenth-Century Concepts
of the English Language

The deeply rooted assumptions which underlay the thinking of the period may be analyzed and summarized as follows:

(1)   That English had no grammar, that is, no codified statement and no rules of right and wrong based upon such a statement. This way of thinking about grammar is only one of its meanings. In another sense, which is better understood today, at least by students of language, English always had a "grammar" because it always had a systematic structure, even when there existed no description of it in writing. But this was not the usual concept in the eighteenth century.

(2)   That the language of the times suffered a decadence from a supposed earlier state of excellence. Thus Dryden (like Spenser) admired Chaucer's English, Swift admired Shakespeare's English, but Samuel Johnson and Thomas Sheridan admired Swift's.

(3)   That the contemporary language was full of corruptions which could be identified, and that the language could and should be purified of these elements of decay.

(4)   That variation was undesirable.

(5)   That language could be made subject to the laws of logic.[2]

(6)   That Latin grammar was a suitable model upon which to base an English grammar.

(7)   That language practice should be controlled by an arbitrary legislative agency.

(8)   That language could and should be fixed beyond the force of change.

---

[2] In the sixteenth century Mulcaster had defended the role of reason in governing the use of language, but the word as he used it meant what we would call "common sense." He retained a high regard for the force of custom.

Some of these assumptions appear at first glance innocent and even desirable, but for the most part they are based upon false concepts of the nature of language, of the way in which it is transmitted from generation to generation, of its versatility in the service of large numbers of people in different ages and environments, and even of the fundamental relationship between language and thought. The appeal to logic, for example, by overlooking the fact that much of what passes for the laws of logic is derived from the analysis of language itself, runs the danger of circular reasoning. But whatever may have been the defects of these attitudes, they were not only commonplace in that period but have been retained by succeeding generations with remarkable tenacity. Even today they direct a large part of the content of school instruction in English.

In accord with these assumptions three goals seemed to many of that period principally worth striving for:

(1) To "ascertain" the language. In this context, the word did not mean to find out, but to settle something beyond doubt or dispute. Ascertainment then looked toward the formation of a standard to which one could turn in doubt or in difference of opinion.

(2) To refine the language, which specifically meant to eliminate terms and locutions which offended the taste of the critical-minded and were therefore accounted "barbarous." Among these were popular terms which have since become quite respectable if not indispensable: *banter, bubble, extra, mob, sham.*

(3) To fix the language in such fashion as to inhibit the changes which we now think inevitable.

Swift expressed the ideal when he wrote in his *Proposal* to the Earl of Oxford that what he had "most at heart is that some method should be thought on for ascertaining and fixing our language forever." Dr. Johnson, however, as a result of his labors in the compilation of his dictionary, was to discover and bear witness to the truth that "sounds are too volatile and subtle for legal restraints; to enchain syllables and to lash the wind, are equally the undertakings of pride, unwilling to measure its desires by its strength." Nevertheless, Thomas Sheridan,[3] who approved Johnson's

---

[3] Father of the playwright Richard Sheridan, and author of a treatise on rhetoric and of a dictionary.

work, was still in midcentury echoing the views of his old patron, Jonathan Swift, in asking "whether many important advantages would not accrue both to the present age and to posterity, if the English language were ascertained and reduced to a fixed and permanent standard?"

"Ascertainment" and the Idea of the Academy

For the realizing of these ends certain practical undertakings arose, one of which was to follow the example of France and Italy by establishing an Academy to rule on all matters linguistic. At one point (1664) the Royal Society made a small provision for such an activity, but since the main interest of its members was in the direction of mathematics and science, nothing came of it. Both Dryden and Defoe supported the idea, but its nearest approach to actual success resulted from Jonathan Swift's *Proposal for Correcting, Improving, and Ascertaining the English Tongue.* In the closing years of the reign of Queen Anne her government was in the hands of the Tories. Swift, himself a staunch Tory, addressed his *Proposal* to Robert Harley, earl of Oxford, then Lord of the Treasury but exercising functions now proper to the Prime Minister. The proposal immediately became a political issue, and, though it was attacked by John Oldmixon for the Whigs, Harley was on the point of establishing the framework of an Academy when his government fell. Queen Anne died, and Swift's proposal was lost. There have been since, and indeed remain today, some few people who admire the French Academy and think we should follow its example. However, since the publication of Dr. Johnson's adverse opinion in the Preface to his *Dictionary* such a project has never had effective support.

Dr. Johnson and the Dictionary

A more fruitful project was the compilation of a dictionary. This turned out to be the greatest achievement of the most influential literary figure in the mid-eighteenth century, Dr. Samuel Johnson. There had, of course, been dictionaries before Johnson's. The earliest of these in the fifteenth century were simple English-Latin glossaries. In the sixteenth century wordlists for the use of foreign students became quite common. In 1658

Edward Phillips moved closer to the modern concept of a dictionary in *The New World of English Words*, which was still further improved upon by Nathan Bailey's *Universal Etymological English Dictionary* in 1721. But even this was not quite satisfactory for the times. Increasing wealth and increasing numbers of the well-to-do middle classes nursed the desire for more authoritative guidance in the social aspects of language, and, of course, printers were ready to supply this demand. Johnson announced a plan for a new dictionary in 1747, appealing to the celebrated Earl of Chesterfield for support—support which in fact he never received. At length, however, the gigantic task was completed and the work appeared in two folio volumes in 1755. It immediately achieved enormous popularity and influence—and understandably so. It was distinguished not only by the great labor devoted to its production but by the great learning embodied in it. Its coverage of the lexicographical material was indeed extensive, and the illustrative quotations were an important contribution to the technique of lexicography. In addition it supplied a very substantial preface which grew out of the author's long involvement with the subject and revealed the intelligence with which he dissented from some of the most persistent misunderstandings of his time.

From our position today it is easy, of course, to find fault with Johnson's work,[4] especially with some of its effect upon the public mind. Also a few of his definitions we find amusing, as when he defines *network* as "anything reticulated or decussated at equal distances between the intersections." His personal resentments appear in his definition of *pension* as "an allowance made to anyone without an equivalent. In England it is generally understood to mean pay given to a state hireling for treason to his country." Or his political partisanship shows through when he defines a *Tory* as "one who adheres to the ancient constitution of the state, and the apostolical hierarchy of the Church of England, opposed to Whig," but limits the definition of *Whig* to no more than "the name of a faction."

More important, however, is a result due less to the intrinsic char-

---

[4] "In general . . . it can be said that the Dictionary was not marked by any distinct originality: neither in preface (with its general observations, history, and grammar) nor in the context itself. Many of Johnson's definitions he took from other sources, and even the use of supporting quotations had appeared in French and Italian dictionaries. But it was an excellent product of the lexicographical thinking of his age, and by far the best dictionary that had ever appeared in English." James H. Sledd and G. J. Kolb, *Dr. Johnson's Dictionary* (Chicago, 1955). See pp. 1–45.

acter of the *Dictionary* itself than to its influence on the public mind. It fostered an attitude favoring strict adherence to traditional spelling, which has given to this subject a dubious importance in the public mind and led to the expenditure of vast amounts of instructional time that, in the opinion of some, might have been put to better uses. A public hungry for direction conceded it the authoritative position of arbiter of usage rather than recorder. This role has been bequeathed to succeeding dictionaries, such as the Webster dictionaries in the United States, with such complete general consent that any effort of the lexicographer to resign the authoritarian position is met with a public clamor even among scholars and historians.

English Grammar

A third undertaking of the age was the compilation of a new literature on the subject of English grammar. We have already referred to the desire among educated men of the eighteenth century for a method of "ascertaining the English language and reducing it to a fixed and permanent standard." To further this end there appeared a series of pioneer works on the subject of English grammar which fostered an attitude quite as uncompromising as that generated by Johnson's *Dictionary*. This movement coincided with and was certainly strengthened by another which is properly part of the history of education, but which cannot be overlooked here.

The earliest school instruction in English consisted mainly of teaching children to read, according to Charles Hoole,[5] who expected children to begin the study of Latin at seven or eight years of age. Protests against the long drudgery imposed upon adolescents in the study of Latin and Greek became very common in the early eighteenth century. The influence of John Locke (*Thoughts on Education*, 1693), who pointed out the inconvenience of the general system of secondary education, undoubtedly gave the subject of reform a degree of respectability, and it was referred to again and again, notably by Addison and Steele. But in this respect, as is usually the case in education, reform was slow. In 1756 Thomas Sheridan wrote a lengthy treatise (*British Education*), in which he included a prefatory essay

---

[5] *A New Discovery in the Old Art of Teaching School* (1659), cited in Rollo L. Lyman, *English Grammar in American Schools* (Washington, 1921).

commending recent innovations at Eton and Westminster which seem to include the study of English. In Book Second of the treatise he enlarged upon the urgent need to give the study of the mother tongue a respected position beside the classics in the education of gentlemen. At all events, views such as this were bearing fruit, if we may judge from the career of the schoolmaster James Buchanan, who not only taught English in the secondary schools of England, but produced a number of works on the subject, one of which, *Linguae Britannicae Vera Pronunciatio* (1757), was a pioneering work among dictionaries of pronunciation.

Meanwhile an event of critical importance had already taken place in the colonies. There in the Academy (later the University of Pennsylvania) established through the energies of Benjamin Franklin, the study of the English language, that is, grammar (with emphasis upon correctness), rhetoric, composition, oratory, and the study of standard English authors, was established as the main substance of education. Franklin's influence here, as in other areas, was powerful. The study of English grammar soon became a common school subject, and as it spread more widely an ever-increasing supply of textbooks followed as a matter of course. The circumstances, then, which surrounded the teaching of English after 1750 became as important to the history of the language as to the history of education. English either replaced Latin or was taught side by side with it, and by schoolmasters whose professional methods had been shaped by their experiences with Latin and who, in many instances, taught English with reluctance.

It is understandable, therefore, that linguistic attitudes and methods peculiar to the study of Latin were transferred to the study of English. The textbook tradition likewise contributed descriptions of English grammatical structure imitated from Latin and concepts of linguistic propriety no longer subject to the pressures of a living language.

PRIESTLEY AND LOWTH

The most influential of eighteenth-century grammatical works was *A Short Introduction to English Grammar with Critical Notes*, published in 1762 by Robert Lowth, later bishop of London and a privy councillor. Lowth had been preceded a few months by Joseph Priestley, the well-known scholar and scientist, who published in 1761 *The Rudiments of English Grammar*. Priestley displayed in this work the same independent quality of mind that characterized his whole intellectual life. It is refreshing, for example, to encounter such practical observations as the following:

> All our grammarians say, that the nominative cases of pronouns ought to follow the verb substantive [*to be*] as well as precede it; yet many familiar forms of speech, and the example of some of our best writers would lead us to make a contrary rule; or, at least, would leave us at liberty to adopt which we liked best. "Are these the houses you were speaking of? Yes, they are *them*. Who is there? It is *me*. It is *him*, etc. It is not *me* you are in love with (Addison). It cannot be *me* (Swift)."⁶

Such tolerance and detachment, however, were not to the public taste, which craved a more uncompromising and decisive approach.

This demand was satisfied by Lowth, who formulated rules based upon his personal preferences, upon notions of logical consistency, or upon idiomatic features proper to his own generation. Where Priestley invoked the example of literary ancestors like Swift and Addison to justify a feature of usage, Lowth cited passages from their works as specimens of "bad" English. For example, of Shakespeare's and Milton's use of the unstressed *ye* in oblique cases he observes that "no authority is sufficient to justify so manifest a solecism" (p. 49).⁷ He had, of course, failed to recognize the survival of the unstressed accusative, [jə], which has been in use from Chaucer's time until our own. He found Addison, Bolingbroke, Swift, and Pope guilty of "great impropriety" in their use of the auxiliary *to be* with intransitive verbs of motion (p. 84). Even the biblical passage in *Genesis*, "This is none other but the house of God," he cited to illustrate the "incorrect" use of *but* (p. 192).

It is true that the "doctrine of usage" as it is recognized today, namely that the current, reputable, and general practice of speakers and writers throughout a speech community is a sufficient guarantee of propriety, was not only perceived by Priestley but explicitly formulated by George Campbell in his *Philosophy of Rhetoric* (1776). But though Campbell's work went through no fewer than thirteen editions by 1850, the implications of his doctrine of usage were ignored or misunderstood by most

---

⁶ Quoted from the edition by J. T. Rutt (London, 1833), p. 69.

⁷ Page numbers refer to the edition of 1783.

people seriously involved with the study and teaching of language, and indeed they still are today.

Lowth's *Grammar*, then, or grammars modeled on it, assumed general acceptance. John Ash's *Grammatical Institutes* (1763) was offered as an "easy introduction to Dr. Lowth's English Grammar." In America the propagation of grammatical knowledge fell to Noah Webster, whose *Grammatical Institute of the English Language*, Part II, was published in 1784. This and other publications of Webster were widely circulated.[8]

LINDLEY MURRAY

However, although the general nature of English study in the schools of England and America remained in the tradition of Lowth and others of his mind, their textbooks were superseded in 1795 by Lindley Murray's *English Grammar Adapted to Different Classes of Learning*. Subsequent editions enlarged upon this early work by the addition of "Appropriate Exercises." In the new edition of 1808, published in two volumes, these exercises occupied the entire second volume. Here Murray popularized the practice of offering "incorrect" sentences to be revised and thus became the ancestor of the current workbook or practice book.

It would be difficult to overestimate the influence of Lindley Murray upon the teaching of English and the shape of public opinion with respect to "good English." Lyman says (p. 80), "The larger books were adopted by the colleges in both countries. It is asserted that his grammatical texts totaled over 120 editions of 10,000 copies each on the average; that more than 1,000,000 copies of his books were sold in America before 1850." It can be said that, despite recent advances in textbook making and classroom methods, the basic concept of grammar and usage as taught by Lowth and Murray has been generally retained.

---

[8] See Lyman, pp. 79–80.

Chapter 19

MODERN LINGUISTIC SCHOLARSHIP

Just about the time when the trend toward prescriptive grammar was at its crest, the stimulus toward a more critical and more objective study of language was being supplied by the exciting suggestions of one Sir William Jones, who had distinguished himself for proficiency in Oriental languages and eventually went to India as a judge. There his judicial and linguistic interests combined to lead him to the study of the native Indian languages. In this pursuit he eventually discovered Sanskrit, the ancient learned language of the Hindus, and the remarkable linguistic studies which the Hindu scholars had devoted to it. The resemblance of Sanskrit to Greek and Latin suggested to Jones a fact but dimly perceived before, that the latter, and other languages as well, were descendants of a single earlier mother tongue. Jones was really not the first Western student to recognize the importance of Sanskrit. It had, indeed, come under the scrutiny of earlier scholars, including Christian missionaries to India, but their observations had led to no continuous line of investigation.

Whether or not Jones realized the full implications of his discovery, they were not lost on other younger scholars, notably Rasmus Rask, Jacob Grimm, and Franz Bopp. Some early investigators of this period thought at first that Sanskrit itself was the mother tongue, but though they were eventually proved wrong, their inquiries originated the study of comparative grammar, the first phase of historical linguistics, through which we have learned to classify languages in terms of their descent from a common ancestor. In the course of continued investigation in comparative

262

grammar, it began to be suspected that Sanskrit was not really the mother tongue but really a cognate language, that is, of parallel descent with Latin and Greek from a much earlier original of which no written record remained (see pp. 79-87).

Such doubts as remained upon that subject were finally settled by the researches of the Italian linguist Graziadio Ascoli, whose views were shared by younger scholars in the universities of Germany. Among these were Karl Brugmann and Karl Verner, who stipulated also a proposition that was to produce a strong reaction among historical linguists, namely, that "sound laws" or descriptive formulas of sound change operated with the regularity of "laws" in the physical sciences. This school of linguists became known among their colleagues in Germany as *Junggrammatiker*, sometimes expressed in English as *neogrammarians*. By the end of the nineteenth century, then, historical linguistics had made important contributions to human knowledge, including besides the comparative method the internal reconstruction of the whole history of recorded languages, phonetics, and dialectology. Nevertheless, this new discipline had made little impact upon the public mind and indeed not much on the teaching of language in the schools.[1]

In the latter nineteenth and early twentieth centuries the historical study of English was pursued on the continent of Europe with great distinction by scholars like Karl Luick of Vienna, Alois Brandl and Wilhelm Horn of Berlin, and the great Danish linguist Otto Jespersen. In England pioneer studies in English phonology were contributed by Alexander Ellis and Henry Sweet. A little later Henry Cecil Wyld opened new and important sources of information on the spoken language in the earlier periods. Meanwhile studies in regional dialects were fostered by the English Dialect Society, under whose patronage Joseph Wright produced his monumental *English Dialect Dictionary* (1898-1905).

The *Oxford English Dictionary*

However, the most practical benefit to students of English contributed by historical linguistics is the *Oxford English Dictionary* and its offspring,

---

[1] Historical linguistics has often been called philology, a quite appropriate term except that it is ambiguous, sometimes being used to refer to the study of an entire culture as represented in its language.

the *Dictionary of American English*. In the words of the editor who saw the first issues through the press, Sir James A. H. Murray, the aim of the *Oxford English Dictionary*[2] was

> (1) to show, with regard to each individual word, when, how, and in what shape, and with what significance it became English; what development of form and meaning it has since received; which of its uses have, in the course of time, become obsolete, and which shall survive; what new uses have since arisen, by what processes and when: (2) to illustrate these facts by a series of quotations ranging from the first known occurrence of the word to the latest, or down to the present day; the word being thus made to exhibit its own history and meaning: and (3) to treat the etymology of each word strictly on the basis of historical fact, and in accordance with the methods and results of modern philological science.

The scope of the investigations for this great production were to cover "all the great works of all ages, . . . all the writers on special subjects . . . , all writers whatever before the 16th century." From this statement it can be understood why the composition of such a project required a large corps of editors and assistants, many of whom donated their services, and a great body of similarly generous readers, whose number rose to 1,300 before the first pages went to press. It is no wonder, then, that, though the proposal was first made in 1857, it was twenty-one years before actual plans for printing could be set up and ten more (1888) before the first volume was given to the public. The last volume of ten was published in 1927 under the editorship of W. A. Craigie, Henry Bradley, and C. T. Onions, its original editor having not lived to see his work completed. Including the supplement issued in 1933, the work required more than three quarters of a century.

Dictionary of American English

Shortly after the completion of the *Oxford Dictionary* its work was further extended by the *Dictionary of American English,* jointly edited by one of the Oxford editors, now Sir William A. Craigie, and James R. Hulbert. This work had begun at the University of Chicago in 1925 and was published

---

[2] First called, and still sometimes referred to as *A New English Dictionary on Historical Principles* (*NED*).

in four volumes between 1936 and 1944. Its purpose was to exhibit clearly "those features by which the English of the American colonies and the United States is distinguished from that of England and the rest of the English-speaking world."

These two dictionaries as well as other special types of more restricted purpose and scope represent the most practical benefits to the general public of the science of historical linguistics. Of the *OED* in particular Baugh has written (pp. 399–400) that the influence of this, "the greatest dictionary of any language in the world—has been far-reaching" and specifically that "it has increased our linguistic perspective and taught us to view many questions of language in a more scientific and less dogmatic way." So far as this judgment refers to the intrinsic value of the *OED*, the appraisal is just. To many, especially professional students of language, the *OED* and *DAE* are indispensable. But of their effect upon the thinking of the general public—even the literate public, including teachers, journalists, and critics—it cannot be said that the lessons imparted have been well learned. Any doubts on this score were surely settled by the public reception accorded to *Webster's Third New International Dictionary*.

Linguistics in the Twentieth Century

First, however, let us return for a moment to the story of the progress of linguistic studies. Two developments which took shape in the early years of this century laid the foundations for a new departure, most commonly referred to as descriptive linguistics. These were the recognition of the importance of applying the principles of systematic linguistic study to the contemporary spoken language and the discovery of the phonemic principle (see pp. 36–37).

One of the youngest of the linguists who had contributed to the advances made by the neogrammarians was Ferdinand de Saussure. Later, as professor at the University of Geneva, his lectures, published posthumously in 1916,[3] established the separate domains of synchronic and dia-

---

[3] *Cours de linguistique générale*, 4th ed. (Paris, 1949). It is perhaps fair to mention here that, just as Jones' discovery of Sanskrit had been anticipated, so also were the advances made by de Saussure. In fact, so important in this connection were the publications of Wilhelm von Humboldt (1767–1835) that de Saussure must have been influenced by them, but Humboldt had not affected the mainstream of historical studies among his contemporaries in the early nineteenth century.

chronic linguistics, the former confined to the state of the language in a single period of time. In this way the characteristics of the contemporary language came under review and contributed new insights of immeasurable value into the nature of language. These investigations of the living language in the field of phonology led to the recognition of the phoneme. The term was used by de Saussure but rather as the equivalent of what we today call the phone. On the other hand, Henry Sweet, the great English phonetician, seems to have recognized the principle without using the term. Perhaps the credit for bringing the two together should go to a pioneer in the field seldom mentioned today, the Slavic linguist Baudowin de Courtenay.[4] At any rate, the new principle became the means by which the structural system of a language could be more satisfactorily analyzed. Hence the term **structural linguistics,** sometimes used as the equivalent of descriptive linguistics.

More recently phonemic theories have been applied in diachronic or historical studies and have provided valuable understanding of the effect of sound change upon a given historic period. In other words, then, descriptive linguistics, in opening a new dimension of language study, has developed concepts and techniques so important that the historical language can no longer be safely explored in ignorance of them.

De Saussure's suggestions were exploited by the great Russian linguist Nikolai S. Trubetzkoy (1890–1938), who became professor of Slavic philology at Vienna in 1922. Together with his friend Roman Jakobson, he was the guiding spirit of the younger European linguists who formed the Linguistic Circle of Prague. In this country the pioneers of the descriptive field took a somewhat independent course, probably owing to the influence of their interest in cultural anthropology and in American Indian languages. The American school found its earliest leaders in Edward Sapir (*Language*, 1921) and Leonard Bloomfield (*Language*, 1933). The influence of the latter upon his pupils and colleagues has been so pronounced that the twenty-five years following the publication of *Language* may be appropriately called the "Bloomfieldian era."

The phonology of American English in this period most often referred to is that worked out jointly by George Trager and Henry Lee Smith (*An Outline of English Structure*, 1951), and though it is by no means final, it

---

[4] Daniel Jones, *The Phoneme, Its Nature and Use*, 3d ed. (Cambridge, 1967), pp. 254 ff.

has been accepted by many publications, such as those of H. A. Gleason, W. Nelson Francis, Archibald Hill, and Charles Hockett.

A significant new venture in syntactic analysis, first suggested by Zellig Harris, was developed by his pupil Noam Chomsky (*Syntactic Structures*, 1957). This is generally known as transformational grammar, or, more comprehensively, **generative grammar.** Chomsky's theories have attracted a considerable following, but their future is not yet determined. However, it is quite clear that the movement toward generative grammar has diverged from the Bloomfieldian school, which was limited by its close adherence to principles of behavioristic psychology. The aim of the generative grammarians is not simply to describe linguistic data, but to discover the rules to which *all the possible* sentences of a native speaker conform. Whatever its future may be, generative grammar has permanently turned the current of modern linguistic studies.

Without attempting to review further the content of descriptive linguistics, we can say that a very important result has been to establish the primacy of the spoken language. Not that this interest implies an assumption that the spoken language is "better" than the literary language, but historical linguistics had labored under the inevitable restriction of dealing only with written records, which testified for the most part to the literary tradition and supplied only a very imperfect image of the spoken language of past times. Now, however, the attention of linguists was directed more than ever before to the whole spectrum of language activity. Among other things, regional and social dialects, commonly labeled "substandard," received renewed attention. In a special way the place of the colloquial, or spoken, language in all its varieties is now more clearly recognized. Unfortunately the exact implications of this new discipline have not yet been fully accepted outside the circle of linguistic scholars themselves. Many even of their university colleagues in related fields have kept aloof. More recently in lower school circles some hopes have been entertained that linguistics will solve old pedagogical problems, but except for a few isolated areas, the interest has remained superficial.

Modern Language Study and the *Third International*

One of the interests closely related to linguistic scholarship is, as we have seen, lexicography. It is not too surprising, then, that when the editors of

Webster's Third New International Dictionary (1961) announced that their editorial principles would be altered to accord with the progress of linguistic knowledge, the public, or at least that part of it which is represented by professional reviewers in newspapers and periodicals, were either confused or scandalized. To many it seemed altogether outrageous that a dictionary should profess to be an index to the total word resources of a language, including words of low social status and dubious novelty, rather than a guide to refined usage, as previous editions were assumed to be.

It is somewhat ironic that publications under Webster's name should have become a public symbol of a prescriptive tradition with which his own theories were somewhat at variance. Though he sometimes rejected pronunciations not in agreement with spelling, he maintained in general a respect for the native genius of the language.[5] He believed that grammars in his time were not altogether good, and especially found fault with their subservience to Latin. He was convinced that grammar should be derived from the language and that language should not be constrained to agree with theoretical grammar. On the basis of his observation of the custom among "men of erudition" he defended the use of *you was* in the colloquial style and of *who* in such constructions as "Who did you speak to?" and "Who did he marry?"

Perhaps for these reasons he was succeeded in popular esteem as a grammarian by Lindley Murray. But he brought the same independent spirit to the making of his dictionary. His own words are not without interest at this time:

> But I am accused of introducing into my Dictionary *Americanisms and vulgarisms.*
>
> This is one of the most extraordinary charges which my opposers have ventured to suggest. I have indeed introduced into our vocabulary a few words, not used perhaps in Great Britain, or not in a like sense. . . . And is this an offense never to be forgiven? Such local terms exist, and will exist, in spite of lexicographers or critics. Is this *my* fault? And if local terms exist, why not explain them? Must they be left unexplained because they are local? This very circumstance renders their insertion in a dictionary the more necessary; for as the

---

[5] See Noah Webster, *Dissertation on the English Language* (Boston, 1789), *passim*. Extracts from this work are printed in Susie I. Tucker, *English Examined* (Cambridge, 1961), pp. 135–40.

faculty of Yale College have said in approbation of this part of my work, how are such words to be understood, without the aid of a dictionary?[6]

Apparently, then, though the editorial policy announced in 1961 professed to be quite modern in its inspiration, the *Dictionary* was returning to a principle set down by its founder a century and a half ago, no doubt equally controversial in its own day.

Like all ventures of a commercial nature with resources limited by the need to make a profit, the new *Dictionary* of 1961 might have been expected, as it certainly did, to make some very human mistakes. But it was not its mistakes that caused the distress so much as its achievement—and this was attributed to the influence of linguistics, generally thought to be pernicious. One clerical reviewer dedicated to the proprieties of good usage found the *Dictionary* to be informed by the "Bolshevik spirit" and closed his patriotic remarks with the entreaty to "include me out."[7] Obviously the misunderstanding was widespread that linguists do not recognize the existence of a literary or cultivated standard, and even that they propose to undermine and destroy such a standard if possible.

True, the general public was being asked to make a radical change in its view of what a modern dictionary ought to be. Nevertheless, it seems remarkable that the most expensively schooled public in history, though it can keep up with breathtaking advances in the physical sciences, should cling with savage bias to the eighteenth-century view not only that the language of the whole of the English-speaking world can and ought to be policed, but that the lexicographer in a particular way has the authority and the duty to execute such a function. There still seems then to be a greater demand for what might be called guidebooks in linguistic etiquette than for complete objective information on the state of the English lexicon. Of course, no reason exists why handbooks of usage should not be avail-

---

[6] Letter to Thomas Dawes in *Monthly Anthology and Boston Review*, VII, 208 ff., reprinted in Mitford M. Mathews, *The Beginnings of American English* (Chicago, 1931), pp. 48–52.

[7] See the very revealing publication by James H. Sledd and Wilma R. Ebbit, *Dictionaries and THAT Dictionary* (Chicago, 1962), in which are reprinted a large number of reviews and other comments. It is interesting to observe the more tolerant tone of the British reviews. For a very competent evaluation of the *Dictionary* see Albert H. Marckwardt, "The New Webster Dictionary: A Critical Appraisal," in W. B. Finnie and Thomas L. Erskine, eds., *Words on Words* (New York, 1971), pp. 138–50.

tongue, is one of the main objects propofed in the following work.

In order to this it will be neceffary in the firft place to afcertain the number of fimple founds in our tongue. And firft I fhall begin with the vowels.

Scheme of the Vowels.

	Firft.	Second.	Third.
	1	2	3
a	hat	hate	hall.
	1	2	3
e	bet	bear	beer.
	1	2	3
i	fit	fight	field.
	1	2	3
o	not	note	noofe.
	1	2	3
u	but	bufh	blue.
	1	2	
y	love-ly	lye.	

Before they proceed any farther, it will be neceffary that all who would readily and clearly comprehend what is laid down in the following treatife with regard to the vowels, fhould get the above fcheme by heart, fo as to be able to repeat it readily in the order in which the words lie, on a parallel, not perpendicular line; as,

	1	2	3
	hat	hate	hall.
	1	2	
	bet	bear, &c.	

in

A page from Thomas Sheridan, A Rhetorical Grammar of the English Language *(1783)*

☞ (559).—Fàte, fàr, fåll, fåt ;—mè, mèt ;—pìne, pìn ;—

FLAGRATION, flå-grå'shǔn. s. Burning.

FLAGSTAFF, flåg'ståf. s. The staff on which the flag is fixed.

FLAIL, flåle. s. (202). The instrument with which grain is beaten out of the ear.

FLAKE, flåke. s. Any thing that appears loosely held together ; a stratum, layer ; a lock of wool drawn out.

FLAKY, flå'kè. a. Loosely hanging together ; lying in layers or strata, broken into lam næ.

FLAM, flåm. s. A falsehood, a lie, an illusory pretext.

To FLAM, flåm. v. a. To deceive with a lie.

FLAMBEAU, flåm'bò. s. (245). A lighted torch. Plural FLAMBEAUX.

FLAME, flåme. s. Light emitted from fire ; a stream of fire ; ardour of temper or imagination, brightness of fancy ; ardour of inclination ; passion of love.

To FLAME, flåme. v. n. To shine as fire, to burn with emission of light ; to blaze ; to break out in violence of passion.

FLAME-COLOURED, flåme'kǔl-lǔr'd. a. (362). Of a bright yellow colour.

FLAMEN, flå'mèn. s. (503). A priest in ancient times, one that officiated in solemn offices.

☞ If there be any case in which we are to take our English quantity from the Latin, it is in words of two syllables which retain their Latin form, and have the vowel in the first syllable long.—See DRAMA.

FLAMMATION, flåm-må'shǔn. s. The act of setting on flame.

FLAMMABILITY, flåm-må-bìl'è-tè. s. The quality of admitting to be set on fire.

FLAMMEOUS, flåm'mè-ǔs. a. Consisting of flame.

FLAMMIFEROUS, flåm-mìf'fè-rǔs. a. (518). Bringing flame.

FLAMMIVOMOUS, flåm-mìv'ò-mǔs. a. (528). Vomiting out flame.

FLAMY, flå'mè. a. Inflamed, burning; having the nature of flame.

FLANK, flånk. s. That part of the side of a quadruped near the hinder thigh : in men, the latter part of the lower belly ; the side of any army or fleet : in fortification, that part of the bastion which reaches from the curtain to the face.

To FLANK, flånk. v. a. To attack the side of a battalion or fleet ; to be posted so as to overlook or command any pass on the side, to be on the side.

FLANKER, flånk'ǔr. s. A fortification

jutting out so as to command the side of a body marching to the assault.

FLANNEL, flån'nèl. s. (99). A soft nappy stuff of wool.

FLAP, flåp. s. Any thing that hangs broad and loose ; the motion of any thing broad and loose ; the noise made by that motion ; a disease in horses.

To FLAP, flåp. v. a. To beat with a flap, as flies are beaten ; to move with a flap or noise.

To FLAP, flåp. v. n. To ply the wings with noise ; to fall with flaps or broad parts depending.

FLAPDRAGON, flåp'dråg-ǔn. s. A play in which they catch raisins out of burning brandy ; the thing eaten at Flapdragon.

FLAPEARED, flåp'èèr'd. a. (362). Having loose and broad ears.

To FLARE, flåre. v. n. To flutter with a splendid show ; to glitter with transient lustre ; to glitter offensively ; to be in too much light.

FLASH, flåsh. s. A sudden, quick, transitory blaze ; sudden burst of wit or merriment ; a short transient state ; a body of water driven by violence.

To FLASH, flåsh. v. n. To glitter with a quick and transient flame ; to burst out into any kind of violence ; to break out into wit, merriment, or bright thought.

To FLASH, flåsh. v. a. To strike up large bodies of water.

FLASHER, flåsh'ǔr. s. A man of more appearance of wit than reality.

FLASHILY, flåsh'è-lè. ad. With empty show.

FLASHY, flåsh'è. a. Empty, not solid ; showy, without substance ; insipid, without force or spirit.

FLASK, flåsk. s. A bottle, a vessel ; a powder-horn.

FLASKET, flåsk'ìt. s. A vessel in which viands are served.

FLAT, flåt. a. Horizontally level ; smooth, without protuberances ; without elevation ; level with the ground ; lying horizontally prostrate, lying along : in painting, without relief, without prominence of the figures ; tasteless, insipid ; dull, unanimated ; spiritless, dejected ; peremptory, absolute, downright ; not sharp in sound.

FLAT, flåt. s. A level, an extended plane ; even ground, not mountainous ; a smooth low ground exposed to inundations ; shallow, strand, place in the sea where the water is not deep ; the broad side of a blade ; depression of thought or language ; a mark or character in musick.

A page from John Walker, Critical Pronouncing Dictionary and Expositor of the English Language (*1791*)

able, but it is not clear why lexicography should be restricted to this pedestrian use.

At any rate, whatever the demand for publications to supply definitive distinctions between "correct" and "incorrect" usage, their effect upon the actual state of the language is relatively small. The standard language existed and served the purposes of literary expression quite well for several centuries before the age of linguistic anxiety. In their fairly long régime the prescriptive grammarians have had only a limited effect upon the literary language and almost none at all upon the popular language. They are not likely to be more influential in the future.

Exercises

1. Look up the history of the *Century Dictionary*. When was it first published? By whom was it edited? What is the latest edition? Describe its contents by volume. (Begin with Arthur G. Kennedy, *Bibliography of Writings on the English Language*, #6584, and Mitford M. Mathews, *A Survey of English Dictionaries* [London, 1933].)

2. What contribution to convenience was introduced by Funk and Wagnall's *Standard Dictionary of the English Language* in 1913? What more recent dictionary has followed this arrangement?

3. Two recent publications are the *Random House Dictionary of the English Language* (1966) and the *American Heritage Dictionary of the English Language* (1969). Construct a bibliographical description of these works: editor, title, publisher, place and date of publication, pages, contents, subdivisions, etc.

4. Make a comparative study of the entries for *advocate* (v.) in

    (a) *OED* (entry for this word was published in what year?)
    (b) *Century Dictionary*
    (c) *Webster's Third International*
    (d) *Random House*

5. Study the facsimile page (this volume, p. 271) from John Walker's *Critical Pronouncing Dictionary*, published first in 1791 and many times later,

and compare its method of indicating pronunciation with that of

(a)   Thomas Sheridan's *Rhetorical Grammar of the English Language* (1783), a facsimile page from which is reproduced in this volume, p. 270;

(b)   current general dictionaries, for example, *Webster's Collegiate* or the *American College Dictionary;*

(c)   special pronouncing dictionaries like those by Jones and by Kenyon and Knott.

6.   Can you determine from examination of the following reference works whether the statements of the authors are influenced by (a) a rigidly prescriptive attitude based upon logic, (b) a respect for the practices of reputable speakers and writers, (c) judgments of variety in usage based upon its history? (The following topics are most likely to supply data for reaching conclusions: Participles and Gerunds [Dangling, Unattached, Fused, etc.], Back Formations, Clipped Forms [Curtailed Words], Case, Sturdy Indefensibles [in Fowler]; also some particular items of usage: *apt-liable, between, each, farther-further, like-as, shall-will, should-would, that-which-who, who-whom*, etc.)

H. W. Fowler, *A Dictionary of Modern English Usage*
Margaret Nicholson, *A Dictionary of American-English Usage*
Porter G. Perrin, *Writer's Guide and Index to English* (third edition, with Karl W. Dykema)
Bergen Evans and Cornelia Evans, *A Dictionary of American Usage*

Part V

ENGLISH IN THE UNITED STATES

Chapter 20

ENGLISH IN THE
UNITED STATES

The English language in this country has been variously referred to as "the American language," "American English," and "the English language in America." All of these terms have their advocates, but the last seems from several points of view the most appropriate.

Earliest Settlements

When the first permanent settlement was established at Jamestown, Virginia, in 1607, Shakespeare's *King Lear* was a new play and just about to be printed for the first time. *The Tempest* was still in the future. When the Puritans landed at Plymouth in 1620, the earliest collected issue of Shakespeare's plays, the First Folio, was yet to come. Ben Jonson was still living at the time of the settlements at St. Mary's (1632), Hartford (1635), and Providence (1636). New York was captured from the Dutch (1664) and Charleston settled (1670) before the death of Milton in 1674, and eight years later (1682), when William Penn founded his colony in Pennsylvania, Dryden was still at the height of his career.

In other words the first colonists brought to the shores of America the English language as we have described it in its Early Modern Period. The earliest of them were born in the sixteenth century and had learned to speak their mother tongue as contemporaries of Shakespeare.

It is obvious therefore why the earliest examples of written English in this country strike us today as somewhat antiquated. The following is from William Bradford's *History of the Plymouth Foundation:*

> But this made them yᵉ more carefully to looke to them selves, so as they agreed to inclose their dwellings with a good strong pale, and make flankers in convenient places, with gates to shute, which were every night locked, and a watch kept, and when neede required ther was also warding in yᵉ day time. And yᵉ company was by yᵉ Captaine and yᵉ Govʳ advise, devided into 4. squadrons, and every one had ther quarter apoynted them, unto which they were to repaire upon any suddane alarme. And if ther should be any crie of fire, a company were appointed for a gard, with muskets, whilst others quenchet yᵉ same, to prevent Indean treachery. This was accomplished very cherfully, and yᵉ towne impayled round by yᵉ beginning of March, in which evry family had a pretty garden plote secured. And herewith I shall end this year. Only I shall remember one passage more, rather of mirth then of waight. One yᵉ day called Chrismas-day, yᵉ Govʳ caled them out to worke, (as was used,) but yᵉ most of this new-company excused them selves and said it wente against their consciences to work on yᵗ day. So yᵉ Govʳ tould them that if they made it mater of conscience, he would spare them till they were better informed. So he led-away yᵉ rest and left them; but when they came home at noone from their worke, he found them in yᵉ streete at play, openly; some pitching yᵉ barr, & some at stoole-ball, and such like sports. So he went to them, and tooke away their implements, and tould them that was against his conscience, that they should play & others worke. If they made yᵉ keeping of it mater of devotion, let them kepe their houses, but ther should be no gameing or revelling in yᵉ streets. Since which time nothing hath been attempted that way, at least openly.

Obviously the spelling in this passage, composed about 1630 or a little later, is somewhat short of our modernized standard, but still it is conventional and therefore does not consistently reveal the exact nature of the sounds. Some words and phrases require careful observation and perhaps some investigation to fix their exact meaning in the particular context in which they occur: *pale, flankers, warding, quarter, quenchet, impayled, secured, remember, passage, keepe their houses, gameing, revelling.*

The grammatical forms, except for the genitive without -*s* in "yᵉ Captaine and yᵉ Governor advise" contain nothing remarkably strange to us. The syntax, however, is more noticeable with the features of word order like "which were every night locked" and a type of sentence organization which today would be regarded as "loose" or incoherent.

A little more than a hundred years later John Bartram was to write an interesting travel book, *Travels from Pennsylvania to Lake Ontario*, which illustrates the changes in style that were taking place in the writing of educated men:

> In the morning as soon as light, I walked out to look at our horses as usual, and close by a cabin spied a knife almost covered with grass; I supposed it lost, but the Indians being not yet stiring let it lie: a little after sunrise I walked there again, and the Squaw being at the door, shewed her where it lay, at which she seemed exceeding pleased, and picked it up immediately. As I came back to our cabin, I spy'd 2 Indian girls at play with beans, which they threw from one to the other on a match coat spread between them; as they were behind our cabin, I turned to see how they play'd, but they seemed much out of countenance, and run off in an instant: I observed that the Indian women are generally very modest.

Apart from a few oddities of spelling, the past tense *run*, and a flat adverb, Bartram's English, unlike Bradford's, is not to our ears strikingly antiquated.

Nothing in the language of this passage would have struck a native educated Londoner of that time as worthy of remark, but in the course of the following decades a number of innovations began to distinguish American usage from that of the mother country. The first to be noticed were lexical and semantic changes like the use of *bluff* to refer to the high steep bank of a river, as commented upon in 1735 by one Francis Moore, who came to Georgia about that time.[1]

Extended observations were made by John Witherspoon, a self-educated Scots clergyman who arrived in the colonies in 1768 to become president of the College of New Jersey, now Princeton University. Witherspoon was singularly free of the patronizing, not to say biased, attitude of most newcomers from England in his time and later. He commented

---

[1] Reported in Mathews, *Beginnings*, p. 13.

favorably upon the comparative homogeneity of the spoken language in America:

> The vulgar in America speak much better than the vulgar in Great Britain, for a very obvious reason, viz. that being much more unsettled, and moving frequently from place to place, they are not so liable to local peculiarities either in accent or phraseology. There is a greater difference in dialect between one county and another in Britain than there is between one state and another in America.[2]

He also recognized the reasonable possibility of a separate American standard—"whether," in his words, "in this new empire, some center of learning and politeness will not be found, which shall obtain influence and prescribe the rules of speech and writing to every other part." His view of those features of language which attracted his attention were, for his time, commendably objective. He attempted to identify Americanisms (a term he himself invented), to distinguish nonstandard American usage from that found in both countries, and to differentiate these from cant, jargon, and simple blunders.

Thereafter the consciousness of a separate American linguistic development began to grow. In 1815 the playwright David Humphries published a play, *The Yankey in England*, to which he appended a glossary. This list, quite different from Witherspoon's, contains a large number of terms chosen from the vulgar, or at least colloquial, vocabulary, many of which reveal the survival of Early Modern forms and pronunciations. *The Vocabulary . . . of Words and Phrases . . . Peculiar to the United States* was published in book form in 1816 by John Pickering, of whom we shall have more to say later. Pickering, whose interests were more elevated than those of Humphries, was more concerned with the meanings of words in literate usage, but his list was a fairly ambitious one. Meanwhile, Noah Webster was pursuing his ambition as a lexicographer. In 1806, he published *A Compendious Dictionary of the English Language, in which 5000 words are added to the number found in the best English compends.* This number of new words was increased to 12,000 when he finally published his great work in 1828, *An American Dictionary of the English Language.* Since many of

---

[2] *Pennsylvania Journal and the Weekly Advertiser*, May 1781; reprinted in Mathews, *Beginnings*, p. 16.

Webster's additions to Johnson's lexicon were Americanisms, the critics of his two dictionaries denounced the intrusion of such novelties.

Webster's purpose, of course, was to produce a general dictionary. Concerning Americanisms in particular, other lists, less important but still useful to the linguistic historian, appeared from time to time, but the first systematic effort to distinguish in full scope the Americanisms in the language appeared in John Russell Bartlett's *Dictionary of Americanisms*, published first in 1848 but much enlarged in 1859. Though subject to the shortcomings naturally to be found in a work compiled before the development of modern linguistic knowledge, Bartlett's *Dictionary* was an ambitious and successful work. With it the study of American English attained respectable stature. It kept its place until the appearance of Thornton's *American Glossary* in 1912, though both are now superseded. The current standard works on this subject are the four-volume *Dictionary of American English* (*DAE*), edited by Sir William Craigie and James R. Hulbert (1938–44), and the two-volume *Dictionary of Americanisms* by Mitford M. Mathews (1951).

British vs. American

In its early years American English faced scornful opposition. Most commentators, especially Britons, were highly intolerant of anything which was, or which they merely fancied was, distinctively American. Even the literary style of prominent American authors was harshly treated by influential journals in England such as the *British Critic*, the *Edinburgh Review*, and the *Quarterly Review*. Thus Jefferson's *Notes on Virginia*, John Quincy Adams's *Letters on Silesia*, and Marshall's *Life of Washington* were judged to be obviously American in language. In particular the attacks of William Gifford, editor of the *Quarterly Review*, were so venomous that when the *Quarterly* offered Washington Irving a hundred guineas for an article, he refused with the response that the *Review* had been "so persistently hostile to our country" that he could not "draw a pen in its service."[3]

Perhaps this hostility was part of the reaction against liberal movements generated by disturbing political and social changes taking place not only in America but also in France, to the consternation of many.

---

[3] H. L. Mencken, *The American Language*, 4th ed. (New York, 1936), p. 21.

Under such circumstances people of a conservative disposition are likely to see subversion in all forms of change, however innocent, as the history of our own times has well demonstrated. Nevertheless, British linguistic snobbery in matters American has long survived the events of the late eighteenth century.

Another and perhaps more essential element in the coolness of the educated classes toward Americanisms was the general acceptance of the prescriptive or normative attitude toward language. Although a legislative academy such as Swift had proposed was never realized, there prevailed a tacit agreement among men of letters that change should be resisted and the "purity" of the language should be jealously guarded. Words and meanings not recognized by the great Dr. Johnson (himself a hopeless bigot toward all things American) were looked upon as unwanted intruders.

In such matters, however, the conservative attitude was not restricted to England. Benjamin Franklin once fashioned a plan for reforming the spelling system, but otherwise, in spite of his general independence of mind, submitted to authority in language usage, as we gather from his deference to Hume, who once took exception to his use of the words *pejorate* and *colonize*. "The introducing new words," he replied, "where we already are possessed of old ones sufficiently expressive, I confess must be generally wrong, as it tends to change the language."[4] An anonymous contributor to the *Royal American* magazine in 1774, although keeping clear of anti-American sentiment by suggesting that the highest perfection of the English language was "perhaps reserved for this land of light and freedom," still held that in general the English language "has been greatly improved within a century." He proposed, therefore, the formation of a society to be called the Fellows of the American Society of Language, whose function would be to correct, enrich, and refine the language "until perfection stops their progress and ends their labor."[5] And John Adams was equally convinced of the value of this already tired ambition:

> The honor of forming the first public institution for refining, correcting, improving, and ascertaining the English language, I hope

---

[4] Quoted in Baugh, p. 442.

[5] Quoted in Mathews, *Beginnings*, p. 40. See also George P. Krapp, *The English Language in America* (New York, 1925), 1: 6.

is reserved for congress; they have every motive that can possibly influence a public assembly to undertake it. It will have a happy effect upon the union of the States to have a public standard for all persons in every part of the continent to appeal to, both for the signification and pronunciation of the language.[6]

The conservative, regulated use of the language was, then, in the end of the eighteenth and the beginning of the nineteenth century the common ideal among the educated classes on both sides of the Atlantic. Among Americans of this persuasion perhaps the most striking example was John Pickering, mentioned above. Son of Timothy Pickering, a distinguished patriot and statesman in the infant republic, John was educated at Harvard and spent some years in the diplomatic service in Portugal and England. He was an assiduous student of languages, even of Oriental languages, the importance of which were in his day becoming more apparent to scholars, and he compiled a Greek-English dictionary. His learning and experience therefore gave a special value to his observations on the English language in America, which he expressed in an essay presented in 1815 in the Memoirs of the American Academy of Arts and Sciences but published separately under the title *A Vocabulary or Collection of Words and Phrases Which Have Been Supposed to Be Peculiar to the United States of America.*[7]

His purpose was to expose and eradicate tendencies characteristically American. Although he recognized that the language had not changed as extensively as might have been expected since the early settlements, yet he insisted that it had "in so many instances departed from the English standard, that our scholars should lose no time in endeavoring to restore it to its purity" (p. 17). His measure of "purity" was, in fact, conformity to the contemporary preferences of English authors:

> As a general rule we should undoubtedly avoid all those words which are noticed by English authors of reputation, as expressions with which *they are unaquainted;* for although we might produce some English authority for such words, yet the very circumstances of their being thus noticed by well-educated *Englishmen,* is a proof that they are not in use at this day in England, and, of course, ought not to be used elsewhere by those who would speak *correct English.*
>
> [p. 18; Pickering's italics]

---

[6] Quoted in Mathews, *Beginnings,* p. 42.

[7] Boston, 1816. Page references cited herein are to this printing.

Pickering's views, which might with some justice be attributed to an invincible cultural colonialism, may fairly be called typical of the educated minority in his time and later. They were reflected in the influential compilation by William Cullen Bryant, the *Index Expurgatorius* (c. 1877), and by various publications of Richard Grant White of the same era, all of which were quite in harmony with the common teaching in the schools established by the textbook heritage of Lowth and Murray. The Pickering attitude, then, has been preserved in American education at all levels and thereby in the state of mind of educated men and women, especially those who shared the insular British hostility toward American features of the language.

American Independence

In all propriety the right of a people to modify its language to serve its needs and to realize its full possibility of expression should not be subverted. At any rate, this right has been fully exercised by the vast independent body of American speakers and in the volume and quality of the authentic American literary voice, especially since the work of William Dean Howells, Mark Twain, and Walt Whitman. But there were also from still earlier times outspoken champions of the American experiment in language, more or less distinguished in public affairs, among whom have been mentioned Thomas Jefferson, Timothy Dwight, William Ellery Channing, Edward Everett, James Fenimore Cooper, James Kirke Paulding, Charles A. Bristed, and others. Bristed, a graduate of both Yale and Cambridge, contributed an essay, "The English Language in America,"[8] of which Mencken (*The American Language*, p. 69) said that "it remains to this day [1936] despite a few aberrations, the most intelligent brief discussion of the subject ever printed."

However, the most stalwart defender of American usage was Noah Webster. In the light of present knowledge we can, of course, point out deficiencies in Webster. Some of his statements about the history and relations among ancient languages are now known to be false. He was also not free from the dogmatic and subjective judgments of usage common in his time. Of *base* as a verb he judged that it was little used and not recommended by necessity or advantage. *Belittle* he considered unautho-

---

[8] *Cambridge Essays by Members of the University* (London, 1855).

rized, though it had been used by Thomas Jefferson, and *progress* as a verb he deemed wholly unnecessary.

On the other hand, as we have described earlier, he had a remarkably advanced conception of the theory of lexicography as well as an almost patriotic zeal for the rights of American ventures in linguistic adaptation. "In this country," he wrote, "new objects, new ideas, and associations of ideas, compel us, either to invent new terms, or to use English words in a new sense."[9] He recognized the inevitability of linguistic variation arising from the separation of communities: "If a perfect uniformity cannot be produced or preserved in two distant counties of England, how is this object to be effected between the English in Great Britain and their descendants in America, India, or New Holland?"[10] The spirit with which he defended Americanisms and in particular his judgment of critics was often expressed in stinging language which earned him a certain degree of unpopularity. To Pickering, in whose *Vocabulary* Webster found some difference of opinion from his own work, he wrote:

> You observe, Sir, under the words *locate* and *location*, in your *Vocabulary*, that the verb, and one of the significations I have given to the latter word, in my Dictionary, are not in the English Dictionaries. No, Sir; and this is one reason why I compiled mine. How can the English *locate* lands, when they have no lands to *locate!*
>
> Under this head may be classed the conversion of nouns into verbs; a practice which has furnished critics, on both sides of the Atlantic, with many bones to gnaw. Nothing excites more rage among the nibbling gentry than to find *test* and *advocate* used as verbs.[11]

Since both Franklin and Pickering had questioned the acceptability of *advocate*, it was perhaps impolitic to classify them among the "nibbling gentry." One need not be surprised, then, that even Jefferson looked upon Webster as a mere pedagogue and a partisan. Nevertheless, history was on Webster's side, undoubtedly because he was right in principle. Like Johnson he was convinced of the folly of attempting to shackle the free

---

[9] *A Letter to the Honorable John Pickering on the Subject of His Vocabulary* . . . (Boston, 1810), p. 8. The entire letter is also reprinted with minor editorial changes in Harry R. Warfel, *Letters of Noah Webster* (1953), pp. 341–94.

[10] *A Letter* . . . *to Pickering*, pp. 28–29.

[11] *Ibid*, p. 8; Webster's italics.

use of words. He believed that custom and habit were, in fact, safer guides than the judgments of academies. Not satisfied with merely defending the special character of American English, Webster went so far as to claim for it a title to superiority in declaring "that the people of America, in particular the English descendents, speak the most *pure* English now known to the world."[12]

Americanisms

Webster had applied himself well to the linguistic knowledge available in his time, but other commentators were less well prepared to speak intelligently on the language they observed. Most of them were convinced of the peculiar excellence of that type of "correctness" which was advocated in the eighteenth century and which the educated minority aspired to practice. Few had any knowledge of the historical evolution of their own language or even were prepared to think of such phenomena. Most, if not all, were limited to casual observation, and, though there is some evidence that the scope and variety of American English were recognized, no systematic search of the data was made before Webster and Bartlett. Consequently, some terms despised in those days as Americanisms have since been discovered to have been current also in England. Finally there was no regular boundary recognized between the requirements of written discourse and conveniences of informal intercourse, nor was there any clear distinction between "vulgar" and "cultivated," though the terms were often employed.

Pickering's observations were less naïve than many. He accepted Witherspoon's classification with the terse statement, "We have formed some *new* words; and to some *old* ones, that are still used in England, we have affixed *new significations:* while others, which have long been *obsolete* in England, are still retained *in common use* with us" (Pickering's italics). Although he did not classify them in his generalization, Pickering included "vulgarisms" in his list, but, for the most part these were simply the varieties of American usage that critics opposed and champions defended.

A number of the disputed features have not survived at all, and for our purposes they may be ignored. Among words now quite well established but formerly viewed as questionable neologisms or at any rate as suspiciously American, Pickering noticed *Americanize, antagonizing, appli-*

---

[12] *Dissertations on the English Language* (Boston, 1789), p. 288.

cant, backwoodsman, barbecue, belittle, caucus, Christianization, congressional, crowbar, decedent, demoralization, departmental, dutiable, evoke, infuriated, insularity, involvement, lengthy, liability, locate, noticeable, obligate, offset, peek, prayerful, presidential, profanity, requirement, romantically, shingle, slump, squatter, stalled, vilification.

He found almost as many familiar word forms with new meanings: *appreciate* 'rise in value,' *authority* 'governing personnel,' *awful* 'disagreeable,' *balance* 'remainder,' *bluff* 'cliff,' *census, clapboard, constable, corn, creek, creature* 'domestic animal,' *depreciate* 'fall in value,' *domestic* 'servant,' *handsome* (generalized), *lot* 'piece of land,' *lumber* 'timber,' *mad* 'angry,' *raise* 'grow, rear,' *rugged* 'robust,' *section* (of land), *tavern* 'inn,' *ugly* 'bad-tempered.' Some familiar words, he noted, were used with functional shift: *advocate* (v.), *appellate* (adj.), *deed* (v.), *test* (v.), *transient* (n.).

Pickering also recognized, as such, survivals in America of provincial words or of words then obsolete in England. They include *checkers, chore, crock, fall* 'autumn,' *fault* 'find fault with,' *freshet, gawky, glut, guess, poke* 'bag,' *progress* (v.), *reckon* 'suppose,' *rungs, sag, scanty, slam, stock* (cattle), *tarry, tidy, wilt.*

Not all of Pickering's judgments were accurate, but they reflected contemporary refined opinion. In fact, some of his proscriptions are not unknown in modern handbooks compiled by authors whom Webster would have termed "the nibbling gentry." But despite the objections of British critics and native "purists," it became increasingly certain that the American people could not face their vast new territory and find there a way of life without discovering and responding to the need for new words to describe their new environment and their experiences in it.

In the introduction to his *Dictionary of Americanisms* Bartlett referred to some of these: *backwoods, backwoodsman, barrens, blaze, cane-brake, clearing, corn-shucking, diggings, dug-out, flat-boat, husking, prairie, reservation, salt lick, squatter,* and others. He pointed out also "metaphorical and other odd expressions, used first in the West, and afterwards in other parts of the country" such as *cave in, flash in the pan, bark up the wrong tree, pull up stakes, fizzle out, tucker out,* and even *chisel* 'to cheat,' often thought to be modern slang.

Foreign Borrowing

As in earlier periods of our language history, a large part of the American additions to the English lexicon consisted of foreign borrowings. For some things new to them, the early settlers took names from one or another of the various Indian languages.[13] To be sure, these borrowings often presented sound clusters which, unfamiliar to English ears, were eventually transformed by the process of folk etymology or other modification. Thus *wejack* became *woodchuck* and *misickquatash* became *succotash*. Other very familiar objects with names of Indian origin are *hickory, hominy, mackinaw, moccasin, moose, muskrat, opossum, pecan, persimmon, raccoon, skunk*.

Contacts with European languages also began early. In the late seventeenth century New Amsterdam, settled by the Dutch, was taken over as the English colony of New York, but many of the Dutch settlers remained and continued to flourish. From them we have *boss, cole slaw, cookie, cruller, dope, patron, Santa Claus, sleigh, snoop, stoop* 'front steps, porch,' *waffle*.

About this time or a little later, refugees from Germany began to settle in America, establishing their remarkably tenacious identity in the rural areas in Southeastern Pennsylvania. Again in the nineteenth century, when a new German immigration began, large numbers of Germans settled in the cities of the Atlantic coast and the Midwest. The culinary art and the festive tendencies of these settlers are reflected in the words we have borrowed from them, such as *beergarden, bock beer, delicatessen, frankfurter, hamburger, lager beer, liverwurst, noodle, pinochle, pretzel, rathskeller, sauerkraut, stein, strudel*.

The French influence upon the English language, as we have seen, has a long and varied history, but in America a new collection of words entered the stream of English speech from contact with the French settlements in Canada and especially in the Louisiana Territory when that large area held by a French-speaking population became part of the United States. To their influence have been traced *bayou, bureau, cache, chowder, depot, gopher, levee, parlay, prairie, rapids, shanty, toboggan*.

As the nation expanded westward, it finally overran the Spanish-speaking centers of California and the Southwest. In the course of time these were officially seized by the United States, and the holdings of the original settlers were expropriated. Nevertheless, the evidences of their

---

[13] For a more detailed account of the additions to English vocabulary resulting from American expansion see the accounts in Mencken and Krapp, and in Albert H. Marckwardt, *American English* (New York, 1958), ch. 3.

culture remained and are traceable in many words that have since spread eastward and gradually become part of the general vocabulary: *alfalfa*, *burro*, *barracuda*, *bonanza*, *bonito*, *cafeteria*, *corral*, *coyote*, *desperado*, *lasso*, *marijuana*, *mustang*, *patio*, *plaza*, *ranch*, *rodeo*, *stampede*, *sombrero*, *vigilantes*.

Evidences of Early Regional Consciousness

Despite these foreign strains, European visitors have often noticed the comparative uniformity of American speech. There are indeed no dialectal differences as striking as those of the regional dialects of England. Nevertheless, Early American varied to some extent according to both region and social class. The testimony of early observers who took occasion to comment upon regional differences is sometimes difficult to interpret, partly because they were not competent to describe sounds accurately, one of the most difficult of all things to describe meaningfully for the general reader, but partly also because we are not always sure what values they attached to their letters.

The provincialisms which David Humphries appended to *The Yankey in England* have already been mentioned. In 1827 Adiel Sherwood, who had come to Georgia from New England and New York, published a third edition of his *Gazetteer of the State of Georgia*, to which he added a list of provincialisms.[14] Bartlett likewise included in the Introduction to his *Dictionary of Americanisms*[15] a "table of words incorrectly pronounced," a number of which are distinguished by region. The pronunciations given in all the lists reveal only a part of the entire phonological system. On the other hand, the features included were more widespread than their authors supposed.

It is important to keep in mind that in those times when spelling pronunciations were becoming frequent among the literate classes, the illiterate or semiliterate, still a large percentage of the population, tended to cling to older habits of speech. Therefore, many of the pronunciations labeled "vulgar" were American survivals of Early Modern sounds and were maintained even by a large number of the conservative or provincial

---

[14] Both lists are reprinted in Mathews, *Beginnings*, pp. 57–61, 118–21.

educated folk. Among these old forms, honorable in their descent, but then falling into disuse, were:

1. Survival of *ar* forms which had replaced ME *er*: *etarnal, consarning, marcy, larning, parfect, presarved, sartin, sarvent, vartuous,* and with excrescent *-t, sarmont* and *varmint.* These pronunciations had remained in quite reputable usage in England to the time of Addison and Pope, but they must have been retained later in America among some educated speakers, since both Webster and Walker[16] found it necessary to denounce them. Somewhat resembling these, but with a different sound history and social status, were the well-known dialectal forms *thar, whar, clar, bar* 'bear,' etc.

2. Raising of *ĕ* to *ĭ* before front consonants: *agin, divil, forgit, frind, gin'ral, inimy, kittle, kiver,*[17] *stiddy;* and conversely, the lowering of *ĭ* to *ĕ* in some other words like *sperit* and *resk.* The raised vowel is still heard to some extent in educated Southern speech.

3. Survival of Early Modern [əɪ] in *ui/oi* diphthongs: *bile* 'boil,' *briled* 'broiled,' *hist* 'hoist,' *jine* 'join,' *iist* 'joist,' *pint* 'point,' *spile* 'spoil.'

4. Variations in vowel length: *eend, leetle, neest* 'nest,' *sheep* 'ship,' *stars,* 'stairs.'

5. Variations in the vowel from ME *ō̩* and in the unrounding of *u: blud, cum, duse* 'does,' *huff* 'hoof,' *ruff* 'roof,' *shuk* 'shook.' Many words of this type retained variants through the nineteenth century. *Aloof, boot, cooper, food, proof* were often pronounced with the lax rounded vowel (as in *foot*) and *foot, stood,* and *took* with the unrounded vowel (as in *blood*). In this connection it may also be remarked that in parts of New England the vowel from ME *ō̩* was raised and shortened as in *hum* 'home' and *stun* 'stone.'

---

[16] John Walker, *A Critical Pronouncing Dictionary* (London, 1791).

[17] The Old French etymon of the word gave two ME forms, *cover* and *kever.* The latter is represented here.

6. Unrounded vowels from ME *ŏ: craps* 'crops,' *drap* 'drop,' *saft* 'soft.'

7. Variations in the development of ME *au*, normally [ɔ:]: *becase, saas* 'sauce,' *sacer* 'saucer,' *sassage, ant* 'aunt,' *hant* 'haunt,' *stanch*. Of these [æ] remains standard only in *aunt*, unless we include the colloquial *sassy* 'impertinent.'

8. Retention of the midfront vowel from ME *ẹ̄*. By the end of the eighteenth century this vowel in most words had been replaced by [i:]. Pronunciations like the following were therefore regarded by Walker as vulgar, but they must have retained for some time a measure of conservative respectability: *rale* 'real,' *railly, rared* 'reared,' *wary* 'weary.' Similar pronunciations were common in *reason, seat*, and *perceive*. Shortened vowels as in *rech* 'reach' were sometimes used also in *appear, beard, fierce, pear*, and *pierce*. Conversely *heerd* and *deef* were frequent. One form, *rare*, as in 'rare beef' has been retained with a modified spelling from earlier *rear*.[18]

9. Early loss of *r* before *s*, which originated in Middle English, was evident in *bust* 'burst,' *cuss, fust, hoss*, and probably also in *mash* 'marsh' and *scace* 'scarce.' The more general vocalization of final and preconsonantal *r* began to spread in standard British usage in the eighteenth century. This development must have had its roots in the southern counties of England and could have been implanted also in the American speech of Eastern New England and the South, its growth paralleling that in the mother country. If so, however, the evidence does not appear in the lists of Humphries and Sherwood, unless we include *hath* 'hearth' and *desput* 'desperate.' The more likely explanation for the vocalization of *r* in American English is the influence of London. In the eighteenth century the upper classes in Boston and the South were much more strongly influenced by London social life than those of Philadelphia, focal center of early

---

[18] *OED*, s.v. "rear," adj. 2; "rare," adj. 2.

Middle Atlantic speech. The preferences of the colonial gentry of these regions were passed on to the common speech and have remained. As the new pronunciations spread, the early grammarians and lexicographers either were too cautious to record them or did not recognize their significance, but the rhymes of poets, as illustrated by Krapp (2: 220–21) point clearly to the facts.

Regional Divisions Today

Many of the early regional features noted here, whatever their geographical distribution, have since been obliterated from the standard speech under the influence of the grammars, spellers, and dictionaries of the nineteenth century. Nevertheless, this influence has not been sufficiently powerful to level all regional differences. Three main divisions of colonial English formed the basis of the present varieties of American speech on the Atlantic coast. Northern American (sometimes called Eastern) includes New England, the Hudson Valley, metropolitan New York, and New York State. Midland is divided into a Northern area which includes most of Pennsylvania and southern New Jersey, and a Southern area (called also Southern Mountain) which extends southward from the Pennsylvania line west of the Susquehanna to include western Maryland, West Virginia, the western section of the Carolinas, and the eastern parts of Kentucky and Tennessee.[19] The Southern region is the coastal area from the lower portions of Delaware and Maryland southward.

None of these three large dialectal divisions is linguistically homogeneous. Eastern New England has features different from inland New England and both of these from the area of New York City. Likewise the metropolitan area of Philadelphia differs in a few respects from that of Pittsburgh. Again, the speech of eastern Virginia is not identical with that of Charleston, South Carolina.

As the nation expanded in the nineteenth and early twentieth centuries, large parts of the population moved westward. Southern speech

---

[19] One of the groups of early settlers not mentioned above were the Scotch-Irish who migrated in restless fashion through Pennsylvania and were responsible for carrying a variety of Midland speech through these Southern parts. From contact with settlers moving westward from the Southern states, Southern Midland acquired some Southern features.

moved across the Gulf states, which are now part of the Southern dialect area, though, as in all three types, the farther west one travels, the greater the intermixture of outside features. A subdivision of Northern speech in western New England and New York State was carried westward and determined the main character of the speech of the Great Lakes area. Between this and the Southern cotton states the westward migration carried the features of Middle Atlantic. Until recently all American speech except Northern and Southern was grouped together as "General American." The progress of research in American dialect study, however, has shown that this is too great an oversimplification to stand, even though the speech of the Middle West and of the Far West shows greater resemblance to Midland speech than it does to Eastern New England or Southern. When current studies in American dialectology are completed it will be possible to describe area characteristics for North Central, Upper and Lower Midwest, Rocky Mountain, Southwest, and Pacific Coast.

The dialect criteria, consisting of features of phonology, morphology, and word use, are too numerous and varied in their boundaries to give in detail here.[20] A few of the more important ones can be stated briefly.

1. Northern and Southern agree against Middle Atlantic and the Western areas in the loss (or vocalization) of r finally and before consonants as in *car* and *card*. This loss of r has modified the preceding vowel in various ways in different subdivisions of the regions. A nonsyllabic ə-glide appears after high vowels as in *ear* [iə] and *poor* [pʊə]. Earlier [ar] became [a:] or [ɑ:], sometimes followed by the ə-glide.

2. The so-called short *o*, derived from ME ŏ and still spelled *o*, as in *odd, cot, drop*, etc., occurs in Midland and Southern speech as an unrounded vowel [a/ɑ], but in parts of New England as [ɔ] or [ɒ]. However, rounded pronunciations are found elsewhere, and in some areas as in eastern Pennsylvania both will be found, such as [ɑ] in *lot, mop*, etc., but [ɔ:] in *dog* and *frost*. The rounded vowel is also common in western Pennsylvania in these words, but is unrounded in some positions, especially before [l].

[20] A good survey of the present state of our knowledge on the subject is that of Raven I. McDavid, Jr., "The Dialects of American English," in Francis, ch. 9. See also Hans Kurath and Raven I. McDavid, Jr., *The Pronunciation of English in the Atlantic States* (Ann Arbor, 1961), and Hans Kurath, *A Word Geography of the Eastern United States* (Ann Arbor, 1949). The place of vowel sounds in the phonemic system of several Eastern dialects is given in Kurath, *Pronunciation*, pp. 5–9. Cf. also Thomas, ch. 22.

3. The tense vowel [e:] occurs in *Mary* in New England and the South, contrasting with [ɛ:] in other regions. On the other hand, in *stairs*, *care*, etc., [æ] is very common in the South and occurs also in parts of New England.

4. In the *r*-less regions [oə] occurs in *door* and *four*. In these areas *hoarse* and *four* with [oə] may contrast with *horse* and *forty* [ɔ].

5. New England has [a] before the voiceless spirants and *n* plus a consonant, as in *half*, *pass*, *bath*, and *dance*.

6. The diphthongs in *twice* and *out* occur in some parts of New England as [əɪ] and [əʊ]. In the South and Southern Midland the diphthong [aɪ] is replaced by [aə] before voiced consonants as in *nine* and *ride*.

British and American Today

What comparison can be made between the English language as spoken today in Britain and in the United States? The latter variety has so frequently been adversely criticized, especially by patronizing British observers, as to exaggerate the real differences between these two varieties of English. It is open to question whether an educated person of, say, Philadelphia or Cleveland would feel that the noticeable differences in RP[21] were more prominent than those he would observe in the cultivated speech of New Orleans or Charleston, South Carolina. In fact, in some important respects Southern speech would seem to him closer to RP than to his own.

Detailed comparison between American and British speech is complicated by the character of the language standard in this country. Here no one regional speech as used by educated speakers has greater prestige than another. A person from the South or the Far West who comes to one of the metropolitan centers of the East does not feel that he must change his speech habits to be accepted in good social and business circles, even though his position demands that he be seen and speak in public. We then have nothing like RP to use as a contrasting system. The comparison, of course, would be much more difficult if we were to take cognizance of the provincial dialects of the British Isles.

---

[21] Received Pronunciation is said, in the words of Jones (*Pronouncing Dictionary*, p. xv), "to be very usually heard in everyday speech in the families of Southern English people who have been educated at the public schools." "Public schools" of course refers to what in the United States are known as independent schools or private schools.

With regard to the latter point, it is helpful to remember that changes have occurred and are still taking place in England which have an important bearing upon regional differences.[22] Two world wars have increased the mobility of the provincial population, thereby weakening the dialect traditions. The older English gentry have at the same time declined in relative economic power and influence. General literacy and the rapid growth of the mass media—movies, radio, and television—have had two opposite effects: more people have become accustomed to RP, especially because of its adoption by BBC, but at the same time the American influence, always deplorable to the conservative, has spread among the younger generation. Equally important, however, are the changes that have taken place in English education. Large numbers of talented sons of the industrial and agricultural classes are now distinguishing themselves not only in the newer "red brick" universities, but in the older institutions as well, and thereby finding their way into professional and public life. A percentage of the "new men" adopt RP or some approximation to it, but others do not conform, so that regional standards are now becoming acceptable to many educated people. It is not certain whether the ultimate result will be the recognition of several standards as in the United States or a modified type of RP.

The RP standard, which, for the time being at least, retains its prestige value and is usually taught to foreigners who learn English in England, resembles Northern and Southern American in the vocalization of r before consonants and in final position. In all of these areas, therefore, a number of vowel clusters occur which are not heard in Midland and Western American (see pp. 47, 184). One consequence of this change is that the linking and intrusive r is as common in RP as in New England speech (see p. 172), but a more important result is that the long vowel [ɑ:] has become much more abundant following the loss of r and is now a relatively prominent feature of RP.

Among the other back vowels the so-called short o as in not and cod is moderately rounded in RP to [ɒ]. In advanced RP [ɔ:] as in all is sometimes raised in the direction of [o:]. Earlier [o:], or its later glide diphthong [oʊ], has now a centered on-glide resulting in [əʊ]. A less prominent

---

[22] An interesting and informative account of this subject for the general reader is Charles Barber, *Linguistic Change in Present-Day English* (Edinburgh and London, 1964). See also Gimson, pp. 81–85.

tendency in this direction is noticeable in the high back vowel, approximating [ɪʊ]. It is interesting to note that a very similar modification of the mid and high long back vowels is taking place in North Midland American.

There is less contrast in the consonants. Intervocalic *r*, however, retains a vestige of the earlier trilled quality and, as we have said, is called by phoneticians a "flap *r*." To American ears it seems to have some of the quality of a lightly articulated intervocalic *d*. In RP pronunciation a fully voiceless, even aspirated, *t* remains in medial position, whereas in American English it is voiced or assimilated as in *latter* [lædɚ] and *granted* [grænɪt]. On the other hand American English is more tenacious of secondary stress, while the British standard tolerates loss of vowel and syllable in words like *secretary* ['sɛkrətrɪ] and *necessary* ['nɛsəsrɪ].

A few incidental differences are associated with length. The suffix -*ile* in *fertile* and *hostile* rhymes in RP with *pile*, but, in conservative practice, -*ate* is short [ɪt] in the nouns *advocate*, *candidate*, and *delegate*. Initial [ʃ] is the rule in *schedule*. A prominent feature of RP but difficult to describe in ordinary discourse is its intonation. Many people feel that the cadences of cultivated British speech are more varied and pleasing than those of American speech, but these judgments are, of course, subjective.

Of rather minor significance are a few points of grammar. British usage does not retain the participial form *gotten*. The American will say *have got* to mean 'have' and *have gotten* to mean 'have obtained.' Where the American says *do not have*, his British friend more often says *have not got*.

The pronunciation of proper names in Britain, formerly a matter of some surprise to the American visitor, is giving way to the tyranny of spelling. These striking pronunciations resulted from phonological changes which were not reflected in the spelling. Some historical place names like *Gloucester* and *Worcester* are, of course, familiar to American ears because of their early use and preservation here. In England the fifteenth-century shift of *er* to *ar* is still heard in *Berkeley*, *Derby*, and *Hertford*, which occur in this country with the modified spellings *Barclay*, *Darby*, and *Hartford*. Phonological modification appears also in the family names *Beecham* (*Beauchamp*) and *Clark(e)* on both sides of the Atlantic. The given names *Ralph* and *St. John* are sometimes pronounced in England as [reːf] and ['sɪndʒən], but not in this country. In a number of place names old pronunciations like ['riːə] for *Wreay* and ['sɪsɪtə] for *Cirencester* are probably preserved by local people but are giving way in more general use to spell-

ing pronunciations; and even the still well-established ['ænɪk] for *Alnwick*
and ['heːzbrə] for *Happisburgh* may eventually follow their example.

Much more noticeable are differences in vocabulary. A rather large
number of commonplace things have names in England different enough
to strike the American visitor. As we have already observed, the American
natural and social environment has given rise to a specifically American
vocabulary. Corresponding terms suitable to the English environment, for
example, *fen, copse, spinney, wold,* are seldom used by Americans and are
encountered only in a literary context, where they evoke a certain respect-
ful attention. To be sure, mass education in this country has for a long
time been widening American acquaintance with British literature, but
the literary language does not very fully reflect contrasts in British and
American usage. In this respect recent light fiction from Wodehouse to
Fleming has accustomed Americans to an amusing, if somewhat dubious,
cultivated colloquial.

The circumstances of two World Wars have altered the world position of the United States, and American prosperity has enormously increased tourist travel in the British Isles. Moreover, critics who suffer
anxiety because of the influence of the American-made cinema on the
English vocabulary may now draw a modicum of comfort from a reverse
trend. For some years actors trained on the British stage have been drawn
to Hollywood in sufficient numbers to make the sounds and cadences of
cultivated British speech quite familiar. More recently movie production
in England has prospered, and the British studios have exposed in America
a small but important stream of technically superb films, in which the
English scene is portrayed in appealing guise and the cultivated speech of
England is heard with full authenticity. All of these new trends form a
rapprochement between the speakers of both English idioms, at least to the
degree of common understanding and tolerance if not of a single standard
of usage.

In this country, at any rate, the usual lists of contrasting British-
American synonyms have now some limitations. According to Barber[23]
radio for British *wireless, movie* for *film, canned* for *tinned, gas* for *petrol, gas
pedal* for *accelerator, elevator* for *lift, rugged* for *robust, automobile* for *car* "are
now often heard in Britain beside the British word." Many Americans,

---

[23] *Linguistic Change,* p. 101.

however, would feel that *film, accelerator, robust,* and *car* have been common here for a long time.

With varying degrees of familiarity Americans would recognize as British certain terms relating to the automobile: *bonnet* (hood), *boot* (trunk), *dynamo* (generator), *hood* (top), *gear lever* (gearshift), *motor car, mudguard, petrol, saloon* (sedan), and *windscreen.* Among items referring to transportation, we should include *booking office* (ticket office), *caravan* (trailer), *goods car* (freight car), *lorry* (truck), *railway, underground* (subway), *roundabout* (traffic circle), *motor way, tarmac* ("black-top" paving), and the word *transport* itself, which is usually *transportation* in the United States.

Among differences in names of foodstuffs are *biscuit* (cracker), *joint* (roast), *porridge* (oatmeal), *sweet* (dessert), *sweets* (candy), *tart* (pie), *tinned goods* (canned food). Other domestic and commonplace terms include *caretaker* (janitor), *cotton wool* (absorbent cotton), *dust bin* (trash can), *fortnight, geyser* (water heater), *gramophone* (phonograph), *leading article* (editorial), *lift* (elevator), *pub* (taproom), *trunk call* (long distance).

Some items of the current American vocabulary which were in standard British use in the eighteenth century or earlier have now been replaced except in some provincial dialects. For example, *cabin, cordwood, drool, tariff* (as 'import duty'), and *wilt* would not be encountered in England today, at least in the same senses as in this country. Likewise in England *chemist* is common for *druggist* (though *pharmacy* is also to be encountered), *autumn* invariably for *fall, flat* for *apartment. Sick* is generally restricted in meaning to 'nauseated,' and *raise* is not applied to children, who are *reared,* to cattle, which are *bred,* or to grain, which is *grown.*

On the other hand, Americans are so familiar to the British public today that Americanisms are accepted quite gracefully, and, as we have been so often reminded, American slang is infiltrating British speech so heavily that we may expect to encounter such expressions in common usage as *ballyhoo, blurb, cagey, cocktail, gimmick, jazz, stooge,* and many others.[24]

One commentator[25] refers to the influence of the American enter-

---

[24] On differences between contemporary American and British usage see further in Mencken, ch. 6; Thomas Pyles, *Words and Ways of American English* (New York, 1952), ch. 9; and the same author's *Origins and Development,* also ch. 9. The latter contains very useful bibliographical notes.

[25] Brian Foster, "Recent American Influence on Standard English," *Anglia* 73 (1956): 328–60.

tainment world on British speech as evidenced by *star, costar, release* (of a film), *fan, feature, natural* (n.), *routine* (as in *vaudeville routine*). But the same writer finds the influence not confined to this field. *Alibi* (an excuse), *rate* (to evaluate), and *transportation* (for British *transport*) are all worthy of his comment. So also are a number of compounds: *bobby-soxer, doubletalk, disk jockey, ghost writer,* and *sports editor;* verb phrases: *build up, get across, put over, break down* (analyze), *beat up, check up on, slip up, get away with, stand for* (tolerate), and *have to* (must); and a number of adverbial idioms such as *right now, that way* (like that), *way down, way back,* and *maybe.*

When all account has been taken, however, of differences between American and British English, it cannot be said that they very greatly impede communication. A number of English purists continue to be annoyed by American lexical aggressiveness, and a number of Americans of provincial temper may perhaps be amused by one item or another of the English vocabulary, but the real obstacles, which occur almost exclusively in the colloquial medium, are quickly hurdled.

In the printed language of serious communication, the British writer, particularly if he is a product of traditional British education, may reveal himself in certain elements of style, but these have no real bearing upon linguistic difference. At any rate the educated American reads many pages of British writing without encountering a form or a meaning the least bit strange to him. It is important to dwell on this point. Thomas Jefferson prophesied that time would separate American and English into different languages. History, fortunately, has proved him wrong. The forces that keep us today in easy communication are stronger than those that separate us.

A Selected
Bibliography

Works useful to the elementary study of the English language, including works cited in this treatise.

Bibliographies

Allen, Harold B. *Linguistics and English Linguistics*. Goldentree Bibliographies. New York, 1966. Contains a bibliography of bibliographies.

Kennedy, Arthur G. *A Bibliography of Writings on the English Language*. Cambridge, Mass., 1927. Reprinted, New York, 1961.

———, and Donald Sands. *A Concise Bibliography for Students of English*. Stanford, 1960. Chapters VII and VIII list important works in French and German, which have been excluded from this list.

Dictionaries

HISTORICAL

Bosworth, Joseph, and T. N. Toller. *An Anglo-Saxon Dictionary*. Oxford, 1882. Reprinted, 1955.

Craigie, Sir William A., and J. R. Hulbert. *A Dictionary of American English on Historical Principles*. 4 vols. Chicago, 1936–44.

Hall, John R. C. *A Concise Anglo-Saxon Dictionary*. 4th ed. Cambridge, 1961.

Kurath, Hans, and Sherman M. Kuhn. *Middle English Dictionary*. Ann Arbor, 1954–

Mathews, Mitford M. *A Dictionary of Americanisms on Historical Principles.* 2 vols. Chicago, 1951. Reprinted in 1 vol., 1956.

Murray, Sir James A. H., and others. *A New English Dictionary on Historical Principles* (*NED*), 10 vols. and suppl. Oxford, 1884–1933. Reissued 1933 as *Oxford English Dictionary* (*OED*) and now universally referred to as such.

ETYMOLOGICAL

Farmer, John S., and W. E. Henley. *Dictionary of Slang and Its Analogues.* New Hyde Park, N. Y., 1966.

Jamieson, John. *An Etymological Dictionary of the Scottish Language.* New ed., Paisley, 1879–82. Abridged ed., Paisley, 1912.

Onions, C. T., G. W. S. Friedrichsen, and R. W. Burchfield. *Oxford Dictionary of English Etymology.* Oxford, 1966.

Partridge, Eric. *A Dictionary of Slang and Unconventional English.* New York, 1967.

———. *Origins: A Short Etymological Dictionary of Modern English.* London, 1958.

Weekley, Ernest. *A Concise Etymological Dictionary of Modern English.* New York, 1952.

Wentworth, Harold. *American Dialect Dictionary.* New York, 1944.

———, and Stuart B. Flexner. *Dictionary of American Slang.* New York, 1967.

Wright, Joseph. *The English Dialect Dictionary.* 6 vols. London, 1898–1905. Reprinted, New York, 1963.

PRONOUNCING

Jones, Daniel. *English Pronouncing Dictionary.* 11th ed. London, Everyman's Reference Library, 1960.

Kenyon, John S., and Thomas A. Knott. *A Pronouncing Dictionary of American English.* Springfield, Mass., 1953.

USAGE

Evans, Bergen, and Cornelia Evans. *A Dictionary of American Usage.* New York, 1957.

Fowler, H. W. *A Dictionary of Modern English Usage.* Oxford, 1959.

Horwill, H. W. *A Dictionary of Modern American Usage.* 2d ed. Oxford, 1944.

Nicholson, Margaret. *A Dictionary of American-English Usage.* New York, 1957.

Perrin, Porter G. *Writer's Guide and Index to English.* 3d ed., with Karl W. Dykema. Chicago, 1959.

LINGUISTICS

Pei, Mario A., and Frank Gaynor. *A Dictionary of Linguistics.* New York, 1954.

General Works

Bach, Emmon. *An Introduction to Transformational Grammars.* New York, 1964.

Barber, Charles. *Linguistic Change in Present-Day English.* Edinburgh and London, 1964.

Baugh, Albert C. *A History of the English Language.* 2d ed. New York, 1957.

Bender, Harold. *The Home of the Indo-Europeans.* Princeton, 1922.

Bloomfield, Leonard. *Language.* New York, 1933.

Bloomfield, Morton M., and Leonard Newmark. *A Linguistic Introduction to the History of English.* New York, 1963.

Bradley, Henry. *The Making of English.* New York, 1904. Reprinted, 1925.

Bronstein, Arthur J. *The Pronunciation of American English.* New York, 1960.

Brook, G. L. *A History of the English Language.* London, 1958.

————. *An Introduction to Old English.* 2d ed. Manchester, 1962.

Brunner, Karl. *An Outline of Middle English Grammar.* Trans. G. K. W. Johnston. Oxford, 1963.

Bryant, Margaret M. *Modern English and Its Heritage.* 2d ed. New York, 1962.

Campbell, Alistair. *Old English Grammar.* Oxford, 1959.

Chambers, R. W. *On the Continuity of English Prose.* Early English Text Society, 191A. 1932. Reprinted, 1957.

Chomsky, Noam. *Aspects of the Theory of Syntax.* Cambridge, Mass., 1965.

————. *Syntactic Structures.* The Hague, 1957.

————, and Morris Halle. *The Sound Pattern of English.* New York, 1968.

Clark, John W. *Early English: An Introduction to Old and Middle English.* London, 1957. Reprinted, New York: Norton Library, 1964.

Crombie, A. C. *Medieval and Early Modern Science.* 2d ed. New York: Doubleday Anchor Books, 1959.

Diringer, David. *The Alphabet: A Key to the History of Mankind.* 2d ed. New York, 1962.

Dobson, E. J. *English Pronunciation, 1500–1700.* 2 vols. Oxford, 1957.

Foster, Brian. "Recent American Influence on Standard English." *Anglia* 73 (1956): 328–60.

Francis, W. Nelson. *The Structure of American English.* New York, 1958.

Garmonsway, G. N., trans. *The Anglo-Saxon Chronicle.* London: Everyman's Library, 1953.

Gimson, A. C. *An Introduction to the Pronunciation of English.* London, 1962.

Gleason, H. A., Jr. *An Introduction to Descriptive Linguistics.* 2d ed. New York, 1961.

————. *Linguistics and English Grammar.* New York, 1965.

Gordon, George. *Shakespeare's English.* Society for Pure English, Tract 29, 1928. Reprinted in the same author's *Shakespearean Comedy*, Oxford, 1944.

Greenough, James B., and G. L. Kittredge. *Words and Their Ways in English Speech*. New York, 1900. Reprinted, Boston: Beacon Press, 1962.

Hall, Robert A., Jr. *Introductory Linguistics*. Philadelphia, 1964.

Haskins, C. H. *The Renaissance of the Twelfth Century*. Cambridge, Mass., 1927.

Hieatt, Constance. *Essentials of Old English*. New York, 1968.

Hill, Archibald A. *An Introduction to Linguistic Structures*. New York, 1958.

Hockett, Charles F. *A Course in Modern Linguistics*. New York, 1958.

Hodgson, Phyllis, and Gabriel M. Liegey, *The Orcherd of Syon. Vol. I, The Text*. Early English Text Society, o.s. 258. 1966.

Hughes, John P. *The Science of Language*. New York, 1962.

Hunter, Edwin R. "Verb + Adverb = Noun." *American Speech* 22 (1947): 115–19.

Irwin, Keith G. *The Romance of Writing*. New York, 1956.

Jacobs, Roderick A., and Paul S. Rosenbaum. *Grammar*. 2 vols. Boston, 1967.

———, and ———. *English Transformational Grammar*. Waltham, Mass., 1968.

Jespersen, Otto. *Essentials of English Grammar*. New York, 1933.

———. *Growth and Structure of the English Language*. 9th ed. Oxford, 1938. Reprinted, 1960.

———. *A Modern English Grammar on Historical Principles*. 7 vols. Vols. 1–4, Heidelberg, 1909–31; 5–7, Copenhagen, 1940–49. Reprinted, London, 1954.

Jones, Daniel. *The Phoneme, Its Nature and Use*. 3d ed., with an appendix, "The History and Meaning of the Term Phoneme." Cambridge, 1967.

Kennedy, Arthur G. *Current English*. Boston, 1935.

Kenyon, John S. *American Pronunciation*. 10th ed. Ann Arbor, 1950.

Kökeritz, Helge. *A Guide to Chaucer's Pronunciation*. New York, 1962.

———. *Shakespeare's Pronunciation*. New Haven, 1953.

Krapp, George P. *The English Language in America*. 2 vols. New York, 1925.

Kuhn, Sherman M. "On the Syllabic Phonemes of Old English." *Language* 37 (1961): 522–38.

Kurath, Hans. "Loss of Long Consonants . . . in Middle English." *Language* 32 (1956): 435–45.

———. "Phonemics and Phones in Historical Phonology." *American Speech* 36 (1961): 93–100.

———. *A Phonology and Prosody of Modern English*. Heidelberg, 1964.

———. *A Word Geography of the Eastern United States*. Ann Arbor, 1949.

———, and Raven I. McDavid, Jr. *The Pronunciation of English in the Atlantic States*. Ann Arbor, 1961.

Lehmann, Winfred P. *Historical Linguistics: An Introduction*. New York, 1962.

Lewis, C. S. *Studies in Words*. Cambridge, 1960.

Lloyd, Donald A., and Harry R. Warfel. *American English in Its Cultural Setting*. New York, 1956.

Long, Percy W. "English Pronouncing Dictionaries before Webster." *Bibliographical Society of America: Papers* 4 (1929): 25–43.

Lord, Robert. *Comparative Linguistics*. London, 1966.

Lyman, Rollo. *English Grammar in American Schools*. Washington: Bureau of Education Bulletin no. 12, 1921.

Malmstrom, Jean, and Annabel Ashley. *Dialects: USA*. Champaign, Ill.: National Council of Teachers of English, 1963.

Marckwardt, Albert H. *American English*. New York, 1958.

———. "The New Webster Dictionary: A Critical Appraisal," in W. B. Finnie and Thomas L. Erskine, eds., *Words on Words*. New York, 1971.

———, and Randolph Quirk. *A Common Language: British and American English*. British Broadcasting Corporation, 1964. (Available through the National Council of Teachers of English. Champaign, Ill.)

Mathews, Mitford M. *The Beginnings of American English*. Chicago, 1931.

———. *A Survey of English Dictionaries*. London, 1933.

McKnight, George H. *Modern English in the Making*. New York, 1928.

Mencken, H. L. *The American Language*. 4th ed. New York, 1936. Supplement I, 1945; Supplement II, 1948. Abridged ed., Raven I. McDavid, Jr., New York, 1963.

Moore, Samuel. *Historical Outlines of English Sounds and Inflections*. Rev. ed., Albert H. Marckwardt. Ann Arbor, 1966.

Mustanoja, Tauno F. *A Middle English Syntax: Part I, Parts of Speech*. Helsinki, 1960.

Myers, L. M. *The Roots of Modern English*. Boston, 1966.

Nida, Eugene A. *A Synopsis of English Syntax*. 2d ed. The Hague, 1966.

Nist, John. *A Structural History of English*. New York, 1966.

Pedersen, Holger. *Linguistic Science in the Nineteenth Century*. Trans. John W. Spargo. Cambridge, Mass., 1931. Reprinted as *The Discovery of Language*, Bloomington: Indiana Midland Books, 1962.

Plummer, Charles. *Two of the Saxon Chronicles*. 2 vols. Oxford, 1892–99.

Potter, Simeon. *Language in the Modern World*. London: Penguin Books, 1960.

———. *Modern Linguistics*. London, 1957. Reprinted, New York: Norton Library, 1964.

———. *Our Language*. London: Penguin Books, 1950.

Pyles, Thomas. *Origins and Development of the English Language*. New York, 1964.

———. *Words and Ways of American English*. New York, 1952.

Quinn, Arthur H., Albert C. Baugh, and Will D. Howe. *The Literature of America*. 2 vols. New York, 1929.

Quirk, Randolph. *The Use of English*. New York, 1962.

———, and C. L. Wrenn. *An Old English Grammar*. London, 1958.

Robertson, Stuart, and F. G. Cassidy. *The Development of Modern English*. New York, 1954.

Robins, R. H. *A Short History of Linguistics*. Bloomington, 1968.

Robinson, F. N., ed. *The Works of Geoffrey Chaucer*. 2d ed. Boston, 1957.

Sapir, Edward. *Language: An Introduction to the Study of Speech*. New York, 1921.

Saussure, Ferdinand de. *Cours de linguistique générale*. 4th ed. Paris, 1949. Trans. Wade Baskin, as *Course in General Linguistics*. New York, 1959. Reprinted, New York: McGraw-Hill Paperbacks, 1966.

Schlauch, Margaret. *The English Language in Modern Times*. Warsaw, 1959.

———. *The Gift of Tongues*. New York, 1942. Reprinted as *The Gift of Language*, 1955.

Serjeantson, Mary S. *A History of Foreign Words in England*. London, 1935. Reprinted, New York, 1962.

Shuy, Roger W. *Discovering American Dialects*. Champaign, Ill.: National Council of Teachers of English, 1967.

Sledd, James H. *A Short Introduction to English Grammar*. Chicago, 1959.

———, and Wilma R. Ebbit. *Dictionaries and THAT Dictionary*. Chicago, 1962.

———, and G. J. Kolb. *Dr. Johnson's Dictionary*. Chicago, 1955.

Stageberg, Norman C. *An Introductory English Grammar*. New York, 1965.

Stevick, Robert D. "The Morphemic Evolution of Middle English *she*." *English Studies* 45 (1968): 381–88.

Sturtevant, Edgar H. *An Introduction to Linguistic Science*. New Haven, 1947.

Thieme, Paul. "The Indo-European Language," *Scientific American* 199, no. 4, October 1958: 63–74.

Thomas, Charles K. *An Introduction to the Phonetics of American English*. 2d ed. New York, 1958.

Trager, George L., and Henry L. Smith. *An Outline of English Structure*. Norman, Okla., 1951. Reprinted, Washington, 1963.

Trevelyan, G. M. *A History of England*. 3d ed. London, 1945. Reprinted, 3 vols., New York: Doubleday Anchor Books, 1953.

Tucker, Susie. *English Examined*. Cambridge, 1961.

Vallins, G. H. *The Pattern of English*. London, 1956.

Waddell, Helen. *The Wandering Scholars*. London, 1927. Reprinted, New York: Doubleday Anchor Books, 1955.

Wardale, E. E. *An Introduction to Middle English*. London, 1937. Reprinted, 1958.

Warfel, Harry R., ed. *Letters of Noah Webster*. New York, 1953.

Weekley, Ernest. *The Romance of Words*. 4th ed. New York, 1922. Reprinted, 1961.

Whitehall, Harold. *Structural Essentials of English*. New York, 1956.

Wyld, Henry C. *A Short History of English*. 3d ed. New York, 1927.

———. *History of Modern Colloquial English*. 3d ed. Oxford, 1936.

Zandvoort, R. W. *A Handbook of English Grammar*. 3d ed. Englewood Cliffs, N. J., 1966.

SOURCES OF THE PASSAGES ON PAGES 237–39

(a) Charles Lamb, "Old China," *London Magazine*, March 1823.
(b) Robert Greene, "The Art of Cony-Catching," in *A Notable Discovery of Cosenage* 1591.
(c) Thomas Huxley, *Autobiography*, 1889.
(d) Samuel Pepys, *Diary*, August 18, 1667.
(e) Winston Churchill, "Harrow," in *A Roving Commission*, 1930.
(f) Philip Stanhope, Earl of Chesterfield, *Letters*, March 19, 1775.
(g) G. A. Alvarez, "Speaking Out," *Saturday Evening Post*, September 9, 1967.

Index

Boethius, 146–47
Book (The) of Troilus (Chaucer), 118
Bopp, Franz, 262
borrowing(s), 13–14, 148
  adverse nature of, 153–56
  in American English, 287–89
  doublets and, 149, 151, 153
  from Dutch, 288
  from French, 146–50, 151–56, 171,
    192, 222, 288
  from German, 288
  from Greek, 17–18, 21
  from Indian languages, 288
  from Latin, 150–51, 154–56, 248
  in ME, 139, 146–56
  from Norse, 152–54
  in OE, 97–98
  from Spanish, 289
bound morphs, 61
boy, as verb, 32
Bradford, William, 278, 279
Bradley, Henry, 29, 30–31, 264
Brandl, Alois, 263
brethren, survival of, 60, 134, 187
Breton, 85
Bristed, Charles A., 284
British English
  adverbial suffix in, 191
  American English vs., 82, 191,
    217, 294–99
  pronunciation: 15, 52; of *a*, 181;
    of consonants, 296; of diphthongs,
    184; of proper names, 296–97;
    regional dialects of, 6, 294, 295;
    of verbs, 206n; of vowels, 41, 170,
    171, 295–96
  word order, 217
British Education (Sheridan), 258
Bronstein, Arthur J., 174n
Browne, Sir Thomas, 204
Brugmann, Karl, 263
Bryant, William Cullen, 284
Brythonic, 85
Buchanan, James, 259
Bulgarian, 84
Bulloker, William, 249
Byron, Lord (George Gordon), 20, 176

c, in OE, 124

Cædmon, 201, 202
Campbell, George, 260–61
Canterbury Tales (Chaucer), 147–48
Canute, King, 102
Carlyle, Thomas, 33
case, *see* declensions; pronouns; *and
    specific case*
Catalan, 84
Caxton, William, 166, 167, 192n
Celtic, 85, 86, 98
Celts, 94
central vowels, 43
centum languages, 86
Chambers, R. W., 243n
Channing, William Ellery, 284
Charlemagne, 101
Chaucer, Geoffrey, 27, 50, 54, 103n,
    172, 254
  and French, 107, 146–48, 150–51
  influence of on language, 30, 111,
    112–13
  personal pronouns in, 193
  pronunciation of, 118–19, 144,
    170, 173, 175, 179
  rhymes in, 130–31
  short vowels in, 117
  stress in, 118–19
  verbs in, 208, 209–10
  word order in, 216, 231
Cheke, Sir John, 248, 249, 250
children, survival of, 60, 134, 187
chisel, meaning of, 29–30
Chomsky, Noam, 65n, 131n, 267
church, influence of on language, *see*
    education, church and
Cicero, 246
classics, influence of, 101, 105, 108–9,
    165–67, 244, 246–48, 250, 252–
    53, 258–59
  see also Greek; Latin
clauses
  adverb, 234
  contact, 231–33
  introductory relative, 230–31
  subordinate, *see* subordination
clipped forms, 18–19
close juncture, 67
Cobbet, William, 227–28
cognate language(s), 79–81